PSYCHOANALYTIC TECHNIQUE AND THEORY

PSYCHOANALYTIC TECHNIQUE AND THEORY
Taking the Transference

Judith L. Mitrani

LONDON AND NEW YORK

First published 2015 by
Karnac Books Ltd.

Published 2018 by Routledge
2 Park Square, Milton Park, Abingdon, Oxon OX14 4RN
711 Third Avenue, New York, NY 10017, USA

Routledge is an imprint of the Taylor & Francis Group, an informa business

Copyright © 2015 by Judith L. Mitrani

The right of Judith L. Mitrani to be identified as the author of this work has been asserted in accordance with §§ 77 and 78 of the Copyright Design and Patents Act 1988.

All rights reserved. No part of this book may be reprinted or reproduced or utilised in any form or by any electronic, mechanical, or other means, now known or hereafter invented, including photocopying and recording, or in any information storage or retrieval system, without permission in writing from the publishers.

Notice:
Product or corporate names may be trademarks or registered trademarks, and are used only for identification and explanation without intent to infringe.

British Library Cataloguing in Publication Data

A C.I.P. for this book is available from the British Library

ISBN-13: 9781782201625 (pbk)

Typeset by V Publishing Solutions Pvt Ltd., Chennai, India

CONTENTS

ACKNOWLEDGEMENTS vii

ABOUT THE AUTHOR ix

FOREWORD
by Neville Symington xi

INTRODUCTION xv

CHAPTER ONE
Listening for the emergence of infantile dependency 1

CHAPTER TWO
"A rose by any other name": working analytically in
  the face of authoritative statements 19

CHAPTER THREE
Some technical implications of Klein's concept of
  "premature ego development" 33

CHAPTER FOUR
Taking the transference: some technical
  implications from three papers by Wilfred Bion   59

CHAPTER FIVE
Excogitating Bion's *Cogitations*: further implications
  for technique   81

CHAPTER SIX
The past presented: bodily centered protections in puberty
  and adolescence   105

CHAPTER SEVEN
"Trying to Enter The Long Black Branches": some
  technical extensions for the analysis of autistic states in
  adults from the work of Frances Tustin   121

CHAPTER EIGHT
Minding the gap between neuroscientific and psychoanalytic
  understanding of autism   147

CHAPTER NINE
Surviving unthinkable trauma: dissociation, delusion, and
  hallucination in *Life of Pi*   173

REFERENCES   195

INDEX   205

ACKNOWLEDGEMENTS

There are so many people who contributed to the making of this volume. The patients who have taught me most of what I've learned over the years deserve my profound indebtedness. They have been truly devoted partners in this work and have often proved to be unusually tolerant of my sometimes protracted learning curve. I like to think that they have gained as much from their efforts as I have.

I also wish to thank my colleagues: the candidates and students and supervisees (many of whom have been my peers) who have shared their own work with me and have challenged me to think beyond what my first-hand experience has afforded me.

There are those who have been invaluable in this effort, supplying much needed encouragement and candid commentaries and holding my feet to the fire when I required an auxiliary dose of reality: among them I owe special acknowledgement to Warren Poland, Yvonne Hansen, Jim Grotstein, and Neville Symington. I am very thankful to my talented colleague Diane Silverman for her photograph of Gradiva, which appears on the cover of this book.

I offer my appreciation to those journal editors who have prodded me to hone my ideas and to further refine my style, and afterward rewarded me by granting my work a place in their volumes, amidst the many well respected and inspiring fellow authors. I especially thank Oliver Rathbone and Rod Tweedy of Karnac Books who have been so helpful, patient, and welcoming of this collection.

Last, and perhaps most significantly, I am eternally grateful to my husband, Dr. Theodore Mitrani, without whom I would never have written a word. He has been my in-house editor, my frequent creditor, and full-time partner in every way.

ABOUT THE AUTHOR

Dr. Judith L. Mitrani is a training and supervising analyst at The Psychoanalytic Center of California. A Fellow of the International Psycho-Analytical Association, Dr. Mitrani's work has been published in seven languages. She is the author of many clinical papers published in both American and international journals as well as the books *Framework for the Imaginary: Clinical Explorations in Primitive States of Being* (re-issued by Karnac in 2008) and *Ordinary People and Extra-Ordinary Protections: A Post-Kleinian Approach to the Treatment of Primitive Mental States* (on the New Library of Psycho-Analysis in 2000). She is also co-editor—with her husband, analyst Dr. Theodore Mitrani—of *Encounters with Autistic States: A Memorial Tribute to Frances Tustin* (1997) and the upcoming *Frances Tustin Today*. Dr. Mitrani is the founding and current Chair of the Frances Tustin Memorial Trust and supervises and lectures internationally on psychoanalytic technique with the infantile transference. She has a private practice in West Los Angeles, California.

FOREWORD

This is not a book to be read; it is a book to be lived. A man teaching scripture to his students made reference to the "Book of Exodus". One student piped up and said, "I've read that". The teacher said, "OK now start living it".

Judith L. Mitrani gives us not discursive theory, but what she has lived and is still living, and we expect future books with yet further development as it is so obvious, from what we have here, that we are in touch with someone who is continuing to develop and expand her knowledge and to deepen the thinking that arises from her experience. Yes, from *her* experience, not from some desiccated piece of discourse on what claims to be psychoanalysis yet is as far from it as cognitive behavioral therapy (CET), or even further. It is what looks like the truth that is furthest from it. G. K. Chesterton gave lucid expression to this when he said "… falsehood is never so false as when it is very nearly true" (Chesterton, 2005, p. 53).

This deepening can be seen in the opening chapter, where Mitrani sees the closeness of analyst to patient as partly determined by the frequency of contact, but in later chapters, especially where she enters a landscape first charted within psychoanalytic discourse by Bion, (I put in the phrase "within psychoanalytic discourse" in order to emphasize that this perspective had been mapped by others prior to the emergence of psychoanalysis) Judith alights on what is "evolving" not just what is there or was there.

A man entered my consulting room once and said, within the first few minutes of the first interview, "I have never been formed." The analysis was the process whereby the unformed began to be formed. This is something that Judith clearly understands and so finds Bion to be an inspiring mentor. But, because this gives expression to her own experience, she in turn becomes an inspiration to us who come into contact with her. Some of us are lucky enough to have had contact with her personally, but those who have not will meet her here in this book.

When I start to read the account of clinical work with a patient I sigh. The patient has been denuded of life and becomes buried beneath arcane phrases whose meaning escape me, but this is not so of Mitrani's vivid vignettes. I come away feeling I know this patient; I have met her. How do I have this sense? It is because Judith's own heart throbs. She lets me feel her pulse; I feel it racing when she is talking about Alex, it slows down as she is with Lily and races again when she is with Cora. She reveals her own charming feminine egotism as Carla enters her room after the weekend. Has she put her mascara on properly? And what about the lipstick? Has she put it on crooked? We all know, even me a man (!), how we feel in the face of someone elegantly attired. But Mitrani, allowing us into her inner chamber, brings these human encounters to life. We are not just in someone's drab consulting room, but in a living wrestling match with humans who test us to the limits; testing not just our emotional strength but also the subtlety of our reflective processes. I say "our" misguidedly. I should have said "her"—Mitrani's—and that this inner manner is then an inspiration to "us".

As all of us who are familiar with Mitrani's work know that a book of her essays will contain an investigation of autism and we are not disappointed. She follows faithfully in the footsteps of Frances Tustin and yet, as in all her essays, she goes further. She truly captures those early traumas in the infant's life and sees, with an acute eye, the way they continue to affect behaviour. Those encapsulated parcels of imprisoned life that although hidden away effect and distort the person's perception and thinking; those sharp icicles that penetrate the heart and prevent that warm outgoing that initiates a relationship before any word has been spoken. Furthermore, she homes in on that elusive thing: what is missing? Why are things not happening in the hoped-for way? The greatest traumas, I am sure, are not the obvious cruelties and abuse so focused upon by the media and by psychologists, but when a crucial emotional element has not been given and that the patient is suffering on account of its absence. Judith is innately sensitive to this. She looks for what is missing and through observing the most subtle bodily cues finds what has never been seen before and, the very act of finding, begins to foster the missing ingredient.

I said at the beginning that this is a book not to be read but to be lived. Interpretations that transform life do not only happen in the consulting room. They can come from the communications of a person in a lecture, in a painting or in a book. There is one thing that Mitrani highlights in this book that struck me in the heart. I understood something that I had not realized before. It was therefore a powerful interpretation. So I know at least one person who has benefitted emotionally from what Judith communicates in this book. Even if it were just one person so affected, the book will have been worthwhile, but I suspect that it will not be just one, but many.

This is a book not to be read, but to be lived.

Neville Symington

INTRODUCTION

Over thirty years ago I read—for the first time and with great interest—a paper by Sigmund Freud (1907) on Jensen's novel *Gradiva*. The name Gradiva means "she who steps along." In Jensen's story, a young archeologist, by the name of Norbert Hanold, suffers from delusions and is eventually helped to unravel the mysteries of his past and of his present. Hanold is convinced that his childhood sweetheart, Zoë Bertgang, is the living embodiment of a work of art he has seen in a museum. Rather than challenging his delusion, Zoë-as-Gradiva "steps along" with Hanold, and thus gradually enables him to disentangle truth from fantasy through what Freud called "cure by love". So it was that Gradiva/Zoë—once felt to be the source of Hanold's malady—eventually becomes the agent of its resolution and his subsequent return to health.

In his paper, Freud artfully made the analogy between the burial and excavation of Pompeii and the expulsion and re-emergence of Hanold's early psychic experiences, all while developing a stunning case for his argument that dreams and delusions are mental events imbued with meaning. What I made of this extraordinary tale, and Freud's telling of it, formed the basis for my concept of "taking the transference", the centerpiece of this book. A replica of the *bas-relief*, shown on the cover of this volume of essays, still hangs in my consulting room, as it had in Freud's own study, as a reminder of what I believe to be a central tenant in my work as an analyst.

By definition, the act of "taking the transference" requires that we attempt to follow, not lead, the analysand through her inner landscape. This requires us to "eschew memory and desire" (Bion) and to suffer the heartbreak (Tustin) that was felt but had never been suffered by our patients. On such journeys, it becomes clear that our intellectual understanding of or even our empathic attunement with what the patient is feeling and experiencing in any given moment is not nearly enough. Like Zoë Bertgang, we need to be able and willing to be cast in the molds determined by the patient's early beginnings, still alive and operating in the present. The analytic function also requires that the we allow for and bear a tentative blurring of boundaries between ourselves and our analysands' internal objects, while at the same time maintaining an acute ability to sustain a sturdy degree of observing ego necessary to implement our interpretive function.

I have been convinced that any conscious attempt at "role playing" or premeditated "going-along" with the analysand is bound to be experienced by the latter as insincere and may even increase persecutory feelings and the defenses against these. Our own "as-if-ness" fosters falseness in the patient. However, the temptation is mighty, for while being "real" with the patient the analyst risks exposing herself to an awareness of her own vulnerabilities and the dangers to herself inherent in such an awareness; being real opens us to a return of those previously buried happenings, memories, and experiences that we had hoped to put behind us. We are also called upon to re-examine our relationship to and identifications with our own parental figures.

On another subject, the reader may notice that I frequently refer to a patient in my interpretations as a "little-he" or myself as a "mommy— or daddy-analyst" and the like. I make use of this language, perhaps because I have found it is helpful when addressing certain aspects of a patient and his experiences, as these are communicated both verbally and especially non-verbally. Indeed, the way in which I intuitively perceive a given patient, at any moment in time, is the product of his attempts to communicate deeply buried states of being. Such communications coalesce into a portrait that takes shape on the canvas of my imagination. Perhaps the more primitive the mode of expression and the more limited the verbal articulation by the patient, the greater the need for the analyst to monitor his inner responses in order to apprehend the *process* as well as the *content* of the analytic moment.

This book, both as a whole and in part, was inspired by the many questions I was required to field in over two decades of teaching Klein and her followers in various psychoanalytic institutes here and abroad. My pupils' enquiries mainly revolved around the "why" of things, and I was challenged to think about and to clearly formulate my reasoning and philosophy—why I did what I did—and to delineate the roots of my personalized version of the analytic method.

What the reader will find in these chapters is not intended to "manualize" the practices or procedures of psychoanalysis. It is rather designed to stimulate questions in, to begin a discussion with, to open the minds of, and to allow the reader to bear witness to one analyst's struggles within her own heart and mind in the course of working analytically. Like the *bas-relief* of Gradiva, it is my hope that my scribbling may afford the reader a multidimensional view of my attempts to circumnavigate the multifaceted domain of the unconscious.

I also hope to illustrate how the art/discipline of "taking the transference" may be put into service from the first contact with the patient onward: to demonstrate that interpretation in the here-and-now does not have to be "premature", whether the patient knows nothing of analysis or even if he believes that he knows all about analysis, and that the wisdom derived from the work with psychotic adults and autistic children—bequeathed to us by the masters Freud, Klein, Bion, and Tustin—can help us to reveal the mysteries that lie in the depths of ordinary souls and may teach us something about the significance of the smallest detail of our work.

I suppose that each analyst, with her own divergent life experiences, might view each patient in very different ways; such is the individual nature of each analytic couple. The value of every permutation of analyst and analysand, like the value of any interpretation, can only be assessed in retrospect and in the light of both the patient's experience and his ever-growing ability to function in post-analytic years. However, I am convinced of the importance of a *willingness and ability to allow ourselves to be transfigured by the patient* as a first step to *transforming his experiences* such that he may become confident enough to suspend the psychic and bodily constraints of omnipotence, originally intended to bind him together; so that he can relinquish a sensation of immortality in exchange for a true sense of humanity among and with other human beings.

CHAPTER ONE

Listening for the emergence of infantile dependency*

> Ultimately, a science stands or falls in proportion as it is a valid technique for discovery, and not by virtue of the "knowledge" gained. This last is always subject to supersession; indeed, supersession of findings by new findings is the criterion by which vitality of the subject is judged.
>
> —Bion, 1957, p. 190

Introduction

During the course of analytic practice—treating patients and supervising other professionals—I have found that, as a rule rather than an exception, the lion's share of today's patients come seeking psychotherapy on a once or perhaps twice-weekly basis, whether or not they are aware that they have been referred to a "psychoanalyst". Few if any

---

*A version of this paper was presented at the fortieth winter meetings of the American Academy of Psychoanalysis in Phoenix, Arizona, on 6 December 1996 and was previously published as "Analytic listening, transference interpretation, and the emergence of infantile dependency: Do we really need to 'educate' patients about analysis?" in 1997 in *The Journal of the American Academy of Psychoanalysis*. Vol. 25 (1): 1–13.

prospective patients know much about "analysis", let alone that it is traditionally conducted four or five times per week, with the patient reclining on a couch, and the analyst seated out of sight behind them. In light of this fact, some analysts seem to suggest that we need to educate patients *about* psychoanalysis in order to encourage them to go along with the program. Some even speak about "converting" a once or twice weekly psychotherapy into a four or five times per week analysis in order to provide a "control case" for the sake of a candidate's training requirements.

However, perhaps by listening to a patient's anxieties and her needs, desires, and fears for and about closeness and dependency, and by interpreting these in the immediacy of *the transference*—and by that I mean the dynamics of the here and now relationship between patient and analyst as it is being transformed moment by moment in the hour, and as it is expressed right from the first hour of contact—we may be able to give the prospective patient a first hand experience of analysis; that is, a sampling of our capacity to closely hold and contain her both firmly and tenderly in mind.

In this manner, we may be able to convey that we *welcome* and thus may *facilitate the emergence* of the infantile aspects of the patient, which are perhaps those dimensions of the personality most in need of contact and understanding. By doing so we may also be able to relieve our new patients of their inclination to hold onto us with their eyes as well as their compulsion to stoically toughen up between what they feel must be infrequent and tenuous encounters with an unknown and unknowable stranger.

Here, I am emphasizing the need for "learning from experience" (Bion, 1962b). This must take place, right from the inception of the analytic process, if there is to be a viable atmosphere in which the patient is truly able to grow; For just as the infant, in the process of discovering the world, can find and move about out of his own sense of agency only when he feels safely held in the attention and gaze of a mother who follows his every move, so the patient in the process of discovering his internal workings—his emotions and his own mind—must feel free to explore without suffering the paralyzing dreads of becoming lost in the act of compliantly following the analyst's lead. For the analysand, knowing "about" must never supersede being and experiencing, just as the analyst's desire to teach analysis must not be permitted to supplant his therapeutic function. In the following clinical examples, I will demonstrate how some patients may come to "feel free" to ask—directly or indirectly—for additional hours, and to wend their way organically to the couch, rather than to be guided there didactically by the analyst.

Anthony

A single man in his early thirties, Anthony was referred for therapy by a colleague. During the course of our first two meetings, which took place on a Monday and Thursday of the same week, Anthony sat in a chair across the room from me. He quite calmly and matter-of-factly presented a very organized history of his "very ordinary" early childhood, education, and career, as well as a description of his relationships up until our meeting. Nearly emotionless, he ended each of the interviews right where he had begun: with a simple statement that he wanted to see a therapist because there was something that did not "feel quite right."

I suggested to him that he might be letting me know that he wished to continue with me for now, although I he did not find me very comforting, "not quite right." He smiled at me in a boyish way, seemingly pleased that I had noticed that he was not "mad about me", that I would take responsibility for bringing this up, and that I was not put off by his lukewarm reception of me.

Anthony seemed to be deeply unhappy and alone, in spite of what appeared to be an uneventful childhood and university experience, and some satisfactory—if not intimate or close—relationships with both male and female friends. I had a discomforting sense that there were some aspects of Anthony's experience that we had not yet arrived to in these interviews, something that he was helpless to "know" and to tell me about. This feeling was especially strong in me at moments when there would be a pause in his otherwise smooth narrative. During these pauses, Anthony seemed to focus his gaze on my couch, positioned to the left of me against the wall opposite from the chair in which he sat. He said he felt "oddly comfortable" with me today, and he wanted to make another appointment for the following week, although he did not know just then what we might accomplish together.

In our very next meeting, he reported the following dream:

> He is sitting in a room when he suddenly notices a baby in the room with him. He feels that he is meant to be watching over the baby as it

is lying in a crib, but he immediately senses that there is something wrong and begins to feel anxious. He notices that the sides of the crib have either been left down or are missing altogether. Only the two ends are in place. He also notices that the baby's head is not supported and it seems uncomfortable to him. He thinks that the baby needs a pillow or a cushion but wonders at the same time if very little babies can suffocate with a cushion. He looks across the room from where he sits and sees a pillow on a couch, but feels suddenly unable to move to reach it. His arms and legs feel weak and unsteady and he knows he needs help, perhaps to pull up the sides of the crib so that the baby won't fall out. He notices a woman sitting in a black leather chair, not far from him. He has some thoughts that she might be able to help, but is unsure that she would want to. He thinks "she would need to carry me over to put the sides up, but what if she doesn't want to, or perhaps she can't". He feels hesitant at first to ask the woman for help. Finally he calls out, but she can't hear him and he wakes up frustrated, crying.

After what felt like an awkward moment, Anthony said that he didn't know what the dream meant. He didn't have much experience with babies. After a brief silence, he said that the black chair in the dream was something like the one that I was sitting in. Then he paused and looked away from me, directly at my couch. He said, "You know, that's an odd piece of furniture! It looks rather like a cot, not like a couch at all". He noticed that there were no cushions at the back, only at one end. He wondered if people really lie down on "those things".

I said that it seemed that, like in the dream, there might be a baby-he who needed watching over, a little one who had suddenly appeared after our encounters last week and who I had left him alone to care for since our last meeting. I added that I thought that perhaps he'd been worrying that this baby was in danger of falling, with only the ends of the week in place. With eyes wide and an upward curve in the corners of his mouth, Anthony seemed surprised and interested in what I was saying to him. I continued, wondering aloud if he might be expressing a wish to ask for my help to secure the baby-he with two more hours per week as a way of supporting his mind and giving him both a sense of comfort and a feeling of safety. But perhaps he was also expressing a concern that I could not nor would not be able to carry him over, and was also somewhat afraid that so much contact between us, like a cushion in the crib, might be too suffocating.

Anthony responded sheepishly, confirming that he had indeed been wondering if anyone ever came to see me that often. Then he had had the thought that he might not be able to afford to come more frequently and that I probably wouldn't agree to adjust my fee to accommodate him. He had also wondered many times during our sessions in the previous week if he could lie on the couch and imagined what it would feel like if he did, but it had seemed too scary then even to ask me about it.

After a pause, Anthony said that he had just remembered something that he had previously forgotten to mention. To my surprise, he told me that, as a baby, he had been adopted. He had been told in his early teens that his birth parents had been too young and poor to keep him and they had given him up at birth. He said that he now wondered why he had not given this much thought over the years until now. It just was what it was and did not strike him as significant.

I told Anthony that perhaps the missing parents of his birth were like the sides of the crib that were missing. Perhaps he might be telling me that we needed all four sides—four hours per week on the "cot" with the pillow—so that he could feel safe with and comforted by me while he gave some thought to these childhood losses, even though it was clear that we would need to be mindful of a baby-he that might be in danger of being overwhelmed, both by such close contact with me, and also by his feelings about what he had missed long ago and was more recently experiencing as missing.

One might see, in this example, how a dream—presented in the very beginning of the treatment—can readily be taken up in the transference; how this works to mobilize additional unconscious material while establishing a closer connection between analyst and patient, thus affording the patient an experience of the analyst's willingness to contend with a burden the patient has felt unable to bear on his own. One can also see how such anxiety-ridden issues of frequency of sessions and the use of the couch might be heard in the patient's material and addressed early on in the work.

Of course, it is not always the case that a desire for greater frequency of hours or a curiosity about the couch will develop this early in the treatment. Many patients work up to this realization more gradually, as trust in the analyst's ability grows slowly. I will now give an example of such a case brought to me for supervision by a colleague.

Cora

Cora was in the process of undergoing intensive fertility treatments—including artificial insemination—when she began analytic therapy twice weekly. Within a few weeks Cora's material began to speak to a desire for "more frequent treatments, which were needed to facilitate conception." The analyst told the patient that she thought that she was also speaking about a felt need for more frequent meetings, in order that the analytic couple might be able to conceive of a baby-Cora that wished to be brought to life in the mind of a mother-analyst. The patient was very moved by this interpretation and the frequency of sessions was subsequently increased to three per week.

During several months of treatment, there was evidence in the patient's material that she experienced herself and her analyst as "growing more and more compatible with each other." The material also spoke to Cora's sense that her analyst was becoming more receptive and "able to conceive" of her. During this time the analyst felt that she could better understand and could now begin to formulate and to transmit in a timely way some rudimentary understanding of her patient's most primitive fears. Each week, over the four-day break, the patient would become seriously depressed and hopeless and the material presented during this time seemed to throw up images of a baby being dropped, aborted, or drained away in a bloody flow.

Cora brought material conveying her sense of a womb that was not adequately constructed to sustain an embryo, which would consequently be "sloughed off soon after conception." Complaints that the fertility treatments were wasted, the money spent on these flushed down the toilet, and the feeling that her fertility doctor was not available when needed, lead Cora's therapist to interpret these communications as expressions of the disillusionment with the analyst suffered by the patient during the too-long four-day weekends, and her experience of the bloody battles that she would attempt to engage her analyst in on Mondays when she returned enraged after the break. This line of interpretation seemed to open the way for the patient to be more direct with her therapist about her discontent, and this new understanding once again seemed to be connected to Cora's request for an additional hour.

Although still sitting up, now Cora began to bring dreams of a baby needing to be held in her mother's lap and in her arms, close to the breast; of an infant with a heavy head, too little to sit up; of fears of predators attacking from behind; of a father who fondled her, and a mother who came at her in a jealous rage with a knife, while she lay prone and helpless in her bed. Taking these dreams up in the transference—as an expression of Cora's wish to be close to her therapist, to lie on the couch, as well as her fears of being vulnerable if she did so—finally enabled the patient to use the couch and the subsequent deepening of the transference relationship, in all its many positive and negative forms, was further facilitated and within a short time the patient requested a fifth hour.

Financial considerations

Next I would like to speak about those patients who quite frequently become aware of their desires for more contact with the analyst early on, just as Anthony did, but who feel financially unable to increase their hours. Some might think of this as an early resistance in the treatment. But I would like to address a different problem: that of resistance in the analyst. At times the analyst may unwittingly avoid addressing such material, especially that aspect of the patient's material that speaks to the need and/or the desire for more contact. When I have pointed this out to my supervisees, they often speak to a concern that, by interpreting their patients' desire or need for more frequent sessions, they might only be tantalizing them.

The following example may illustrate the importance of "telling it like it is" with respect to our patients' psychic reality, regardless of the external reality of their situation, since an enormous amount of work can and must often be done to remove adjunct obstructions to increased contact, as these are interwoven into and bound up with an external fiscal reality. In the process, financial impediments may also be ameliorated, as it was the case in the analysis of a patient I call Lilly.

Lilly

A twenty-eight-year-old graduate student, Lilly entered therapy on a once-weekly basis, referred by the clinic. However, it soon became apparent, in the material presented in the first few hours of the treatment, that the chronic depression of which the patient complained was characterized, in part, by hopelessness about the prospect of ever achieving a close and caring relationship. The contemporary version of what I took to be an early hopelessness was expressed in terms of her relationship with a man whom she had been seeing for a number of years. She had hoped, almost from the beginning, that this relationship would lead to marriage and "having a baby". However, we soon came to understand that this also represented a deep unconscious longing for such closeness with me—a steady, analytic marriage and the creation of an analytic couple that might be capable of conceiving of and bringing to life a baby-Lilly who could then develop and grow into a creative individual. Just as Lilly's paramour had shied away from serious considerations of marriage and children because of financial deficits, seeing her only once a week, Lilly feared, in the transference, that I too might refuse to commit to a true couple-ship and to participate with her in parenting the baby-her.

My interpretation of Lilly's need and her fear that it would never be met, because she felt she had too little to offer me, seemed to diminish her sense of helplessness, and within weeks she was able to see her way clear to obtain a second part-time job in order to pay for an additional hour each week, which she also felt encouraged to ask for.

Now Lilly began to speak about her parents, who partially supported her in her graduate studies. Although she was in contact with them, she actively avoided and therefore had little to do with her younger sister, who had a lengthy history of depression and eating disorders with multiple suicidal attempts for which she had been frequently hospitalized. I took this up as pertaining to a feeling that I was only partially supporting her, referring to the two hours per week, and her feeling that this situation left a very ill sister-half of herself un-helped, left out of touch in the treatment along with a profound sense that it was I who wished to avoid contact with that part of her.

Although Lilly had at first only briefly referred to her sister and the intense nature of the competition between them, dreams as well as some memories unearthed by or alluded to in the analysis of the transference now began to aid us in fleshing out some of the complexities of this relationship with the sister and its numerous unconscious internal counterparts enacted in the transference relationship.

For example, during one Monday hour, Lilly was telling me about a growing sense that her boyfriend did not like babies. This was troubling, as it seemed just one more piece of evidence in support of her fear that she would never have the baby she so wanted. When I pointed out to her that she might perhaps be in despair over the suspicion, which had grown in her over the breach in our contact, that I did not like the baby-her and how unwanted she had been made to feel by me, she recalled that she had never had a baby-doll when she was a child, and had been afraid to ask her parents for one. This thought reminded her that she had not been allowed to see her baby-sister until the sister was old enough to walk, and she had taken this to mean that her parents were fearful that she might harm the new baby in some way. Over a number of hours we came to understand that she had been convinced that it was dangerous for her to come directly into contact with a helpless, needy baby-part of herself, and that she had been keeping this baby-she out of sight and out of mind for protection. However, it seemed that in spite of this, there was also a Lilly who wanted to have contact with this baby-doll-sister, but was afraid to ask for it, just as she was afraid to ask for more contact with me.

Lilly went on in the same session to say that she had been grocery shopping when she noticed a girl. From behind, this girl looked so thin and emaciated that Lilly thought to herself that she must be very ill. Once the girl turned around, Lilly recognized her as her own sister, but was so taken aback by her frail condition that she hid herself from view until her sister left the store. Lilly's report of this incident lead us to better appreciate how persecuted she felt by the sight of or insight into the state of that baby-her, starved and neglected over the years, and of how she continues to hide from this aspect of herself, which perpetuates her terrible sense of guilt.

Following this session, Lilly reported a dream in which hundreds of little mice were running loose in a diner or market in which she worked. In the dream she was ordered by her "boss" to destroy the mice with a broom. At the counter was a customer playing a game of tiddledywinks. She was angry that this customer just wanted to talk, but would not help her to eradicate the mice. She was able to kill one of them, but the others got away. It soon became apparent to me, and thus I said, that Lilly was quite angry at me for not helping her to kill off her mousy, run-away infantile feelings of hunger and dependency, which a very bossy part of her orders her to destroy, and that she felt my desire to talk with her about these feelings was like some wasteful and idle game I wanted her to play with me, but that I would do nothing to help her with her task.

One week after this session it became more clear that Lilly's sister also represented a psychotic, out-of-control, and suicidal part of her that she was terrified to associate with and was painfully ashamed of; an envious, greedy usurper that threatened to take away or, more accurately, to takeover her creative capacities; as well as a stunted or as-yet-undeveloped part of Lilly that was always holding her back.

In the transference, I soon became all of these things to Lilly. During this period, she often feared she would destroy me with her hatred; that I would take away some good experience, which she'd had in school; that she would be made to feel ashamed if someone found out that she was in treatment, or that I was holding her back in her progress in the analysis due to my incompetence. Associated with the latter, was a maternal transference in which Lilly experienced herself either as a "smart baby" who had to take care of a feckless Mother-me, educating and organizing me as well as picking up after me in my mindless incompetence, or as a "stupid, ugly, messy baby", unwanted, abandoned and neglected by the Mother-me. In this way Lilly seemed to fend off anxieties related to envy of her caretaking object (when she could experience me as dependent upon her), as well as the pain of gratitude (when she could feel that I had drained away all of her resources).

I was also experienced at times either as a diabetic Father-analyst in a state of self-inflicted coma: unconscious, mindless, and speechless (especially during my silences) or as a cruel, heartless, erratic, and incomprehensible Father-analyst (when she experienced my interpretations as abusive and meaningless). Lilly's reluctance to expose hostile feelings toward me seemed to stem from some early experience with her father who seemed to be quite authoritarian as well as physically abusive with her. On one occasion, Lilly had struck back at her father during a particularly cruel incident in which he had pushed her to the floor and kicked her. Lilly's attempts at defending herself served only to arouse further violence on the part of the father. It seemed that, during this period, Lilly's silences served as a means of protecting herself from those interpretations felt to be violently attacking of her.

Now it appeared that Lilly's initial inability to be direct with me—regarding her needs and wants and also feelings of rage in the face of the inevitable frustrations inherent in the analytic setting and the limits of the relationship—seemed to be related to a well-remembered prohibition by her mother against "drinking directly from the milk carton." Lilly's oblique style of reporting material and responding to interpretations seemed to resemble the bent straw in the glass from which she recalled being made to drink her milk as a child. During this period, she would often report that whenever she would call home to speak to her mother, her father always answered the phone and thus she had to pass by him to get to her mother. This seemed to be a current-day representation of Lilly's sense of a circuitous contact with her mother, which always had to be screened by the father and could proceed only with his consent. It was clear that her experience of me as unavailable echoed an early experience in which the mother was compelled to put the needs of the father, as well as those of the new baby sister, ahead of the still dependent little-Lilly.

In spite of such barriers to our connection, around the anniversary of the first year of the treatment Lilly began to bring material related to themes of containment. For example, she reported seeing a "baby bag snow suit for sale in an L. L. Bean Catalogue," which approximated her dreams of being safe and warm. She imagined that there might be a feeling of claustrophobia or some constriction of movement associated with this suit, as there did not seem to be space for the hands and feet to move about freely (i.e., no adequate articulation), but mostly it just seemed to her to offer safety and warmth.

Soon Lilly began to express not only her angry feelings toward me, but also the sense that I could contain some unbearable excitement that she had experienced regarding some very positive developments occurring at that time in her life. She seemed to be increasingly able to differentiate the me she experienced in the transference from the me she experienced as a new object who could be trusted to articulate and to contain rather than to distort or restrict her experience and her development.

Lilly's feelings of being held in a caring and safe ambiance in the analysis lead to an increasing awareness of her dependency upon me. In turn her increased longing for more closeness with me brought her nearer to those feelings of emptiness and loneliness and of having nothing inside during my absence. At first, Lilly dealt with this "empty feeling" by filling up her schedule, especially letting things pile up until the weekend so that she had to work around the clock to complete her school and work assignments. Although this served as an efficient way of warding off the terrifying feelings of falling to pieces, placing enormous pressure on her—like the constricting baby-bag snow suit that seemed to act as a second skin (Bick, 1968) that held her together—a now exhausted Lilly, feeling even nearer to the point of collapse, and she began to binge on food, which helped her to feel full inside.

Around this time, there also appeared a delusional jealousy toward the baby-Lilly that could depend upon me, as well as toward the adult-Lilly who was engaged in a creative intercourse with me in the analysis. This jealousy seemed to be located in that part of the patient that felt consistently left out and ignored, having to fend for and feed herself: a part of her that was so angry that she often refused my attention and availability. This refusal often took the form of the sort of silence that seemed to help Lilly to feel "hard and mean", rather than soft, vulnerable, helpless, needy, and defenseless.

Another aspect of Lilly's history now surfaced to present a complicated technical dilemma. For example, as her parents had not allowed Lilly to ride a bicycle or to cross the street by herself, she always felt left calling out for help, unheard and unattended to, but also prohibited from helping herself. Indeed Lilly felt that she had not been allowed to fall—or perhaps to fail—in the normal ways children do, so that she could have an experience of being picked up and of being capable of picking herself up when she did fall. Thus, falling—stunted in its early infantile form—remained a terrifying threat to her, and she seemed to have inherited her parents' fears on top of her own. Lilly thought that her parents—and myself in the transference—needed her to be safe for them, in order that they might be shielded from re-experiencing their own dangerous childhood traumas.

In part this experience of hers—that the parents needed her to protect them from an awareness of their own childhood experiences—seemed to be at the core of her identity and was indeed her reason for being, so much so that she seemed compelled to forfeit her own needs, including her need for more analytic hours, in favor of obligations and duties toward others. At the same time, it seemed that such rigidly adhered to commitments functioned as a secure and reliable structure, omnipotently created (Symington, 1985), within which Lilly could feel relatively safe from an overwhelmingly intense fear that "the world would otherwise come to an end." Without this preoccupation with the needs and desires of others she was faced with an empty space to be filled with "who-knows-what."

Possibilities were unbearably frightening for Lilly and she now experienced my silences as "the dangerous unknown." Many times I felt compelled to say something before I even have time to know what I was thinking or experiencing with her. It seemed that she merely needed to hear my voice in order to allay her fears that I was no longer there. Perhaps this was in part an expression of her need to have me fill up the spaces between us at times when she felt she might float away off the face of the earth into nothingness. My voice was felt to hold her together at such times, regardless of the content of my interpretations (Mitrani, 1992). My understanding of this, coming just prior to a holiday break, seemed relieving to her and lead to her admission that she hated to be aware that I was so important to her, since this awareness left her feeling unglued in my absence.

This period of the analysis seemed to free Lilly to think more and more clearly about her own needs, and seemed also to increase her sense of herself as a valuable person who deserved more than she had allowed herself. Subsequently she was able to seek and to find more appropriate and profitable employment and, with a dramatic increase in her income as well as her self-esteem, she was able to ask me for two additional hours.

Conclusion

In concluding this chapter, I wish to briefly say something about another category of patients who not infrequently come to us: those patients who bring us the remains of a previous analysis that has ended badly, either prematurely interrupted or in a state of impasse or stalemate. In these cases we must often be prepared to be the inheritors of a ready-made negative transference, which may act as a hard and impermeable protective barrier against further analytic contact, which carries with it the threat of still more disillusionment. Such prior disappointments in analysis dare us to try to explain them away, and the pressure from the patient to do so can be intense. However, if we get caught up in that challenge, all our efforts to reassure the patient—that this time will be different—usually fall flat. The patient who comes for "therapy" to heal the wounds of a "bad experience" in analysis needs to experience the difference between past and present, rather than be told about it.

Indeed, only by sustaining a tolerant attitude and by paying meticulous attention to gathering in the negative transference right from the first encounter with such patients, can we hope to win back their confidence in analysis once this confidence has been betrayed. These last examples will perhaps serve to get my point across.

Marc

Marc was referred for therapy after the termination of very long analysis. This was all I knew of him prior to his arrival—exactly on the hour—for our first session. When I introduced myself at the door to the waiting room, Marc was speechless and sullen. He walked past me through the hall, ricocheting off the walls. He seemed to be worried that he would come too close and touch me as he passed over the threshold. Eyes downcast, Marc sat in the chair across from mine, facing the couch, appearing quite depressed, emotionally beaten, battered and bruised by experience. I feared that he might be too sore to be touched.

Marc began by explaining that his former analyst's announcement of her intention to retire had precipitated his decision to end the analysis when he did. However he wanted me to know that he had terminated, not because his analyst was ending her career, but because he had become aware that the analysis itself had effectively come to an end many years ago.

Marc explained that he was married and that he and his wife had a new baby. He had begun dating his wife soon after ending a long relationship with another woman, which had been based upon and sustained by little more than an intense sexual attraction. He had not been attracted to his wife in the same way as he had been attracted to this woman, but had liked and admired her, feeling her to be a good person. He then said that although he loved his child, he thought that he should never have become a father. He often felt neglected by his wife and resented that there seemed to be no time for him to have a life—with or without her—since the birth of their baby. He added that, when his wife went out, he enjoyed the time alone with his child, although he resented that his wife seemed to be able to continue on with many of the activities she had engaged in before the baby's birth, while he, in contrast, felt stuck. Marc had not felt psychically alive for many years. He also experienced himself as a failure in his profession. He had often considered having an affair with his former lover so that he might feel at least physically alive. However, he was afraid this would mean the end of his marriage.

The patient concluded his monologue, telling me that a friend who was a colleague of mine and who had been impressed after reading a book I had written had informed him about my work. However, he warned that he still did not have much faith in anyone being able to help him. He also mentioned that he did not like the idea that my husband shared my office suite.

Over time I said to Marc that I thought that he was telling me that, on one level, he could not feel any strong emotional attraction to me and did not really feel capable of fathering the baby-he. He was afraid to be stuck in yet another dead relationship, like his previous analysis or the way he currently experienced his marriage. However, he seemed also to be afraid that if he did come to feel alive with me, that it might lead to the end of his marriage. I added that he might also be fearful that, should he begin to feel strongly about me, he would be vulnerable and might suffer devastation on the weekends when I go off and am felt to betray him with another, depriving him of life (just as he feels betrayed by his wife when she goes off with his child, or in identification with his baby, when she goes off leaving them both alone).

Marc looked pained and said that he thought that this was true, after which the pained look turned to one of extreme disturbance and agitation and he hastily added that he had "been fooled before." There was a brief silence after which he said that he had been thinking of a story he'd read in the newspaper about a good Samaritan who'd been in the wrong place at the wrong time and had suffered a fractured skull at the hands of a madman. He said that when he'd read this story, he'd felt oddly guilty for what had happened. I felt here that I needed somehow to address Marc's painful disappointment in psychoanalysis and the rage that was secondary to this disappointment, palpably seething underneath the surface of every word he had uttered. I told him that I thought that he was letting me know how crushed he'd been by the realizations about his previous analysis that had failed to bring him to life after so many years, and that he was afraid that, although on the one hand he sensed my intentions to be benign, he was so sore and raw that my words had been felt as incredibly painful and maddening and that he, in turn, now wanted to break me, and was feeling guilty and ashamed about that.

Marc left that first hour seemingly relieved and asked to begin twice weekly meetings the following week. Subsequent hours were filled with material that revealed a preoccupation with the physical qualities of my office and of myself—particularly my "large breasts" and the way my room was decorated—and his fear that he would not know if I were the wrong analyst for him. Phone contacts—initiated by the patient in a panic between these sessions—lead me to convey to him my sense of a little-he who was sticking to me for dear life, and in so doing, had lost his capacity to distinguish between the way he experienced me and the way I experience myself. It also seemed that my body—my physical presence or perhaps my "body of work"—so impressed him that he was afraid that he was attracted to this, rather than anything inside my mind that he could perceive through the way in which I spoke to him. Regarding my room, we came to understand that he was worried that if I was coordinated and pulled together thoughtfully, that I could not understand or might be put off by a little-he who was disorganized and in pieces and all over the place much of the time.

In one hour, Marc said he was not sure that he could see any difference between his former analyst and me and confessed that he was "always looking." I said that I thought that he felt he must keep an eye on me, to be sure I was not his former analyst. He laughed and said that he had thought, as I said this, that he did not wish to lie on the couch because he might forget who he is and get lost in a deep regression in yet another bad analysis. He added that he felt always "stuck up a horses ass, his head in shit." I said that perhaps he felt stuck with his head in my book, and that he sensed this was the wrong place for him. Perhaps he feared that I would not be able to generate any new thoughts just for him and in response to him. He was worried that I might treat him "by the book" and felt that he had to stay vigilant and keep his guard up. In the next session to my surprise, Marc decided to lie down on the couch, and soon afterward asked to increase his hours to four times per week.

Nell

Like Marc, Nell came in complaining of her former analyst's behavior, which she described as "manipulative and intimidating" and which she had remarkably endured under constant protest for a dozen years. She said that she thought that the analyst's "religion" and hers could never be compatible. Then she reported a dream she had on the previous night:

> She was at a party in a church and the people there were all in costume, like the masked ball in the *Phantom of the Opera*. They were not Catholics like herself, but actors. The Pope was there watching the people as they received the sacrament and took the Eucharist. Nell walked to the aisle to go up to receive the blessing and the Eucharist when she saw a man in a gold and diamond robe walking toward her. They walked up to the altar together. He looked like Christ but he was just an actor. Nell realized that he planned to desecrate God by taking the Eucharist away with him and not swallowing it and she cried out in an attempt to stop him.

Nell's association to her dream was that her former analyst had tried to take away her faith and that, although she knew that I too was an analyst, she had only come for therapy and was only interested in coming once per week. Although I also recognized and kept in mind the many implications of this dream, perhaps forewarning of a part of Nell that might only appear to take in what I might give her, and in so doing would desecrate our work together, I chose to say that I thought the dream was communicating strongly how she had lost faith in analysis and suspected that I was no "savior." I added that it seemed to me that she feared that not only would I be antagonistic toward her religion, but that analysis was merely an act of desecration against a personal God, perhaps some way of protecting and nourishing herself that she had organized throughout her life (Mitrani, 1995). She was fearful that I would not respect her or her means of surviving, but would merely use and exploit her for my own purposes, which were not her own.

Soon after this hour, Nell seemed to be able to let go of her preoccupation about her former analysis and took up a new process with me when she discovered that I might be capable of sufficient respect and adequate attention to all of her experiences and past discontents expressed in the present context of our relationship.

Such experiences, discussed in this chapter, have convinced me that careful analytic listening and consistent interpretation of the patient's experience in the here-and-now of the hour, right from the beginning, can facilitate the emergence of the infantile transference and obviate the necessity for "educating the patient" about psychoanalysis.

CHAPTER TWO

"A rose by any other name": working analytically in the face of authoritative statements*

When beliefs need some modification,
We make it with much trepidation,
For our world is then new, things seem all askew,
'Til we're used to the new formulation.

—Arnold Tustin, 1984, *personal communication*

Introduction

In Chapter One, I have written about beginning a therapeutic process with individuals who have little knowledge, if any, about psychoanalysis: those who have no notion of frequency of sessions or the use of the couch, nor any idea of the intimate relationship that can evolve within the bounds of what we call "the transference." In that chapter, I advocated listening for and addressing those unconscious communications of infantile happenings coming from the patient, and for indications

---

*A version of this paper was presented at a scientific meeting on 23 January 2014 by invitation of The New Center for Psychoanalysis, Los Angeles.

that such happenings are being relived in the immediate relationship with the analyst, right from the very first contact and onward.

However, in this chapter, I shall attempt to demonstrate some potential hurdles to beginnings with individuals who seem to "know all about" analysis, but who have yet to experience one. It might be said that beginning an analytic process, under any circumstances, is risky business for both analysand and analyst. As Bion put it,

> When two personalities meet, an emotional storm is created. If they make sufficient contact to be aware of each other, or even sufficient to be unaware of each other, an emotional state is produced by the conjunction of these two individuals, and the resulting disturbance is hardly likely to be regarded as necessarily an improvement on the state of affairs had they never met at all. But since they have met, and since this emotional storm has occurred, the two parties to this storm may decide to "make the best of a bad job." (Bion, 1979, p. 247)

Bion also warned that:

> Human beings clamour for some kind of authoritative statement to take the place of both ignorance and the exercise of curiosity; they hope, in that way, to put a stop to disagreeable feelings of ignorance and the repetition of the questions. The repeated questions may even be what is known as the repetition compulsion. But *repetition compulsion may in fact be a spark of human curiosity*, which has hitherto failed to be extinguished by any authoritative statements from whatever source. (Bion, 1979, pp. 229–230, my italics)

On the one hand, Bion seems to be suggesting that there is an aspect of human nature that is actively and quite insistently involved in a quest for psychic truth. I imagine that this is precisely the part of the patient with which the analyst, if he is so inclined, may be able to form a working alliance (Zetzel, 1956). On the other hand, Bion points out that there are disagreeable feelings—what he calls emotional turbulence—that are provoked by not knowing and by the "exercise of curiosity" motivated by the awareness of not knowing. Relative to this, there appears to be another aspect of human nature that strives to restore a sense of comfort, cutting off further enquiry by offering "authoritative statements." Indeed, both aspects of the personality can be found in analyst and patient alike.

It is also important to realize that each member of the prospective analytic couple comes complete with their own quota of authoritative statements. These may materialize in the form of preconceptions about anything and everything. Some of these preconceptions—the analyst's beliefs and past experiences, along with the significance and meaning we attribute to them—can often overlap with those of the patient, forming blind spots that occlude the opportunity to learn from experience.

I believe that a patient's "job description" includes the existence of a fair amount of conscious as well as unconscious preconception, bias, predjudice, and misunderstanding that may have at one time been useful, or he would not have lived to tell the tale to an analyst. However, with time, these protective barriers may have worn thin, becoming outdated, and as such may now fail to serve an individual as well as they once did, causing pain and suffering in the present. Thus, it comes to pass that these preconceived ideas call for some "modification."

However, in contrast, the analyst's job description calls for her own preconceptions—her pet theories, beliefs, and experiences—to be rendered more or less conscious, such that she has come to possess both a quantity and quality of awareness regarding their possible impact upon others. To put it another way, preconceieved notions in the mind of the analyst might best be harnessed in service of the analytic process, as they can rarely-if-ever be eradicated. Perhaps my experience with the patient whom I call Alex might clarify these points and may serve to stimulate the reader.

Alex on self psychology

Alex was a forty-eight-year-old married man and a mental health professional in training. He was referred to me for analysis many years ago by his former therapist, Dr. X, who had moved out of the area. Alex confided, in our first meeting, that his initial reason for beginning therapy with Dr. X (and his motive for eventually changing professions) was connected to the loss of his position in law enforcement when he was apprehended while taking advantage of female detainees, forcing them to disrobe in front of him in the course of their arrest.

This man was also quite candid about his desire for *anything but* a "Kleinian analyst" and expressed apprehension about the possibility that I was one. He knew that my institute had a reputation as, what he called, a "Kleinian bastion" in contrast to other analytic institutes in the area at the time. He clarified that he had been engaged in a "self-psychology treatment" with Dr. X, a man with whom he had felt very much at ease.

Alex somewhat bashfully confessed that before Dr. X had referred him to me, he had sent him to a candidate in training. Reportedly, this analytic candidate told Alex, after several sessions, that she was in supervision with one of the Kleinian training analysts at her own institute, and this analyst had recommended that she not accept Alex as a "control case," since he did not wish to be treated by a Kleinian. At this point, I had to wonder, why was Alex here? He assumed that I *was* a Kleinian, which was what he professed not to want: "anything but," he had said.

Not surprisingly, as I continued to listen to his story, I felt more and more "unwanted." I also felt uncharacteristically dull-witted and increasingly uncertain that anything I had to say would be of much value to Alex. As I sat stiffly in my chair, I was aware that I was feeling unusually self-conscious about my clothing, about the books on my sheves and the art on my walls, while this rather good-looking man—well dressed in a suit and tie—gazed about my room with a certain insouciance, speaking fluidly and with an air of confidence. It seemed that there was a particular atmosphere being created, which I came to suspect was contributing to my state of mind.

Just before the hour ended, I enquired with Alex if it was possible that, deep down, he might be *unbearably afraid* that I would reject him should he fail to meet my expectations. His response could only be described as a double take. His facade began to soften and before he left me that day, we had arranged to meet four days per week.

Immediately after that first interview, and in spite of my initial discomfort, I found that my impression of this man was strangely sympathetic: an impression that went a very long way toward mitigating the less than benevolent feelings I was to experience down the road, when it became clear that Alex often lied, fabricating material as bait, perhaps even seeking "Kleinian" interpretations by-the-book. At times, especially in the beginning months, I found myself falling into the traps he'd lay for me, which seemed to result in the destruction of any sincere emotional contact that had been established between us. By this I mean that Alex tended to respond to what I came to realize were my too-pat interpretations of his too-free-and-easy associations in a way that led nowhere, but which seemed to serve to tentatively put both of us at ease.

It did not take too long for me to realize that this was the point of the whole exercise. Alex would show me *what he wasn't*—perhaps his shell (Tustin, 1990a)[1] or his false and compliant self (Winnicott, 1956)—and I was supposed to chip away at this protective decoy such that his most genuine and painful experiences could remain intact, undisturbed and untouched.[2] We would go nowhere, inseparably stuck together in a state of at-one-ment that precluded any growth of the mind, but rather insured a sensation of suvival. As Bion reminds us, "The patient, especially if intelligent and sophisticated, offers every inducement to bring the analyst to interpretations that leave the defense intact" (Bion, 1970, p. 90).

During this period, we discovered that, *at least for Alex*, a "self-psychological analysis" represented a kind of pseudo-analysis, which might shore up and reinforce his failing defensive organization and restore his psychic equilibrium (Joseph, 1992),[3] while keeping at bay the terrors of the awareness of separateness and loss. When I wised up to this ploy, I learned to wait—in spite of intense pressure from the patient—until something that was new, both to myself and to Alex, could emerge. As I resisted Alex's nudge toward addressing the content of his associations rather than the process actually developing in the moment: when I gave myself the time to base my interpretations upon a carefully examined and well worked over bit of countertransference, set against the *context* of the session and woven out of threads of language *derived from* the subject matter of his narrative, Alex and I began to achieve some moments of meaningful emotional contact.

At first Alex appeared to experience these moments as shocks to his system. He was seemingly unable to respond to my interpretations with his customary compliance. Often I suspected that I had hit pay dirt when he was silent—almost dumb struck—after one of my infrequent-if-mindful and heartfelt comments, because he did not respond in his usual rapid-fire and obliging way, as if knowing in advance what I would say and how he should respond.

Alex's definition of a "Kleinian"

Now Alex was certain that I was a "Kleinian." At this point, the term Kleinian could be understood to mean one who does not mirror the patient's conscious thoughts; who does not act as a self-object: that is, who fails to interpret along those lines that are predictable and that feel smooth and easy; one who has something to say that the patient has not already consciously been thinking. When it seemed to Alex that I did not subscribe to his "orientation," he would object vigorously.

Much of the time, during this phase, Alex behaved as if he hated and feared me. Even so, he would intermittently bring material expressing an emerging sense of closeness to me and a feeling of conflict stirred up by the discrepancy between his analysis with me and his former therapy. This conflict was frequently expressed somatically. For example, he would often get "Charlie horses" that seemed temporarily to grip him, painfully interrupting the contact between us.

During the week prior to the sessions I will recap, Alex and I discovered yet another idiosyncratic meaning of the "Klein/Kohut" controversy that existed in his mind. At times, it seemed that I was perceived as the strong Kleinian/Mother-analyst who had my own thoughts and who left him longing for the kindly Kohutian Father-therapist he had lost. He was also convinced that, as a woman, I could not possibly understand and reflect his male existence. Alex was certain that only a man could "mirror" and provide the acknowledgement and validation he needed for his experiences.

As a "Kleinian mother", like Alex's own mother, I was seen as parochial and adamant about my views being the "correct" ones. He said that his mother had robbed him of his manhood. In the transference Alex often felt belittled by me, and his protection against this terrible feeling was to belittle and denigrate me in return: to "dress me down" and to "expose me" as a weakling. This was achieved in part as I had agreed to see him at a reduced fee. After some time, I came to learn that I had unwittingly colluded with his belief that I was "not worth much" and also that he was a "poor thing." However around the time that the following conversations took place, Alex discovered that I was published and had acquired copies of some of my papers from the hospital library.

The following excerpts are from the eighteenth month of Alex's analysis. They represent the Tuesday, Wednesday, and Thursday hours after a Monday holiday break that followed a week when the contact between us had been unusually lively and moving, if difficult to achieve. Relevant to the encounters as I recall them, it might be noted that Alex's sessions were scheduled at 2:15pm on Monday, Wednesday and Thursday and at 2:pm on Tuesday.

Tuesday: off balance or in the grip

The patient came two minutes before time on Tuesday, which was noteworthy as he generally arrived ten to fifteen minutes early in order "To think about what is on [his] mind and to prepare [himself] for the hour." When I went to collect him from the waiting room, he seemed surprised and a bit startled to see me. As he passed through the waiting room door, he looked me in the eye and exclaimed, "Oh!" with an awkward smile and a heavy sigh. "I guess I'm on Monday."

Once settled on the couch, he muttered the word "startled" followed by a long silence. Then he offered, "I'm thinking that you must be thinking 'what an unconscious idiot Alex is'". After a pause he said, "Well, I worked hard over the weekend. Still not enough got done, not enough time." It became apparent that Dr. Z [Alex's dissertation advisor] had called, and Alex was embarrassed that he'd neglected to return an earlier message. "I felt caught off balance," he explained.

I said that I thought perhaps he was also indicating that, when I came to get him from the waiting room, I had startled or even humiliated him, as if to intentionally remind him of our missing Monday hour, which he may have been working very hard not to notice as this left him feeling an idiot with little time to reconnect with either himself or with me.

Alex then put his hands over his forehead and there was a moment of silence, after which he said, "Funny, when you said that, I remembered wanting to call you to …" At this point the patient let out a earsplitting yelp and he cried, "Oh no! A cramp. Oh no!"

As the pain seemed to persist, I said "Could it be that, when you had the urge just now to reach out to me, just as you had over the weekend, some private 'advisor' cruelly punishes you, reinforcing the feeling of being an idiot. As this advisor tightens its grip on you, our delicate connection is broken."

As if to illustrate the process, Alex sat up to flatten out his cramping foot. When the pain subsided, he returned to his prone position and began to speak again. However his tone of voice had changed, he spoke quietly, dispassionately, nearly flat about his upcoming oral exams, the conversation with Dr. Z, and how he had been asked to go and talk to students in various classes at his graduate school to tell them about a clinical placement, which his advisor headed up.

Alex also spoke about two women with whom he was chummy at the hospital and about his sexual attraction to them, and also about one of his patients. He used the phrases "you know" and "I've talked to you about this before" several times in this rambling, undifferentiated report of the weekend's events. Finally, he recounted a conversation with one of my husband's patients, a woman whom he had met in the waiting room that my husband and I shared. This woman had been waiting for Alex to return from the restroom with the key, and had spoken about her new marriage and her upcoming move to another town.

Remarkably, in the telling, Alex had referred to my husband by the diminutive "Teddy," although I was certain that they had never been introduced. I felt irrationally irritated with Alex. I thought to myself "He's showing off, sounds arrogant, self-aggrandizing and cocky. Isn't he getting a little too familiar?" Then I wondered if he might be unwittingly baiting me to persecute him with some interpretation about how he belittles me.

Alex said, "Timmy called me over the weekend. I think you might recall that I've spoken to you about him before. He's that kid I see. A real burden. He went on and on with me. I finally had to cut him off. He made an emergency call to tell me that he had been pushed into a pool over the weekend and almost drowned. He said it was black and scary until someone pulled him out." After a pause Alex added. "You're silent, not saying anything. Now I'm worried about what you're thinking."

I said, "I wonder if you might be letting me know that you have no choice but to rescue yourself by clinging to familiar things and people that you can feel you know in order to keep your head above water while you wait for me to rescue you, perhaps with my words, from that scary black pool, the too-long weekend, where I left you unseen and unheard. Perhaps, when I opened the door to the waiting room, you suddenly realized what day it was and may have felt that, to add insult to injury, I was pushing you back into that black pool with a silent reproach."

Here Alex cut me off saying, "I just forgot." I said, "Perhaps it seems that I still don't understand how I cruelly cut you off, forgot about you and dropped you, which left you feeling that you must be a real burden to me."

With what sounded like a lump in his throat, Alex said, "When you don't say anything I get really anxious." He seemed thoughtful and even moved for a moment. Then suddenly he cried out, "Shit! I just remembered, I had a dream on Saturday. I was bending over a pool, I think trying to pull a drowning baby or a really little kid out of the water. The pool was one of those pools that's painted black, like a lagoon with rocks instead of tile and coping. The water was murky. Maybe the dream had something to do with the call from my patient."

I agreed and added, "I think you are also letting me know how black and foreboding some unfamiliar and murky part of your mind seems to you. Perhaps you're convinced you must rescue that baby-you from the darkness, the unknown aloneness in which you are afraid you could drown if you fall into it. You must pull yourself out of it right now, just as you did over the weekend and in your dream. It's dark and scary and you cannot see into it."

Silently wiping away his tears, Alex walked to the door when I indicated that it was the end of the hour, but he returned to takes some tissues from the box at the head of the couch and smiled at me in a sincere way before turning to leave.

Wednesday: the "pissing contest"

When I went to get Alex from the waiting room, he hesitated to get up, stretching nervously as he stood. He shuffled through the door with his head down, eyes averted. On the couch he said, "Didn't want to come in. (long pause) I was really angry about something that happened on the way over. I was driving on Charleville. I passed a van going in the other direction. I heard the driver shout 'Hey' so I stopped the car. He backed up and said, 'Wanna buy some speakers?' Shit!! I know all about that scam and I told him so. I yelled, 'I hope the cops get you!' Then he yelled back, 'Fuck-off, asshole' and he peeled off."

After a few moments of silence, Alex shook his head and went on to tell me about how well he had done at work with his patients, how he had seen things in them that reminded him of what he was going through. Then he reported having interpreted something about the weekend separation with Sammy, the boy who had fallen into the pool over the weekend: something that I had been telling him about himself the previous day. There was a certain arrogance in his tone, which was a marked shift from the first moments of the session. He commented on my silence with overt sarcasm and said that he wondered if he hadn't expressed himself well enough for me to make anything out of what he had said.

After a long pause the tone of his voice shifted back demonstrably. Any sense of condescension disappeared as he returned to the story of the van and the man who had attempted to sell him the stolen speakers. I felt just out of reach of what he was expressing, but had a strong sense that it was linked to what I had begun to address in the previous hour.

Alex exclaimed, "Oh hell, I guess I'm sort of ashamed that I got into a pissing contest with the guy." After expanding on that interchange he said, "I don't know why I'm so preoccupied with this shit." I said, "It seems you're quite embarrassed about another scam; perhaps one which a delinquent-you tries to perpetrate, that 'you' who is felt to be in some sort of pissing contest with me, perhaps in competition to see which one of us will gain access to the baby-you who was drowning over the weekend. It speaks to you, beckoning you back away from our connection. But it seems there is also a you who really hopes that I will 'catch' the thief who steals my interpretations and tries to sell them to you as your own."

After another long pause, Alex said "I don't know why, but I'm thinking about the route I take home from here. I always pass by the house of a friend I had in elementary school. I used to stay with him. He was bigger than me. A tough kid. I thought he'd protect me from the other kids that made fun of me at school 'cause I was short, but I never really felt good about him. We even slept in the same bed, but I always felt separate and alone. I'm also thinking about when I go back to the hospital after I leave you. I just flashed on Mindy. I think I was having a sexual phantasy about her, undressing her." When he goes on and on about this, I feel baited, even titillated. He sounds pulled together again and far, far, away.

I said, "Perhaps you're helping me to understand that what I just said let you down. Rather than protecting the little-you from that tough guy with whom you bunked-in overnight to keep you from feeling so lonely and unprotected, I may have left you exposed and ridiculed in my silence."

Alex seemed to want to respond to this as he turned his body toward me at first. Then he wrapped his arms around the pillow, silent, as if hugging a grudge. I said "I wonder if you might be silently dressing me down, perhaps needing me to know just how it feels to be the naked one who is powerless, vulnerable and alone? Maybe, for a moment, you were in contact with your loneliness, but when you feel exposed as the hour ends, I leave you no choice but to turn to something else, something that makes you feel tough and covers over your vunerability and tender feelings."

As it was the end of the hour I had no choice but to wait until Thursday for my patient's response to my attempt at understanding his experience.

Thursday: the pigeonhole

Alex began the hour by saying "When I came in just now I smelled something good. A really good smell of something cooking, and I think you—your perfume. It's a comforting feeling, being close to you." The sense of his contentment only lasted a few moments. Suddenly he cried out, "Oh Shit! Here it comes." He sits up with a cramp in his foot and, flattening it on the floor, trying to work out the knot in his muscle. When he lies back on the couch once again, his tone of voice is flattened.

"I was just thinking of this woman at school, Julie. She's thinking of coming over to our program. I was telling her about it. I really like her. She's in analysis. But I have some doubts about her too. I get the idea she's very Kleinian. Yesterday I was in the supervision group with Dan. I was a real motor mouth. I was very honest about what I sensed was going on, about my perception of the situation, my feelings about the case we were discussing. I couldn't stop making comments. I felt kinda funny. I made some comment about smearing faeces and I got sanctioned by the group."

I said, "I wonder if perhaps you were being sanctioned a moment ago by an inarticulate you who feels uncomfortable and embarrassed when you're open and honest about what you perceive here, about how you feel, even that sense of goodness you can have with me at times."

Seeming quite sincere, Alex said "Yeah. I really get on myself. Like this habit I have of picking my nose. Like some kind of little monkey. Huh! That's what my mother used to call me, little monkey. She says I liked to handle my food and stuff—that kind of shit. I don't know why I'm telling you all this. Maybe I think a Kleinian would like that stuff. You know, I've read some of your papers. And I feel kind of ashamed and humiliated to say that I just don't know what you are! I guess I've tried to pigeonhole you."

Although I felt some pressure to say something about how Alex was smearing me with good "Kleinian" stuff in a sort of pissing contest, and I was momentarily tempted to interpret in terms of Alex feelings of envy of my good smells, I believe this may have been a call to collude with an aspect of Alex that attempts to get me to sanction him, to take up the role of that aspect of his mind that ridicules and humiliates him, as the mother with the little monkey. However by doing this, I would have failed to sanction (in the alternative meaning of the word) that aspect of Alex who had loving, good, and close feelings, which were very present at the beginning of the hour.

Experiences with this patient had taught me that he tries to eliminate any feelings of closeness and goodness in our connection at the end of the week, perhaps because he believes that by doing so, it will be easier for him to contend with his awareness of separateness and loneliness over the weekend, by canceling out my goodness and capturing me in a pigeonhole through which he has some continuous access to me.

On the other hand, I was also aware that there was a certain tone of genuineness in his attempt to give me "good Kleinian associations" and so I said, "Perhaps you perceive that I've given you something good this week, something sweet and fresh, some good thoughts. It may well be that what you say about pigeonholing me is true, especially when you wish to keep tabs on me, to make sure I cannot get away from you. Might it be that you try to pigeonhole me so that you will know where to find me?"

A nod prompted me to add, "It may be that there is also a 'you' who would like to give me something good in return for the goodness you feel you receive from me. You try to give me some good Kleinian stuff, but you end up feeling humiliated by me—like a little monkey or a little baby—convinced that you don't have anything near as good to give as you get from me, which leaves you all the more embarrassed and mortified."

After some period of silence, Alex said that he just remembered something that happened that morning. "Mindy came into my office. She wanted my advise on a difficult case. She needed to unload. I rubbed her shoulders while we talked. It felt good that she looked to me to help and soothe her." I did not comment on this material, although I thought that, in the silence, he had found a way, by conjuring up the memory of Mindy, to once again transform those feelings of humiliation, which he finds so unbearable. I believe that my words had given him good reason to believe that he could pacify me as well.

Alex continued telling me that he was worrying about what he had said. "I wonder what you think of me. I'm afraid you think I'm trying to compete with you. Dr. X used to say I did that all the time. I had supervision with 'B' today. She was worried about having made some soup in the office for lunch. She said the smells remained in her office afterward. She was afraid it was unprofessional and told me how she tried to cover them up with perfume." Alex laughed at this thought, perhaps making some connection with my food and perfume smells. Then his voice dropped to a much lower register, his lip quivered, and he covered his face with his hand, wiping a tear from under his eye.

I said that I wondered if perhaps, as nice as it was to feel me with him, I also caused him to feel small by comparison. Alex nodded and there was a moment of genuine contact, after which he rolled onto his side and curled up tight. Some time passed and I said, "So, perhaps thinking about feeling big and important with Mindy helps to 'cover up' those painful feelings of shame and humiliation." But it also seems that you soon become fearful that I'll turn on you, and you're left saddened and hopeless that there's nothing good to take away with you—nothing to savor over the break in our contact.

Alex turned his face toward me and shouted "God, it is Thursday! This week felt so short." I said to Alex that I thought that, as we run out of time, he's letting me know that the "feeling" that I'm too small either to hurt or to help him is not only of his making, but a part of the reality of our too short week, which is not enough to sustain him over this weekend.

At the door, Alex asked with a sincere smile, "What's in a name? A rose by any other would smell as sweet. I don't know why I thought of that. Is it Shakespeare? Whatever! Next week, could we talk about arranging a fifth hour?"

Conclusion

Indeed, especially in the beginning, the analyst needs to be able to remain curious to discover "what's in a name." That is, what are the various latent meanings of what the patient tells us from the start—how he "names" himself, his former analyst/therapist, and how he categorizes us, even before the first contact and onward. What are we to make of our reaction, our first impressions? What interpretations can we construct and convey that will be useful to the patient in his endeavor to get to know his own mind as well as ours?

I will conclude with one last quote from Bion, who writes: "In psycho-analysis, when approaching … what we do not know, not what we do know—we, patient and analyst alike, are certain to be disturbed. ... In every consulting room there ought to be two rather frightened people: the patient and the psychoanalyst. If they are not, one wonders why they are bothering to find out what everyone knows" (Bion, 1976, pp. 4–5).

Notes

1. In earlier papers (Mitrani, 1992, 1994), I have expanded on the idea that rigidly held beliefs and intellectual functioning may be employed by adult patients as a "protective shell" in Tustin's sense of the term.
2. This false self is no doubt an aspect of the true self. It hides and protects it, and it reacts to the adaptation failures and develops a pattern corresponding to the pattern of environmental failure. In this way the true self is not involved in the reacting, and so preserves a continuity of being. This hidden true self suffers an impoverishment, however, that results from lack of experience.
3. "The patient consciously wishes to change, but dreads any disturbance to his sense of equilibrium, the way in which he deals with anxieties and defenses, the organization which he regards as best—this is his vertex" (Joseph, 1992, p. 237).

CHAPTER THREE

Some technical implications of Klein's concept of "premature ego development"*

> One could think of separation as the cause of the first idea of union; before this there's union but no idea of union, and here the terms good and bad have no function. For union of this kind, so important for the foundation of the mental health of the individual, the mother's active adaptation is an absolute necessity, an active adaptation to the infant's needs which can only come about through the mother's devotion to the infant. Less than good-enough adaptation on the part of a mother to her infant's needs at this very early stage lead ... to the premature ego-development.
>
> —*Personal communication from*
> D. W. Winnicott to M. Milner, 1952

The phenomenon of premature ego development was first introduced in Melanie Klein's (1930) seminal paper on the importance of the symbol forming function of the mind. In

---

*An earlier version of this chapter was read at the second international conference on the work of Frances Tustin in Caen (Normandy), France in April 2005 and was published in 2008 in *The International Journal of Psychoanalysis*, 88 (4): 825–842; published by John Wiley & Sons.

this chapter, I will first introduce several developments in modern, post-Kleinian thinking since the publication of that paper, which can be seen as offshoots of or complements to Klein's work. Included are my own thoughts, firmly rooted in that same discipline, on the specific link between this sort of precocious development and the deficiency of the experience of what Bion termed the "containing object."[1] Second and most significantly, as the main contribution of this work, I will put forward several implications for psychoanalytic technique with patients who suffer as a result of this aspect of early development gone awry and who have thus become difficult to reach. Throughout, I will present detailed clinical vignettes to demonstrate the ways in which my particular line of thinking takes shape in the analytic setting.

Klein's analysis of an autistic child

In her paper "On the importance of symbol-formation in the development of the ego," Klein (1930) presented findings from the analysis of a four-year-old boy that she called Dick. Although, at the time Klein analyzed Dick, Leo Kanner's (1943) seminal work on early infantile autism had not yet been published, one can ascertain from Klein's keen observations, which paralleled Kanner's to a remarkable degree, that indeed Dick would have been diagnosed on the autistic spectrum.

Klein introduced the concept of "precocious ego development" (Klein, 1930, p. 244) to sum up Dick's dilemma. She described this child's precocity as a case of "pre-mature empathy" (p. 244) for and "pre-mature and exaggerated identification" (p. 241) with the mother.[2]

> ... The genital phase had become active in Dick prematurely ... [Sadistic phantasies] were followed not by anxiety alone, but by remorse, pity and a feeling that he must make restitution. (Klein, 1930, p. 244)

Here Klein seems to posit that Dick suffered as a result of a far-too-early onset of what she would later call the "depressive position" (1935). In other words, in the transference, Klein observed and inferred Dick's untimely concern, as a very young infant, with issues related to the survival of his mother.[3] Although Klein had posited the existence of an ego from birth, and even before that in utero, in this work she made an important discrimination between normal healthy ego development on the one hand and premature pathological ego development on the other.

Additionally, something else quite remarkable stands out in Klein's narrative of Dick's case. Here she seems to explicitly appreciate and she clearly takes into account the impact upon the baby-Dick, for better or for worse, of environmental influences that coalesce with those constitutional factors[4] that are the predominant focus of her metapsychology and her specific model of the mind, that is, the role of innate envy, of the baby's congenital intolerance of frustration and of an in-born tendency to rely upon primitive omnipotence as a defense against elemental anxieties.[5] Elsewhere, in the more formalized and oft re-stated outline of Klein's model of the mind and its dynamics, the role that she accorded to environmental influences is not always apparent, and mention of these factors are generally relegated to a few footnotes or relies upon the reader's ability to read between the lines in the clinical material. All the same, these peripheral notations are especially significant and are relevant for the understanding of the plight of and the psychoanalytic work with the patients I discuss further on in this paper.

Nevertheless, a careful review of Klein's paper suggests that she thought that little-Dick's difficulties were the result of an "exceptionally unsatisfactory and disturbed time as a sucking infant" (Klein, 1930, p. 240). Additionally, Klein pointed out that although "[Dick] had every [physical] care, no real love was lavished on him, his mother's attitude to him being, from the very beginning, over-anxious" (ibid).[6] In this chapter I will return to this problem of maternal anxiety and will further extend Klein's work by linking this to a failure in the development of the containing function necessary to ongoing mental and emotional development.

Environmental impact

Additional examples of Klein's consideration of the impact of the mother's mental state upon the development of the infant's ego can be found in her 1952 paper on "Observing the behavior of young infants" in which she wrote that:

> Recent studies of prenatal modes of behavior ... provide food for thought about a rudimentary ego and the extent to which constitutional factors are already at work in the foetus. It is also an open

> question whether or not the mother's mental and physical state influences the foetus as regards ... constitutional factors. (Klein, 1952, p. 116)

Further on she concluded that:

> Feelings of frustration and grievance ... often focus in retrospect on privations suffered in relation to the mother's breast. (Klein, 1952, p. 117)

I believe that Klein's use of the word "privation" in relation to the mother's breast, rather than *deprivation* in relation to the breast-as-internal-object, indicates her cognizance of a primary deficiency in some essential environmental component necessary to the process of normal ego development and the establishment of the good internal object at its core.[7] Additionally, Klein's many references to the importance of "reality testing", for example in her 1963 paper "On loneliness", seem to attest to her conviction that the ongoing beneficent nature of the real external object provides an essential proof of the enduring existence of the good internal object, not only in infancy but into adulthood as well.

Furthering the study of premature ego development

Following on Klein's work, Martin James (1960) specifically defined premature ego development as a reaction to a mother who is experienced as preoccupied either by circumstance or by nature. James suggested that this prematurity is often manifested in a taking over of the maternal function in actuality, or starting out as though to do so, at a time when the mother is experienced as emotionally inaccessible. To illustrate his point, James wrote about an infant whose mother, while mourning the death of a brother, was unable to be affectionately and mindfully present with or to take delight in her baby. Thus the infant cried inconsolably, could not relax, and exhibited extreme hypersensitivity to her environment.

James emphasized that, while this mother was overwhelmed with and could hardly contain her own experience of grief, loss, and anxiety, she was unable to provide an effective filter for her baby's earliest experiences of loss. Thus, her infant had been prematurely pushed to identify with her in her state of mourning. This identification led to an extreme physical and emotional adaptation, a shell of pseudo-maturity behind which the once vulnerable infant retreated. Unfortunately James' patient, like Klein's Dick, was developmentally unprepared to deal with the complex anxieties associated with the experiences of guilt and loss encountered in a *pre-mature depressive position*, as such preparedness requires the aid and support of previously well established "good internal objects" at the core of the ego.

Indeed, Klein (1930) noted that amongst Dick's symptoms was the development of a "premature defense against [normal infantile] sadism" (Klein, 1930, p. 241). She underscored Dick's "severe incapacity to tolerate anxiety, such that he was incapable of any act of aggression" (ibid). This defense against sadism, in turn, led to a cessation of Dick's phantasy-life and a withdrawal from any ordinary means of reality testing. Klein concluded that any further moves toward development became inhibited when Dick retreated within the sensuous world of "the dark, empty mummy's body" (Klein, 1930, p. 245).

Now, one might ask what is the significance of all of this? I believe that it is important to remember that the infant's "normal sadistic impulses" (or what Winnicott (1946) called "pre-ruth": a term he used for developmentally appropriate "ruthlessness") give rise to paranoid-schizoid anxieties, which in health are dealt with by increasingly complex phantasies. Initially these phantasies are those of splitting and projective identification, later on developing into displacement and symbolic equation. The latter eventually form the basis for the baby's increasing interest in new objects and his ability to symbolize. I propose that the "infantile sadistic act of aggression" is not only the evacuative act of intruding into the mother's body that constitutes the elemental phantasy that we know clinically as *projective identification,* but also the corresponding introjective phantasy connected with sucking and with feedback coming from the mother.

One can infer, from the material presented by Klein, that Dick may have accurately perceived that his mother, in her over-anxious state, was unable to receive and to deal with his own infantile anxieties. Under these circumstances, what Dick may have re-introjected was an object that had little mental space, one that could not take-in and accommodate his primordial anxieties. When this state of affairs persists chronically, not only does the infant take back his own undigested fears, but some of the mother's conscious and unconscious fears as well, resulting in what Bion called a "nameless dread."[8]

Dick apparently experienced this nameless dread as a mother in bits, the consequence of his biting orality. This situation was reflected in his early feeding difficulties, his refusal to suck from his mother's breast, and later on, his rejection of any foods that required aggressive acts such as biting and chewing. It appeared that Dick's nascent phantasies of both projective and introjective identification had to be curtailed almost from the start. Thus, his internal world of objects became severely limited, experienced as the "dark empty mummy's body" (Klein, 1930, p. 245).

Clearly one can see that both the projective and introjective forms of identification are essential to normal mental and emotional development. The build up of the internal world of objects, the ego, and the capacity for symbol formation all depend upon these identificatory processes proceeding without undue inhibition (brought into play on behalf of the mother's survival). With this assumption I will now return, as earlier promised, to the problem of maternal anxiety, which is an essential factor at the root of the inhibitions that contribute to the hampering of projective and introjective identification. I will also link this to the failure in the evolution of what Bion called the containing function of the mind.

Bion's model of container–contained

In 1946, Klein defined splitting and projective identification as the developmentally normal aggressive means by which the newborn relieves itself of unwanted affects, objects, and parts of the self and through which he takes control of the mother in phantasy. Later on, in 1957, she introduced the notion that the phantasy of projective identification—when fueled by unconscious envy—serves to destroy the object of that envy.

Then, in 1959 Wilfred Bion began to expand and extend Klein's notion of projective identification to include normal non-verbal and pre-verbal forms of *communication* between mother and infant, something he referred to as "realistic projective identification". In one of his *Brazilian Lectures*, Bion said:

> Let us imagine that the baby is very upset and feels afraid of an impending disaster like dying, which it expresses by crying. That language may be both comprehensible and disturbing to the

mother .... Suppose the mother picks up the baby and comforts it, is not at all disorganized or distressed, but makes some soothing response. The distressed infant can feel that, by its screams or yells, it has expelled those feelings of impending disaster into the mother. The mother's response can be felt to detoxicate the evacuation of the infant; the sense of impending disaster is modified by the mother's reaction and can then be taken back into itself by the baby. Having got rid of a sense of impending disaster, the infant gets back something that is far more tolerable. Susan Isaacs has described a situation in which the baby could be heard saying something like "oo el, oo el", which the mother recognized was an imitation of herself saying "well, well". In that way the infant was able to feel comforted by a good mother inside, and could make reassuring, comforting noises to itself exactly as if the mother was there all the time. (Bion, 1974, pp. 83–84)

I believe that this is the essence of Bion's concept of the maternal containing function, which has been widely adopted in contemporary Kleinian circles and is, by now, well-known (see Mitrani, 2001). Furthermore, Bion's model of the container and the contained (1962a) helps us to further appreciate the importance of both projective and introjective identification in the development of the ego and implies that the mother's state of mind—and perhaps most of all, her capacity to deal with her own as well as her infant's anxieties—is the fulcrum upon which the baby's future mental health and his sense of autonomy pivots. In the interest of clarity, I will elaborate upon this model, as I understand it, and will elucidate its relevance to psychoanalytic technique.

Three essential components in the process of "containing"

In Bion's model, the mother—in a state of what Bion called "reverie"—first receives and takes-in those unbearable aspects of the infant's self, objects, affects, and unprocessed sensory experiences that have been projected into her in phantasy. Second, she bears the full affect of these projections on her mind and body for as long as need be in order to be able to think about and to understand them—a process that Bion referred to as "transformation." Next, having transformed her baby's experiences in her own mind, she gradually returns them to her infant, in due time and in detoxified form, as demonstrated in her attitude and in the way in which she handles him. In analysis, Bion referred to this last process as "publication," or what we commonly refer to as *interpretation*. Perhaps an example of this entire process may be helpful here.

Carla

In the third year of her analysis I noticed that, almost invariably when my analysand Carla returned from the weekend breaks, she would greet my arrival at the waiting room door with a warm and enthusiastic smile. Then she would scan my face quite intensely, passing through the doorway on the way to my consulting room. The intensity of Carla's scrutinizing gaze often left me feeling unusually self-conscious. Carla was very beautiful and always perfectly made-up when she came for her sessions, and frequently I was given over to wondering whether my lipstick was on crooked, whether I had forgotten to powder my nose, or perhaps had applied mascara to just one eye and not the other. These banal ruminations were discomforting and intractable, and I found myself tempted to dismiss them as irrelevant. However, as these were uncommon if not altogether absent preoccupation with others of my patients, I opted to allow them to brew a bit to see what percolated out of them. This lead to the emergence of some fleeting thoughts: might I be envious of this young and beautiful girl? Might Carla be looking for something in my face that might reflect her own feelings? Was I felt to be failing her in some way that was both disconcerting and implacable?

No matter how many times this sequence would occur, by the time my patient had settled on the couch, I noticed that her enthusiasm for me and her analysis had suddenly been transformed into a tough, leathery air of indifference and disgust, as if she resented having to submit to *my* "rigid requirement for yet another hour and another week."

One day I had the opportunity to turn our attention to this shift in her attitude toward me from waiting room to couch. I said that I wondered if the change might somehow be connected to feelings and thoughts provoked in her by what she seemed to see in my face when I came to the door. She replied with despair, "It could be, but I can't think how. After all, *you always look the same.*"

Carla then went on—as if changing the subject—to tell me that she had been happy that she'd managed to arrive in plenty of time to get to the restroom before her session. However when she found that "it was all locked up," she was left feeling as if she might burst open.[9]

Then, by way of denying the urgency of her need to relieve herself and the significance of her disappointment, she added resolutely that it was "*really* OK."

At that moment, it seemed to me that the story of the locked restroom contained clues to the meaning of her radical transition from joy in the waiting room to disdain on the couch. I now considered that Carla had been filled to bursting with positive feelings about our connection, feelings that she could barely hold inside when she arrived. However, she had soon been disappointed when she felt me to be emotionally shutting her out—just as she had felt shut out of the restroom—as she searched my face for signs of *my own joy* as evidence that I might have been open to the overflow of her excitement, that I might therefore be able to provide her with some relief from these as well as other (perhaps less positive) overwhelming feelings. Instead, she seemed to find me "… always … the same" or locked-up.

When I conveyed my thought to her, she nodded in agreement, so I continued, telling her that I thought that she might be bringing to our attention a very little-she, unable to bear that feeling of disillusionment, a thin-skinned little one who had consequently resolved to toughen up for fear of bursting open. Carla responded by saying, quite poignantly, that she had only hoped that I would be as happy to see her as she was to see me. I acknowledged her hope and also added that she seemed to need to feel that a flowing-over and joyous baby-she could be seen and held in my facial expression, so that she would not spill away and be lost again. I also offered that I thought that this need to be held together might be felt as so intense and urgent that—when it seemed to her that I *could not* reflect and reciprocate her joyous feeling for me—that she was compelled to transform herself to "match" what must have felt to her to be a locked-up, leathery-tough, mommy-analyst.

After a few moments passed during which Carla was silently licking her lips (as if after a satisfying feed), I went on to say that I wondered if this transformation was intended to enable her to create a sense that she could catch and hold herself by bringing us closer together with no gap in between. She wept softly and finally told me that, as I was speaking, she had flashed back upon the image of her mother's face looking just as it had when, as a very little girl, she would watch her with loving admiration as she sat before the mirror on her dressing table. After another, much longer pause, Carla then told me—for the first time—that when her mother was a child she had been disfigured in a terrible automobile accident and, as a result, her face had always looked strange, disgusted, and remote, with a leathery skin full of scar tissue resulting in a frozen, unchanging expression of disdain. Carla then tearfully expressed the painful realization that she could never tell if her mother really loved her.

It seemed to me that—in some dimension of her experience—the baby-Carla may never have had the experience of being lovable or of being held lovingly, safely, and responsively in her mother's gaze, as Mother's unalterable expression might have hindered her own ability to reflect her daughter's joyous states of ecstasy, admiration, and love for her and may have failed to adequately reflect Mother's own loving feelings.

Unfortunately for Carla, the ecstasy of oneness with the mother (Tustin, 1992) may well have been left uncontained, rebounding off the expressionless surface of her mother's face, an ecstasy apparently experienced as un-reflected in the mother's sense of herself. Here I am reminded of a passage by Winnicott (1967), who was admittedly influenced by the work of Lacan (1949) on ego development when he wrote:

> What the baby sees [when he looks at the mother's face] is himself or herself. In other words the mother is looking at the baby and *what she looks like is related* [in the baby's phantasy] *to what she sees there*. Many babies ... have a long experience of not getting back what they are giving. They look and they do not see themselves. There are consequences. First, their own creative capacity begins to atrophy ... most mothers can respond when the baby is in trouble or is aggressive, and especially when the baby is ill. Second, ... perception takes the place of apperception ... [it] takes the place of that which might have been the beginning of a significant exchange with the world, a two-way process in which self-enrichment alternates with the discovery of meaning in the world of seen things. (Winnicott, 1967, pp. 112–113)[10]

I could also imagine that Carla's mother—grief-stricken, abandoned, and betrayed, with little in the way of self-esteem and self-love to reflect back to her daughter—may have failed to confirm the little girl's *experience of her mother's inner goodness*. Thus, Carla's faith in and appreciation of *her own* inner goodness and beauty—lacking resonance with a sense of a good internal object—may have dissipated and faded away over time and she was left to contend with what had been registered as an obstructive and unaffected presence.

Carla's perception that I "always look[ed] the same" seemed to evoke, in the transference, these very early and ongoing painful feelings of being unlovable. At the same time, I became the receptacle for that inner maternal object with the frozen, disfigured face that manifested itself in the countertransference as my extreme self-consciousness and obsessive doubts about my make-up being lop-sided or missing, and indeed may well have affected my facial expression, contributing to a vicious cycle.[11]

As our understanding of Carla's experience deepened over time, the ways in which we saw each other and ourselves shifted. She began to feel better about herself and our connection, and we could begin to touch upon some of the omnipotent phantasies that contributed to the untoward sense of guilt and shame against which she so mightily defended herself.

Fuller (1980) reminded us that the negative of the *aesthetic* is the *anesthetic*, and he suggested that the aesthetic emotion is connected to primal experiences of the self submerged in its environment, with the subsequent gradual differentiation of the self cut from it. I believe that a premature or abrupt loss of that early fleeting experience of "at-one-ment with the beauty of the world" often leads to states of anesthesia, in which little can flow in or out. The most extreme consequences of such disruptions might be seen in those cases of infantile autism described by Tustin (1992) wherein the natural processes of projective and introjective identification have been massively truncated. Indeed it seemed that, at best, all that my patient Carla could gain for herself, in adhesive identification (Bick, 1968) with her mother, was a tough, leathery protection against that penetrating disillusionment that threatened to puncture and deflate her own beautiful baby-buoyancy.

Carla's situation may be seen to exemplify Bion's description of the sequence that follows a failure in maternal containment:

> The infant takes back into itself the sense of impending disaster that has grown more terrifying through the rejection of the mother and through its own rejection of the feeling of dread. This baby will not feel that it gets back something good. but the evacuation with its badness worse than before. It may continue to cry and to

> rouse powerful anxiety in the mother. In this way a vicious cycle is created in which matters get worse and worse until the infant cannot stand its own screams any longer. In fact, left to deal with them by itself, it becomes silent and closes within itself a frightening and bad thing; something that it fears may burst out again. In the meantime, it becomes a "good baby", a "good child." (Bion, 1974, p. 84)

This fragment of my work with Carla demonstrates the sequence of reverie, transformation, and publication that, for me, constitutes the ongoing process of containing the patient in analysis. As I have previously written (1999, 2000, 2001), the act of "taking the transference" is essential to what Bion called the maternal function of reverie: that attentive, actively receptive, introjective, and experiencing aspect of the container. To my mind, this function does not merely entail a cognitive understanding of or an "empathic attunement" with what the patient is feeling toward and experiencing with the analyst in any given moment. It also refers to the unconscious introjection, by the analyst, of certain aspects of the patient's inner world, and a resonance with those elements of the analyst's own inner world, such that she is able to *feel herself to actually be* that unwanted part of the patient's self or that unbearable object that has previously been introjectively identified with.

In a personal communication, Theodore Mitrani recently called my attention to a paper by Enid Balint (1968) in which she addressed this as a feature of what she termed the "mirror technique." Of this technique, recommended in 1912 by Freud and elaborated upon by Ferenczi in 1919, she wrote:

> It is a biphasic attitude in which the analyst first identifies with the patient and then, by his interpretations, shows what the patient's thoughts and ideas 'look like'. ... As I see it, the stress is on the assumption that the analyst's ideas and thoughts do not distort or colour the picture he reflects back to the patient. This assumes a high degree of identification by the analyst and a minimum of projection. (Balint, 1968, p. 58)

I propose that the act of introjecting the patient may be the most difficult aspect of our work, as it is not a matter of good will or good training, but an unconscious act governed by unconscious factors. An example of what I am trying to convey might be helpful.

Hendrick

A markedly depressed and angry man in his late forties, Hendrick was referred to me for analysis many years ago. That first day, I found him standing up in my waiting room, a physically imposing, raw-boned, six foot six inches. Upon introducing himself to me, he lumbered into my consulting room with an air of menace and sat, stoop-shouldered and sullen, inspecting the premises with suspicion. His face bore the scars of a hellish case of adolescent acne that, together with his enormous feet and hands, gave him an awesomely scary appearance. His expression was brooding and, although his posture was slumped as he sat in the chair, he appeared ready for combat, fists clenched and eyes scanning my room as if for an opponent.

In contrast to his impermeable countenance, Hendrick poignantly confessed to feelings of extreme loneliness and confided that he was on the verge of being dismissed from his position for belligerent behavior toward female co-workers, many of whom he had reduced to tears on more than one occasion. In part, Hendrick was seeking help because he was apprehensive about his professional future, fearing that he might be labeled "unemployable" if he could not learn to control his interactions with fellow workers, which he characterized as "bullying and intimidating." However, he was equally troubled by the poverty of his personal life and it came to light that Hendrick's human contacts outside those at work were limited to his immediate family of origin. He briefly referred to his mother as "a zero," said little about the remainder of his family, and did not recall anything about his father, who had died when Hendrick was fifteen, leaving him to fill his shoes as the man of the house.

Hendrick also disclosed that he had never been able to consummate a sexual relationship with either a woman or a man, although he had lived with one woman and her young son for a brief period some twenty years prior. Although their relationship was platonic, Hendrick had been content to be "the man of the house" by providing this woman and her son with some of the comforts she could not otherwise afford. They had reportedly enjoyed each other's companionship until she abruptly broke off their relationship after an incident in which he had become uncontrollably enraged at her child for "drinking up all the milk in the refrigerator."

While hearing this, I felt I was being privileged to a glimpse of a very-little-Hendrick who, while failing to connect in a deep emotional way with his parents, subsequently consoled himself with the benefits of a prematurity that functioned to cover over his infantile despair, disappointment and wrath. Hendrick also mentioned in this first meeting that prior to and for some years after this woman had ended, he spent nearly all his weekends engaged in anonymous sex-play with "parts of people" through what he called "glory holes" in public restrooms, and he lurked on the periphery of school playgrounds with fantasies of dominating young boys. Although he never acted-out these fantasies, Hendrick damned himself as a pedophile. I understood this behavior as an expression of his need to distance himself from the pain of longing for real relationships and to gain dominance, if only in phantasy, over those vulnerable aspects of his child-self.

Of interest to my discussion of "taking the transference" is something that occurred at the end of this initial interview, when Hendrick stood over the chair in which I sat and extended his hand in such a way that I felt he was both challenging me to shake it and daring me not to. I sensed that either way I would be faulted and condemned to death. In spite of the fact that I desperately wanted to find some hole in the floor to crawl into, I responded by taking Hendrick's hand in mine. In his iron grip, I felt terribly small, frightened, helpless, vulnerable, and yes, bullied and intimidated.

The remainder of that week was no less disturbing, as Hendrick repeatedly cursed at me in a booming baritone voice about everything from my physical appearance, to the layout of my room, my reserve, and the fees he had agreed to pay me. Although I could well understand why several other analysts that Hendrick had interviewed before me had refused to take him on, I was also struck by and greatly appreciated this man's unconscious cooperativeness and his immense capacity for communicating his most primitive experiences to me.

When I recovered my wits long enough to think about my experience of these events, I sensed that Hendrick was unconsciously attempting to get across to me some sense of what it was like to be a very little child, perhaps under threat of abandonment by a mother on whom he depended for survival and especially his need to take cover from that threat. Taking this up directly in terms of our connection—his unbearably painful and the humiliating need for me to help him, his unthinkable terror that I would reject him out of hand, as well as his inclination to hide his vulnerability from me within a cloud of intimidation—proved quite relieving to this man and eventually led to the spontaneous recovery of his early memories of Mother.

Apparently when Hendrick was just a year old, his mother was gravely ill subsequent to the birth of a second child who was congenitally impaired and who eventually died. Mother's "sickness" was characterized by frequent and violent fits of rage, which erupted with verbal assaults aimed at a little Hendrick and culminated in bouts of vomiting and vegetative depression. Thus, I inferred that, while helpless to do otherwise, Hendrick was compelled to develop prematurely, to toughen-up in order to with-stand both his own and his Mother's fears of death, as her uncontained and unbearable grief and rage overflowed into him as an infant and toddler.

I think that in this example one can see how the analyst's capacity to introjectively identify with the patient can lead to an organic "learning from experience" for both members of the analytic couple. Through this exchange, the patient learns that his earliest experiences are not so *frightening and bad* as he had once been led to believe.

Alongside these situations, in which the baby develops prematurely as a means of protecting itself, premature ego development may also be set in motion in response to the mother's need for protection.

Next, I will speak to this motive for such aberrant development.

Premature ego development in response to the experience of mother's needs

In London, Pricilla Roth (1994) identified another manifestation of precocious ego development in one patient whose apparent falseness and shallowness offered many obstacles to real emotional contact in the analysis. Roth discovered that, in the case of her patient, these "as-if" characteristics had to do with the presence of these qualities in the original object. She observed,

> In analysis it gradually emerges that the patient correctly perceived the primary object not only to have been false, but also to have been utterly dependent upon its illusions of goodness being maintained.
> (Roth, 1994, p. 394)

Roth implied that what is recognized quite early on by the baby in these instances is the *mother's need* to sustain an illusion of herself as ideally good. Along with the perception of mother's need is the baby's own compelling need to maintain a sense of unity with the mother by responding to her need that unfortunately takes priority over the baby's own valid perceptions and experiences.

Roth went on to write that, in defense of the mother, the baby's idealizations run amok the moment it begins to accurately perceive the mother in moments of disappointment with her. I would suggest that, in these situations, *splitting*—which in normal development will evolve into a mature process of discrimination—is instead recruited *in the service of preserving the belief in and integrity of the external mothering object*, as well as the internal object, and actually becomes a weapon turned against the baby's own nascent capacity to perceive and to be aware of the truth, which further hampers normal development. An example from the analysis of the patient I call Chloe may serve to demonstrate how this situation can be played out in the analytic relationship and how it may become attenuated through the process.

Chloe

Three years into her analysis, Chloe, a young woman in her mid-thirties, had recently married and was attempting to conceive a baby. After the last session of one week, I re-thought the sequence of the hour and I felt certain that I had misinterpreted Chloe's expression of improvement in her feeling state as a manic defense against the week-end separation.

Sure enough, in the following Monday hour, Chloe was able to convey to me how she had dealt with the anger and disappointment she might otherwise have felt toward me. She began the session by telling me that her housekeeper had been steeling painkillers from her medicine cabinet. The moment she began to feel angry and betrayed, she quickly split herself in two, bestowing upon her husband the role of the angry, hurt, and betrayed party who was adamant about dismissing the housekeeper, while Chloe became forgiving and seemed unbothered by the theft.

I was struck by the possibility that I, like the housekeeper, had robbed Chloe of her good feelings at the end of the previous week. Additionally, since I found her lack of anger toward me personally relieving on some level, I considered that Chloe might have been unwittingly responding to her sense that I was unable to tolerate persecution and thus was attempting to relieve me. Like this maid who steals her means of coping with pain—I was experienced by my patient as a thief rudely and illicitly depriving her, not only of her positive feelings about herself, but also of her way of defending herself in my absence.

Just before the hour ended I managed to say that I thought it must be very painful and difficult for Chloe to bear feeling so betrayed by me on Thursday, when she may have felt that I was attempting to erode her self-confidence and her growing sense of hopefulness and security. The next day she began the hour by informing me that she had "calmed her husband down," by "obtaining a confession from the housekeeper, who promised never to take anything again without first asking for permission." However, she knew that their trust in this housekeeper had been damaged and she feared that her husband might eventually ask the housekeeper to leave. She thought it "too bad," as this woman had been good to her and Chloe felt that, if she were to give birth, she would need her more than ever. Furthermore, Chloe was dismayed by the prospect of dismissing the housekeeper as she sensed that this woman "felt really unlovable at the core" and she did not wish to add to such feelings by letting her go.

At this point I felt resigned to the possibility that Chloe might well fire me! I was also able to recognize my own tendency toward feeling unlovable, and acknowledged to myself that I might have undermined my patient's positive feelings when any sign of her development threatened to leave an unlovable-me in danger of abandonment. I recalled how Chloe had seemed wary of me as she arrived to the session that day, although she *seemed* to have pushed aside her more overtly angry feelings about that me who was experienced as preying on her nascent good spirits *by turning my interpretation into a confession*.

With this in mind, I said that although there was a she who, perhaps for my benefit, had put aside her anger and who no longer seemed to mind that I had robbed her, she was letting me know that there was also an enraged-she who felt irreparably betrayed, was furious with me for depriving her of her means of dealing with acute and overwhelming pain, and who was trying to put off a demand for my resignation. Although Chloe nodded, I sensed that she was trying too hard *not* to dismiss what I had said, so I added, "I wonder if you may be attempting to quell your inclination to dismiss me, when you can also feel gratitude toward me, may still need me, and perhaps—although I can't be sure of this—might perceive me to have some deep-seated sense that I am unlovable and are right now trying to shore me up in order to protect me from what you fear to be my inevitable collapse."

As my formulation was confirmed over the next several hours, it became clear that Chloe—who had been born to a manic depressive father and a severely depressed and passive mother—had recreated a situation (with my unwitting assistance) in which she precociously took responsibility for the parents[12] who were demoralized, guilt-ridden and grieving over the death of her elder brother, a child that she had been conceived to replace. It was only when I was able to comprehend and communicate to my patient what had been enacted between us in the transference relationship, and what Chloe had made of this, were we able to move forward.[13]

Technical considerations

In concluding, I would offer—as the primary contribution of this chapter—several technical considerations that may be helpful in the analysis with patients in whom ego has developed prematurely. I hope to have been able to demonstrate through clinical example some of the manifestations of these precocious tendencies in our patients, running the gamut from the somatic to the psychic. They can vary within and between individuals anywhere from Bick's muscular or behavioral "second skin" (1968) or what Tustin (1990a) called the "autistic shell" of auto-sensuality, to the many varieties of what Steiner (1993) called "psychic retreats" or what earlier Kleinians have termed "pathological", "narcissistic" or "defensive organizations." In each of these cases, the baby has been moved to develop such survival mechanisms when the mother is unable to satisfactorily perform her function as a filtering container for his experiences. Subsequently, we can anticipate that these protections will come into play in relation to the analyst in the following ways.

First, it may be important to take into consideration that, since these patients have managed to psychically survive infancy by such means, it follows that their earliest sense of themselves, their core identity, and even their reason for being is rooted in pseudo-maturity. This means that their basic sense of going-on-being is felt to be dependent upon maintaining their pseudo-maturity. Consequently, *they often tenaciously and repeatedly fend off our attempts to reach, to be in touch with, and especially to put them into contact with those nascent experiences of vulnerability* that have early on been rendered alien.

When this occurs in the analysis, the analyst needs to be able to bear the pain of being pushed away and must "keep on going forward" as Tustin liked to put it. We must be prepared to bear and to digest our own feelings of rejection while remaining vulnerable if we are to do this, while the patient defends his fortress of pseudo-maturity mightily through the use of projective identification. When we succeed, the product of our emotional and mental digestive processes is an interpretive understanding of the plight that the patient, one that had previously been felt as unbearable. This understanding may be further used by the analytic couple to weave a more thoroughgoing and genuinely coherent narrative, one that has the potential to relieve the patient of an unremitting experience of the black hole of depression and the absence of a common sense.

Second, in the transference, the patient's built-in assumption of the analyst's vulnerability—for which patients can frequently find evidence—often results in the patient's exaggerated *fear that the analyst will come in contact with the baby-self* that has previously been experienced as a "frightening and bad thing"; An internal reality that needs to be kept silently closed off or encapsulated. *The need to remain the "good baby" in order to prevent the analyst from becoming overwhelmed*, motivates the patient to work overtime to modulate both his affectionate and aggressive feelings toward us. When we collect up and explicitly interpret the patient's unconscious expressions of these passionate emotions in the relationship with the analyst, we *demonstrate* both our desire for contact the patient and our capacity to bear the "torrential overflows" of emotionality that have been dammed up deep inside, or diverted into present-life tributaries along with aspects of the patient's infantile self that have been damned and alienated.

A third set of considerations regards the analyst's countertransference. These considerations (or perhaps precautions) may be helpful to keep in mind as they regard pitfalls frequently encountered in work with the patients I have described who, *more so than others, not only resist interpretations that address the immediate positive or negative infantile transference relationship, but who are also extremely adept at stimulating the analyst's own resistance to being in contact with states of maximal dependence and vulnerability* through this very rejection, as exemplified in the case of Chloe.

At times, the weight of this coercive stimulant may be so great that the analyst might unwittingly collude with the patient by hardening herself. In other words, the analyst may become relatively insensitive at that crucial juncture when what the infant-in-the-patient communicates threatens to resonate too strongly with what the infant-in-the-analyst has experienced.

This resonance may evoke a range of countertransference reactions rooted in happenings from the analyst's own beginnings, and complicated by those happenings in the early life of the patient as these are communicated unconsciously and often non-verbally.[14] Ordinarily, we can use these reactions as tools for understanding. However, when we are not sufficiently mindful we may be prompted, in identification with the pseudo-mature patient, to use our adult experience and competence, our training and most especially our theories, to avoid these feelings. Unfortunately, such protections may lead to misunderstanding the patient or to interpretations that lack contact on all but an intellectual level.

Along these same lines, we may be nudged by the patient to address the current situation of his life outside the immediate transference happening, or his childhood history, or the dynamics of his internal world. However, in turning our interpretive attention to current external events or toward the historical past, we may be perceived as pushing certain infantile aspects of our patients' experiences away from us, just as we may be felt to be altogether abandoning the infant-in-the-patient when we choose to discuss intellectually—with these precociously adultified patients—their internal conflicts. This may lead to a fortification of the patient's defensive structures rather than a relaxation of these structures that might facilitate a resumption of previously hindered mental and emotional development.

A fourth related feature encountered in the work with such patients is the appearance of strenuous resistance, in both members of the analytic couple, against unforeseeable happenings. This resistance can take form as an unflinching effort to endlessly reproduce the "familiar". In the patient this may become manifest on the sensual level, in their tendency to pay attention to the tone of the analyst's voice and the sound of words rather than their meaning.[15] Put another way, patients may treat our words as if they are made solely out of their musical and rhythmical components and not as a result of the symbol-producing process that we call thinking.

As I have demonstrated in some of my clinical work, the corresponding problematic in the analyst may appear in a tendency to rely on "memory and desire" (Bion, 1967), which often appears as an adherence to the theoretical orientation in which we have been "trained". The soothing nature of this theoretical "pacifier" is seductive. Thus it takes a concerted effort to remain in the unknown and in the unfamiliar long enough to hear something new and unexpected in the patient's material when the pressure to interpret prematurely is stimulated by our own as well as the patient's need to survive.

These points bring me back to what James (1960) wrote about babies that *start out as though to take-over the maternal function*, at a time when the mother is experienced as emotionally inaccessible. It follows that patients who have developed prematurely, at a time when the mother was experienced as emotionally inaccessible, may well *start out in analysis as if to take over our function*. At this critical time when these patients appear to be unresponsive to our efforts to connect with them through transference interpretation, the danger lies in the inclination to withdraw or refrain from interpretation or to defensively interpret the patient's lack of cooperation as a usurpation of or envious attack on the analytic "breast". If the analyst takes either road, a vicious cycle can be set in train with the analyst withdrawing or attacking and the patient now *accurately perceiving* the analyst to be emotionally inaccessible. Either way, our ability to notice when things go well or when they go awry will be impeded, which may lead to an arrest in our capacity to find better ways of addressing the patient.

On those occasions when I was faced with such difficulties, Frances Tustin (1987) encouraged me to find a way to "keep on going forward", to continue to seek out those communications from the baby-in-the-patient whose screams were long ago felt as unbearably "frightening and bad" and were silenced and closed off. If we can consistently pick up these often muted or distorted screams, we might be able to help them burst out once again.

Notes

1. The link I am making between "precocious ego development" and deficiencies in the Bion's "containing" function of the mind is complementary to, but not synonymous with, the link that Winnicott (1949) made between the development of a "pathological enemy-mind-psyche"

that takes over the function of caring for the baby's "psyche-soma" and deficiencies in the "holding" function of the mother. Although Bion's concept of containing function overlaps considerably with Winnicott's "holding" function, the latter places emphasis on the physical and biological elements of the emotional contact between mother and infant, while the former emphasizes the emergence of or the impediments to the healthy development of the capacity for thinking thoughts, as it emerges from emotional experience and in the process of mental development. Additionally, one might say that "holding" is a necessary component of "containing."

2. The English analyst Margaret Wilkinson notes, "Klein impressed on us the importance of what might be thought of as the genetic predispositions that the baby brings to its way of experiencing the world, but neuroscience has made clear that this only becomes activated by environmental experience" (Wilkinson, 2006b). She also hypothesizes that, "What may seem to present in the consulting-room as a premature arrival at the depressive position sometimes may not actually be that at all, but is rather a noxious identification with the mother's own disturbance, which occurs as the baby's growing brain literally mirrors that of the mother. This is perhaps at the nub of the development of the adaptive, false, coping self. I am thinking of the mirroring of the mother's brain that occurs in all infants and that, in a healthy two some, would reflect good feelings and allow for the 'getting to know each other' of two beings, as against the mirroring of a less than healthy mother's brain/mind that has no room for her baby as a separate being, a mind that may be filled to overflowing with anxiety, rage, or depression that then determines the growth patterns of the baby's brain–mind" (2006a). Wilkinson also quotes Decety and Chaminade (2003) whose research indicates that "The understanding that others are like us at the psychological level develops as one represents the mental activities and processes of others by generating similar activities and processes in oneself ... What is so striking about this for therapists and analysts is that it provides a sound neuro-scientific basis for the transference/countertransference process and establishes an indissoluble link between those processes and the earliest development of mind" (Wilkinson, 2007, p. 231).

3. Hinshelwood's *Dictionary of Kleinian Thought* (1989) simply defines "Persecutory anxiety [as] a fear for the ego, and depressive anxiety is a fear for the survival of the object." Klein suggested that the former developmentally precedes the latter, with movement to and fro continuing throughout the life cycle. However in some infants, autistic

maneuvers appear to develop as a protection against falling into a state of despair and hopelessness, which dates from an infantile experience of a mother who is depressed and therefore unable to deal with her own or her baby's fears of death and dying. In such cases, a pattern may be observed wherein babies who are born highly sensitive and intelligent, and with a great lust for life and beauty, often become overwhelmed with depressive anxiety when their preconception of a lively, responsive, and caring object (i.e., the mindful breast) fails to materialize at a time when they are as yet psycho-biologically unprepared to deal creatively with such anxieties. While in a state of "normal infantile omnipotence" (Winnicott, 1945) these infants may hold themselves responsible for this disturbance in the mother, which leads to an attempt to protect her by omnipotent means. However, the eventual failure of such an attempt triggers a shift from trust in the ordinary human object to reliance on the sensational "hard-object" (Tustin, 1980) that is often created through obsessional activity and that is used to escape from the terror of hopelessness and non-being.

4. Although the scope of this paper addresses environmental factors rarely emphasized in the Kleinian literature, I wish to direct the reader to Hinshelwood (1989, pp. 272–277) for a most interesting synopsis of Klein's view of the role of constitutional/biological factors that influence the development of the internal world of objects and also to the work of Allan Schore (2003) describing the negative impact of relational trauma on the developmental trajectory of the right brain. Shore offers a model of the intergenerational transmission of a predisposition to psychopathologies of self-regulation, including various personality disorders. Both the classical Kleinian view and the modern neuro-psychoanalytic view must be taken into consideration in any thoroughgoing clinical approach. It is surely a topic for further discussion as to how the analyst determines the weight of each factor and its influence on the development of the individual patient. "LeDoux (2002) emphasized that genes only shape the broad outline of mental and behavioral functions, that inheritance may bias us in certain directions, but that many environmental factors, most particularly the primary care-giver, affect how one's genes are expressed" (Wilkinson, 2006a, p. 35). My own experience has shown me that those patients who have been predominately affected by environmental factors may respond more readily to a good-enough-analyst-containing-object, while those with a predominant biological pre-disposition toward intolerance of anxiety, frustration, and mental pain may appear to be less responsive to and more demanding of the analytic process.

5. Parenthetically, Winnicott (1945) recognized the essential role of the experience of normal infantile omnipotence as necessary for healthy development.
6. In light of this observation of Klein's, it might be of interest to note that Bion once said, "Understanding is a function of love." The current author hypothesizes that, if this is true, when we are able to understand our patients adequately, and if over time there is a steady trend toward growth (including an increasing capacity to bear the emotions provoked by ordinary human experiences, including separations and reunions) then we might be able to infer that there is evidence for a deficiency in the original environment (relative to the individual's need and resilience), rather than an innate deficiency in constitutional make-up.
7. Schore states, "Such environmental influences are embedded in the attachment transactions with the primary object, the mother. These affect communicating and affect regulating transactions are too frequently psychobiologically missattuned and unrepaired in insecure attachments. The caregiver's inability to receive and interactively regulate negative affect, including both fear states and depressive affect, triggers the infant's characterological use of auto-regulation" (i.e., Tustin's autistic maneuvers). The prime example of this auto-regulation is dissociation, a primitive defense against unbearable affect, frequently adopted in insecure disorganized/disoriented and insecure avoidant attachments. Chronic stress in the first years of life is associated with the characterological use of dissociation, which in turn negatively impacts the experience-dependent maturation of the major regulatory systems of the right brain in its early critical period of growth. At later points of object relational intersubjective stress (e.g., the transference–countertransference relationship) such individuals access an immature right brain regulatory system, which is dominant for survival functions and inefficient in regulating both depressive and fearful affect states. They over-regulate (i.e., shut out) affects via over-inhibitory circuits of the right brain, the biological substrate of the human unconscious. This right lateralized deficit is also expressed in a lack of empathy, for both other and self. In this manner, "the lacking bio-neurological development that makes it untenable for the neonate to bear the sort of anxiety inherent in the depressive position." (Schore, 2006, personal communication).
8. Bion coined the term "nameless dread" to denote the severe psychic consequences of the failure of the environment not only to provide the "realization" of what has been naturally "pre-conceived" by the baby, but also by adding insult to injury: by stripping its sense impressions of any and all rudimentary meaning analogous to the

psychic-skin (Bick, 1968). Unfortunately, like some classical analysts and ego-psychologists who take a good-enough infancy for granted, many classical Kleinians often take for granted the development of the "container" as well as "the contained" from the moment of birth or even in *utero*. However, such crucial developments *cannot* be taken for granted, as these are dependent upon both innate and environmental factors.

9. Over the weekend, prior to this hour, the management of the building in which my office was situated installed locks on the public restroom doors on each floor to discourage transients. The keys for the restrooms were readily displayed in my waiting room, although I had not had the opportunity to inform patients of this change.

10. Kohut also discussed mirroring and mirroring transferences as "the therapeutic reinstatement of that normal phase of the grandiose self in which the gleam in the mother's eye, which mirrors the child's exhibitionistic displays, and other forms of maternal participation in and response to the child's narcissistic-exhibitionistic enjoyment confirm the child's self esteem and, by gradually increasing selectivity of these responses, begin to channel it into realistic directions" (Kohut, 1971, p. 116). However, I believe that Winnicott and Kohut did not directly address the conflict between the infant's pre- and post-natal experiences of the mother's mental/emotional and physical presence, and its attempts to sort out and derive some meaning from these as they affect its developing sense of self. Neither did they directly address the issue of the mother's self-esteem nor how this affects the infant's self-esteem as well as the build-up of its internal world of objects and self-representations and the emotional links between them.

11. With respect to the controversy regarding the relationship between a given transference–countertransference constellation and the so-called "real" interaction with the primary external object, I would suggest that such clinical moments such as this one with my patient Carla (and others about which I have previously written) may convince some that there are indeed incidences of accurate perception on the part of the infant/child, and that these perceptions are frequently recorded in some area of the psyche-soma that may be re-enacted in the analysis in such a way that the analyst may, in time, come to intuit the substance if not the specific details of the actual events. The sort of validation obtained through specific recovered memories by the patient (when spontaneous and unsolicited) may lend further credibility and clarity to such intuitions. I am also reminded of Fairbairn's (1952) model of the mind, wherein the beginning ego, and thereafter the central ego, is (in health) capable of realistic perception.

12. Fairbairn's (1952) model of the development of the "moral defense" is clearly related to these dynamics. Even though its full consideration exceeds the limits of this paper.
13. Joseph (1984) extended Klein's original notion of transference of "total situations" from the past relived in the present, as well as the transfer of emotions, defenses and object-relations, emphasizing that the patient's acting out in session is a rich source of information about his internal world, his object relations and his history. In this model, the patient is thought to live out his earliest history in ways that go beyond verbal associations and that are communicated through the pressures that are unconsciously brought to bear on the analyst. Joseph suggested that "transference [is] a relationship in which something is all the time going on, but we know that this something is essentially based on the patient's past and the relationship with his internal objects or his belief about them and what they were like" (Joseph, 1984, p. 164).
14. Such collusion/collision relates directly, and in a deep sense, to Freud's original understanding of the countertransference.
15. Clearly, alongside the content, the phonetic dimension of language and of live communication is an organic factor that impacts the listener and that triggers a variety of emotional responses, as this factor affects different areas of the brain (Schore, 2003). However, in the context of the present paper, I focus on the defensive phenomenon of splitting of the patient's/listener's attention. From the perspective of neuroscience, we may consider that this condition may suggest a suppression of the cognitive frontal lobe function of linear logic.

CHAPTER FOUR

Taking the transference: some technical implications from three papers by Wilfred Bion*

> It is no good anyone trying to tell you how you look at things, or from where you look at things—no one will ever know except you.
>
> —Bion, 1976, p. 245

In this chapter, I will flesh out my concept of "taking the transference" as introduced in the previous chapters, and I will outline a model for conceptualizing the process of establishing a "containing object" in the mind of the analysand throughout the course of analysis. The technical implications offered in this model derive mainly from concepts and notions put forward in three papers by Wilfred Bion and explicated by the present author: "A theory of thinking" (1962a/1988), in which Bion emphasizes what he calls "realistic projective identification," which functions as an unconscious form of communication

---

*The original version of this paper was published (2001) in *International Journal of Psychoanalysis*, 82 (6), pp. 1083–1104 published by John Wiley & Sons. A later version was also published as 'Taking the transference" In: C. Mawson (Ed.), *Bion Today*. London: Routledge.

to and calls for understanding on the part of the analyst that is aimed toward the development of thoughts and an apparatus with which to think thought; "Notes on memory and desire" (1967/1988), in which he sets forth some "rules" for the analytic work that is centered on the "here and now" of the evolving therapeutic interaction; and his paper on "Evidence" (1976/1987), wherein he focuses on the "fact" of the individual analyst's emotional experience. I will attempt to demonstrate, through the presentation of detailed vignettes, some of the ways in which the analytic process may fail or succeed, highlighting the import of the analyst's capacity for "reverie," "transformation," and "publication"—all aspects of the containing function. In addition, she further expands upon Bion's work with a discussion of the essentials of "taking the transference" and differentiates between two main dimensions of interpretation, "projective" and "introjective."

Introduction

Early on, Freud (1901) observed that patients suffer from amnesias and then invent paramnesias to fill the gaps. However, as Bion pointed out near the end of his life, "It would be so nice if it were only patients who did it, and so fortunate if we did not" (Bion, 1976/1987, p. 243). Bion even went so far as to consider the possibility that our analytic theories, indeed "the whole of psychoanalysis [might turn] out to be one vast elaboration of a paramnesia, something intended to fill the gap—the gap of our frightful ignorance?" (p. 244). In his theoretical papers, Bion intentionally left his concepts "unsaturated"—full of gaps or perhaps, more accurately, open spaces to be filled in, not by each individual analyst's paramnesias, but by her own individual thoughts derived from the process of "learning from experience" in analysis. In this manner, Bion hoped that each analyst might be more able to forge "for himself the language which he knows, which he knows how to use, and the value of which he knows" (Bion, 1976/1987, p. 242).

Not unlike a "good" analyst or supervisor, Bion's body of work has provided a source of inspiration for analysts, especially with regard to their efforts to develop, for themselves, models that conceptualize the analytic process. In constructing my particular model, I have taken into consideration certain aspects of three papers by Bion: "A theory of thinking" (1962a/1988), "Notes on memory and desire" (1967/1988), and one of his last papers, on "Evidence" (1976/1987). From my point of view, these papers—when considered together—generate some technical implications for Kleinian as well as non-Kleinian analysts, which I will endeavor to outline here.

Throughout this chapter, I will underscore several aspects of each of these papers, drawing a few very tentative conclusions from them, and elaborating on those concepts of Bion's that I find central to my personal way of working. As I go along I will attempt to demonstrate a number of these ideas with clinical vignettes, emphasizing the importance of the development and handling of the earliest infantile transference encountered in the treatment of the sorts of patients that I believe are ordinarily seen in many analytic practices.

Bion's thoughts on thinking thoughts

Daring to disturb one of the centerpieces of Klein's theory (1946), Wilfred Bion courageously expanded and extended the notion of "projective identification as a defensive phantasy" to include its function as a normal, pre-verbal form of communication between mother and infant. Most notably in his 1962a paper, Bion outlined a "theoretical system" (p. 178) that he was convinced might apply in a significant number of cases. He began by suggesting that "thinking" is dependent as much upon the successful development of thoughts as it is upon the growth of an apparatus for thinking these thoughts. Along the lines of Kantian philosophy, Bion considered that thinking is called into existence to cope with thoughts, that thinking is "a development forced upon the psyche by the pressure of thoughts and not the other way around" (Bion, 1962a, p. 179). As cryptic as this may at first appear, Bion explains himself further on in the paper as he tells us how thoughts first come into being.

Bion clarifies that the baby's inbuilt expectation (or what he called a preconception) of the existence of a satisfying breast, when mated with an experience approximating this preconception (which he called a realization), results in a conception (or an as-yet-unnamed concept). Thus, he concluded that a conception is always found in the presence of an actual emotional experience of satisfaction.

In contrast to this situation, the mating of a preconception with a negative realization results in the development of a bad object: a "no-breast" (Bion, 1962a, p. 180) or the "presence of an absence" that frustrates. The resultant feeling of frustration—when sufficiently tolerated—leads to the birth of a thought. So here we can see that, according to Bion, a thought is born of frustration that is sufficiently tolerated, or what he later called "tolerated doubt." Additionally, since thought acts as a bridge between a felt-want or desire and the action necessary to obtaining satisfaction, the "capacity for tolerating frustration thus enables the psyche to develop thought as a means by which the frustration that is tolerated is itself made more tolerable" (ibid).

Bion observed that if tolerance of frustration is inadequate, evasion of frustration, rather than its modification, would be the outcome. In other words, frustration, rather than leading to the development of thoughts, will result in the development of a "bad object" fit only for evacuation. Now here is where Bion tells us that the mother—the external object—comes into the picture right from the start of the baby's life, and since I am referring to the beginnings of mental life, it is important to consider that the mother plays a significant role in this respect even before birth at around twenty-six to thirty weeks of gestation. For more on this topic, I recommend the work of Mauro Mancia (1981), who has extensively reviewed research regarding the pre-natal mental life of the foetus and its impact on the mental life of the newborn infant.

Regarding the role of the mother, Bion specified that the preconceptions of the baby are concerned with its own survival. However, while noting that the baby's own personality is one factor that impacts its survival, he clarified that:

> The personality of the infant, like other elements of the environment, is [ordinarily] managed by the mother. If mother and child are adjusted to each other, projective identification plays a major role in the management; the infant is able, through the operation of a rudimentary reality sense, to behave in such a way that projective identification, usually [thought of as] an omnipotent phantasy, is a realistic phenomenon. ... As a realistic activity it shows itself as behavior reasonably calculated to arouse in the mother feelings of which the infant wishes to be rid. (Bion, 1962a, p. 182)

Parenthetically, the reader may notice that this view of Bion's resonates with what Winnicott (1960a) called the area of normal omnipotence and speaks to the latter's notion that there is no such thing as a baby without a mother. To illustrate Bion's concept, I will present an example of realistic projective identification from a case brought to me in supervision by a candidate in training.

Dr. A and Cora

In the first chapter of this book, I introduced Cora, who was undergoing intensive fertility treatments, including artificial insemination, when she began analytic therapy twice weekly with Dr. A. Almost from the start of the therapy, one could detect Cora's desire for more contact with her therapist, not only in material that spoke to the need for "more frequent treatments, necessary to facilitate the conception" of the baby to whom the patient desired to give life, but also in Dr. A's experience, which appeared to be a derivative of her countertransference. During this initial period in the treatment, Dr. A either reported that she often had great difficulty recalling her sense of the sessions long enough to write them up for supervision, or she complained that she did not have enough time to do so. When she could write up an hour or two, she realized that she had not registered the transference significance of her patient's communications until well after Cora had left the room, which by then was "too late."

With some encouragement, Dr. A was eventually able to interpret the patient's repetitious material, in the context of her own unsettling experience, as an expression of Cora's need for more sessions so that the analytic couple might be able to conceive of a baby-Cora needing to be brought to life in the mind of her analyst. The patient was quite moved by this line of interpretation and eventually pursued a more direct request for two additional hours per week.

During the next several months of the treatment, there was evidence in the patient's material that she experienced herself and Dr. A as "growing more and more compatible with one another." The material also revealed Cora's sense that Dr. A was becoming gradually more "able to conceive" of the baby in the patient. Indeed my supervisee felt, during this time, that she could formulate and transmit, in a more timely way, some rudimentary understanding of her patient's most primitive fears.

However, Cora's dread of the weekend breaks appeared to increase in direct proportion to her experience of being understood by her therapist, which led to an increase in Cora's dependence upon her. This extreme dread began to take its toll on Dr. A's capacity to tolerate and contain such intense separation anxieties. For example, this dread was expressed in one Thursday hour, the last session of the week, when Cora came in and spoke directly of how relieved she had felt by the end of the previous hour, although her voice was flat as she reported this improvement.

Following a long silence, she added that she had felt "still" all morning long while awaiting the time of her session. Dr. A was at a loss to understand this mixed communication and became quite anxious as Cora went on to say that she was wondering if, in the previous hour, she had been accurate in her perception that Dr. A had tears in her eyes. She further explained that she recalled feeling touched when these tears appeared, as it meant to her that Dr. A might really be willing and able to feel something of what Cora was going through. However, the patient was also disturbed when this positive feeling was suddenly followed by an awful thought: that the tears were merely a part of the therapist's technique. With no immediate response coming from Dr. A, Cora emphasized that she really needed to know if the tears were real or an aspect of technique.

As Dr. A remained silent Cora reiterated, with some urgency, that she thought it important for her to know whether or not her initial perception regarding the tears was correct. However, while feeling under extreme pressure to say something, Dr. A could not make head or tail of her patient's material. At this point, Cora's tone changed to one of despair, followed by an air of icy indifference as she announced that she was aware that even if Dr. A could bring herself to confirm the genuineness of the tears, she probably would not believe her anyway.

As Dr. A remained unresponsive, Cora went on (as if to change the subject) mentioning that she was having qualms about the week's fertility work. She had undergone three inseminations so far that week and, although she had been more hopeful than usual after Wednesday's procedure, she now felt doomed, afraid that, like all the other times, the embryo had failed to implant itself in the womb and she would surely begin her menstrual period, with the little embryo sloughing off, draining away into nothing; she said "It's such a pity, so much money, so much pain and hard work flushed down the toilet like nothing."

By now Dr. A could feel her patient slipping away and she grew desperate to give Cora something to hold on to. She thought about the up-coming weekend and decided to take up Cora's questions as the patient's way of making herself "still" and deadening her feelings about the break by rendering the analyst's interventions over the previous three sessions inconsequential. She suggested that Cora was "sloughing off" or "flushing" them down the toilet like so much waste, and went on to point out to her how this "wasting of the analytic week" left the patient in a state of despair, which was then covered over with an air of icy indifference.

Cora quickly reacted to this line of interpretation with overt rage, telling Dr. A that she couldn't really speak to what she was feeling about the "damned weekend." She could only say that she was growing less and less certain that the therapist would be there for her by Monday. Then she added, "In fact, I'm not even sure that I will be here on Monday."

Clearly frustrated, Cora now demanded even more forcefully to know the answer to her original question. Under still more pressure, Dr. A said that she wondered what might lie beneath the patient's question. Understandably, this tactic only served to provoke more frustration in the patient. She replied defensively that she was sure that if she said anything more about why she needed to know the answer or what she herself thought or felt about the question, that she could never be certain that Dr. A was answering truthfully about the tears; that she would never know if her therapist was being real or if she "was just using a technique." As they were out of time, Dr. A ended the session and the patient left in an angry huff, slamming the door of the consulting room loudly behind her.

In our supervisory hour, which took place Monday shortly before she would see her patient, Dr. A reported that after the session she had felt terribly anxious and upset. She simply "could not get her patient out of [her] mind." She was afraid that when Cora said that she was not even sure that she herself would be there on Monday that the patient was planning to break off the treatment. Subsequently, the candidate not only feared that she had lost her patient forever, but she was also left feeling abandoned and at a loss to understand what had gone wrong.

Dr. A confided that she had examined these feelings of abandonment in her personal analysis and had found that these were somewhat related to her own analyst's upcoming holiday. However, as this insight afforded Dr. A little relief from her anxiety about her patient, she hoped that I could help her to trace what she might have missed with respect to Cora's experience in the Thursday hour.

It seemed to me that in the beginning of the Thursday hour Cora may have been trying to express how hopeful she had been when it had felt to her that she and Dr. A had been able to "conceive" of the patient and her difficulties in the previous three sessions—just as she had felt hopeful after the three inseminations that week. However, it appeared that Cora was also attempting to let Dr. A know, by the tone and shape of her voice, that this hopefulness had begun to flatten out or perhaps that it had begun to wear thin by Thursday morning prior to her session, as she was already beginning to experience the impending weekend as a dangerous discontinuity in their contact.

Here we could see that Cora was not just fearing the future separation from the therapist, but was already actually feeling herself as "still" or perhaps "stillborn" in the present. Apparently unable to breast her analyst's silence, Cora seemed to reach for the memory of the tears she had seen in Dr. A's eyes, which she had taken as a sign of emotional contact: proof that Dr. A really did exist. Her enquiry may have been an attempt at testing the reality of this perception in the hope of obtaining validation of her sense that Dr. A had indeed taken her in throughout the week. However, the wait for some understanding was clearly too long for this patient at this time, and her anxiety proliferated.

To complicate matters, Cora's overflowing fear was clearly more than Dr. A could contain, while encumbered with her own as-yet-unconscious anticipation of loss. Unable to tolerate doubt long enough for intuition to shed light on the evolution of the session, Dr. A missed the significance of her own experience of "her patient slipping away" and her "desperate need to give Cora something to hold on to." Instead Dr. A grasped for general theory upon which to base her interventions. The ensuing all-too-pat interpretations, regarding what she assumed to be Cora's omnipotent denial and denigration of the value of the analytic work, only served to provide confirmation of the patient's sense of "mis-conception."

In this example, I believe one can appreciate Cora's attempt to communicate—through realistic projective identification—something about the deepest level of her most troublesome state of mind as it was being experienced in the immediacy of the session. While feeling "sloughed off" waiting for her Thursday hour, she seemed to be prematurely losing the experience of the analyst's containing presence gained in the three preceding hours, which she subsequently feared was "merely a technique," not unlike the insemination "technique" that had thus far failed to lead to the conception of the "baby she wanted so much to give birth to." I would suggest that Cora was not only experiencing the loss of the mother-analyst, but also the loss of that embryonic self, which had just barely been conceived through the first three sessions of the analytic week.

Without sufficient time in which to build up and firmly establish a consistent and enduring experience of herself safely ensconced in the mental womb of the mother-analyst, a "containing object" was yet to become securely implanted in Cora's own mind. Thus, Dr. A's silences and her "mis-conception" of Cora's dilemma threatened to abort the beginnings of this internalization process and Cora began to slip away in the Thursday session. As if in a last ditch attempt to re-establish contact with Dr. A, Cora seemed to slam herself into her analyst's mind, just as she had slammed the door to the consulting room. Through her use of such realistic projective identification, we can observe how Cora succeeded in making a place for herself during the break, since Dr. A truly "could not get her patient out of [her] mind" all weekend long.

The situation I have just described was eventually resolved, albeit with much effort on the part of both members of the analytic couple to preserve and expand the meaning of the projection. However, Bion depicted a "worst case" scenario, wherein a pathological form of projective identification is set in train.

> If the mother cannot tolerate these projections, the infant is reduced to continue projective identification carried out with increasing force and frequency ... [that] seems to denude the projection of its penumbra of meaning. (Bion, 1962a, p. 182)

Bion points out that, subsequently, the process of reintrojection results in an internal object that strips of its goodness and tentative meaning all that the infant receives and gives, starving its host of any understanding that is made available.

In other words, there are severe long-term consequences for the normal development of thoughts and thinking when there is "a breakdown of interplay through projective identification between the rudimentary consciousness [of the infant] and maternal reverie" (Bion, 1962a, p. 183). In such cases, "The tasks that the breakdown in mother's capacity for reverie have left unfinished are imposed on the [baby's] rudimentary consciousness" (ibid), which is omniscient and omnipotent by nature—leading to the "establishment internally of a projective-identification-rejecting-object ... This means that instead of an understanding internal object, the infant has a willfully misunderstanding object with which it is identified. Further, its psychic qualities are perceived by a preconscious and fragile consciousness" (Bion, 1962a, p. 184). I have found that often times such an internalized object figures into most unresolvable impasses and may be the product of more than one generation of breakdown in the interplay, through projective identification, between the rudimentary consciousness of the baby and the reverie of the mother.

Bion's model of the "containing" object helps one to further appreciate the importance of both projective and introjective identification in normal development, and implies that the mother's state of mind—most of all her capacity to deal with her own as well as her infant's anxieties—is the fulcrum upon which the baby's security and thus his mental health pivots. So, in the interest of clarity, I will take a moment to elaborate this concept, as I understand it, and will try to highlight its influence on my analytic technique.

Mother as containing object

In his model, the mother—in a state of what Bion called reverie—first receives and takes in (or to use the prevailing lingo "introjects") those unbearable aspects of self, objects, affects, and unprocessed sensory experiences of her infant that have been projected into her in phantasy. Second, she must bear the full affect of these projections upon her mind and body for as long as need be in order to be able to think about and to understand them, a process that Bion referred to as transformation. Next, having thus transformed her baby's experiences in her own mind, she must gradually return them to the infant in detoxified and digestible form and (at such time as these may be of use to him) as demonstrated in her attitude and the way in which she handles him. In analysis, Bion referred to this last process as publication, what we commonly refer to as interpretation.

As one can readily see, the ability to "contain" assumes a mother who has boundaries and sufficient internal space to accommodate her own anxieties as well those acquired in relation to her infant; a mother who has a well-developed capacity to bear pain, to contemplate, to think and to convey what she thinks in a way that is meaningful to her infant. A mother who is herself separate, intact, receptive, capable of reverie, and appropriately giving, is thus suitable for introjection as a "containing" object, and, little by little, over time, the infant's identification with and assimilation of such an object leads to increasing mental space, the development of a capacity to make meaning (what Bion called alpha-function), and the ongoing evolution of a mind that can think for itself. Should such a description seem idealized, I would suggest that it corresponds to Winnicott's (1960a) ordinary devoted mother in his model of mental health.

I believe that Bion's use of the term reverie—for the attentive, receptive, introjecting, and experiencing aspect of the container—refers also to the function on the part of the analyst that is analogous to what I call taking the transference (Mitrani, 1999). To my way of thinking, the act of taking the transference is a necessary and indispensable step on the way toward the interpretation of the transference, especially when dealing with primitive mental states.

The inability on the part of the analyst to "take" the patient's material in the transference and its consequences can perhaps be readily traced in the following example from a case presented to me, with much candor, by a senior colleague in Israel who wished to learn how the way in which she worked might have contributed to a premature interruption in this analysis. The reader may note, in this example, a marked difference between Dr. A, who was able to "take the transference," but who did not quite know what to do with it (much like a mother who is capable of "reverie" but whose capacity for transformation is deficient or as yet undeveloped), and Dr. B whose capacity for reverie seems to have been obstructed with this particular patient.

Dr. B and Gaila

Dr. B presented material from one of the last sessions with Gaila, a female patient near her own age. It may be important to note that both analyst and analysand shared a similar history as children of Holocaust survivors. Gaila returned, after a weekend break in the second year of treatment, complaining that she had not been able to sleep since their last session. She then reported that X (a friend) had told her about a conference held in a fashionable resort where she had heard Dr. B and her husband presenting. Gaila said that X had commented on "what a handsome couple they made, so well suited to each other." Gaila then mentioned another friend, Y, who had miscarried her baby over the weekend. She criticized Y for smoking during the pregnancy and felt strongly that Y had clearly not taken into consideration the effects of this dangerous behavior upon her foetus. Gaila said that she thought that Y did not really wish to have a baby, as she seemed to be much more interested in her successful career and in continuing a carefree lifestyle with her husband.

Dr. B took up this material as the expression of an "old hurt" stemming from Gaila's childhood experience of her mother who had been negligent and irresponsible, smoking during her entire childhood, which made mother seem negligent and disinterested, and left Gaila feeling that she had been "miscarried" and therefore unloved by a mother who did not want her. The patient responded to this interpretation with the telling of a dream:

> She was in a hospital and the doctor attending her bedside was not taking her complaints to heart. Gaila thought in the dream that the doctor might think she had something contagious and was thus keeping some distance from her and so was having difficulty diagnosing the problem. The patient knew she had a brain tumor as a result of some shrapnel embedded in her head when it had ricocheted off the chest of another soldier. She thought how unfair it was since it was not her war, but rather belonged to the dispute between older generations. No one took responsibility for the conflict and she was fearful that she was going to die as a result.

It appeared that Dr. B had overlooked the possibility that Gaila might have been making reference to her sense that the analyst chose to resume her career and her carefree life with her husband over the weekend break, leaving Gaila feeling unwanted and aborted. In this context, the dream seemed to suggest that the genetic interpretations made by the analyst may have left the patient feeling further pushed away and was contributing to the doctor's difficulty in understanding her dilemma, which was linked to the older generation who could not take responsibility for their own experience, instead passing this on (perhaps through projective identification) to the younger generation.

Dr. B had thought at the time that she was being empathic when she took up the dream as an expression of Gaila's experience of being made to suffer due to her mother's lack of responsibility and from the aftermath of the war, especially the Holocaust, which belonged to her mother's generation and not to her own. The analyst was unable to imagine that the patient might have been attempting to call her attention to the miscarriage that was occurring in the analysis at that very moment, the sense that the analyst-mother was deflecting the transference, including the patient's sense of being dropped and therefore mortally wounded.

As one often observes when misunderstandings occur, the patient was unresponsive and nothing Dr. B could subsequently say served to reach her. Gaila remained mute until finally she said:

> I've been thinking of changing jobs. My employer treats me unfairly. She goes over my work and when I get it back, it's such a mess, it's unrecognizable. She always blames me for everything that goes wrong. It doesn't matter what I do. I try to take responsibility to put things right again, but she never considers her part, and I feel hurt and resentful. I've been sick more often on this job than any other. I feel trapped. It's a bad job. I know I can leave, but where would I go? I'm unqualified for other work.

Painfully, Dr. B continued to address how trapped Gaila felt with the mother she was born to—that she could not bring herself to leave her mother, and the various effects upon her of Mother's Holocaust experiences—while the patient continued to fall deeper and deeper into despair, silent through to the end of the hour. This pattern is one that is frequently found in the sort of impasse where the unifying thread is a coincidence of vulnerability between analyst and analysand, resulting in a kind of transference blindness. In the case of Dr. B and her patient Gaila, their shared vulnerability was stimulated but not responded to, as both members of the therapeutic couple were trapped in the same post-traumatic experience (the Holocaust like the "bad job"), unable to find refuge from the psychic shrapnel that may have bounced off the protective shielding of their respective parents (the other soldier), with each suffering the trauma that rightfully belonged to "another generation." The patient had attempted once again to reach the analyst when she spoke of the "bad job" and the "blaming employer" who did not take responsibility. However, in the absence of one who could contend with the pain and frustration, Gaila retreated into silence.

In the transference enactment of this situation, the analyst (as the doctor in the dream) was felt not to be taking the patient's complaints to heart (that is, she did not take up the complaint as an indication of how the patient may have felt about her analyst). The resulting silence may have been an indication of the death or deadening of that communicative aspect of the patient. Here we can see that what Dr. B interpreted was the content of Gaila's material and the link to the genetic situation (in the past), while the essential experience of her analysand in the here-and-now of the negative transference was bypassed rather than taken in, resulting in a repetition of the original trauma: that of being in the care of a mother who, while filled with her own unbearable and undigested suffering, was unable to bear feeling her baby's suffering in relationship to her own human failings.

The primitive, infantile, unmentalized experiences (Mitrani, 1995) of helplessness, terror and loss, when reactivated by the Holocaust experience, often prove so horrific for some that much of their emotional charge has been foreclosed from the mind of the parent, and later the analyst, in the service of survival. In the case of Gaila and Dr. B, just as the analyst had unwittingly abandoned the transference in the interest of her own psychic survival, so did the analysand eventually abandon the analysis, disillusioned and hopeless about her "qualifications for other work."

As one can see, the act of taking the transference does not merely entail a cognitive understanding of or an empathic attunement with what the patient is feeling toward and experiencing with the analyst in any given moment. It also refers to the introjection by the analyst of certain aspects of the patient's inner world and experience, and a resonance with those elements of the analyst's own inner world and experience, such that the latter is able to feel herself to actually be that unwanted part of the patient's self or that unbearable object that has previously been introjectively identified with.

This may be one of the most difficult aspects of our task, as it is not a matter of goodwill or adequate training, but an unconscious act governed by unconscious factors in response to an emotional experience. Bion (1976/1987) considered the emotional experience to be the only "fact" (Bion, 1976, p. 242) or true evidence upon which we may reliably base our interpretive interventions. The examples in Chapter One, of the patients I refer to as Hendrick and Anthony, may also highlight Bion's notion of evidence in the psychoanalytic conversation. Not unlike Hendrick, the earliest happenings in Anthony's life had been left to the devices of his "rudimentary consciousness."

While working with patients such as Hendrick and Anthony, one is struck by how essential it is to resist the pull toward reliance upon memory of theories or to be influenced by the desire to give a patient something when we are faced with doubt and uncertainty. The transference must be taken and the emotional experience had and tolerated by the analyst in order for her to make optimal use of such realistic projective identification. This brings me to Bion's recommendation that we attempt to work without memory and desire. I will address this curious and often misunderstood notion of Bion's and what I believe to be its main technical implications.

On evidence, memory, and desire

In one of his most controversial papers, "Notes on memory and desire", Bion (1967/1988) gave me food for thought regarding issues of technique in analysis. In this compact communication, not much more than a thousand words, Bion made a plea for the analyst to eschew memory and desire deriving from sensuous impressions of "what is supposed to have happened" (Bion, 1967, p. 17) and of "what has not yet happened" (ibid), in favor of the reliance upon an emotional experience or "feelings," which he designated as the only "facts" we analysts have to base our interpretations upon (Bion, 1976/1988).

Bion further argued that memory is misleading as it is always distorted by unconscious processes, and desire interferes with the capacity to observe, which is essential to sound judgment. In support of a technique utilizing here-and-now interpretation, Bion stated that, "Psychoanalytic observation is concerned neither with what has happened, nor what is going to happen, but with what is happening" (ibid). Both Cora and Gaila may serve as reminders of the need for attention to this way of working. It is perhaps essential to note that Bion encouraged the analyst's at-oneness with her intuition, insisting that what is already known is obsolete. Only the unknown is relevant and "Nothing must be allowed to distract [us] from intuiting that" (Bion, 1976, pp. 17–18).

Next, in what may be the centerpiece of this paper, Bion wrote:

> In any session, evolution takes place. Out of the darkness and formlessness something evolves. That evolution can bear a superficial resemblance to memory, but once it has been experienced it can never be confounded with memory. It shares with dreams the quality of being wholly present or unaccountably and suddenly absent.

> This evolution is what the analyst must be ready to interpret. (Bion, 1976, p. 18)

Bion cautioned that when memory and desire occupy the mind of the analyst, this evolution is missed while it is taking place. He acknowledged that adherence to this "rule" would certainly lead to increasing anxiety for the analyst; anxiety that accompanies a state of experiencing and of "not knowing" on the way toward intuiting evolution. However, he assured us that the pay-off will come with signs of progress in each meeting, where the tempo of each and every session quickens, the "number and variety of moods, ideas and attitudes" (ibid) increases, and the repetition in the material decreases. Additionally, Bion promised that the analyst's interpretations would "gain in force and conviction—both for himself and for his patient" (Bion, 1976, p. 19)—when these are derived from emotional experience with a unique individual rather than from generalized theory.

Since Bion suggested that the technical implications of his rules "can be worked out by each analyst for himself" (ibid), I will share my thoughts on the subject and hope to stimulate discussion. First, it is my understanding that Bion uses the term "evolution" to indicate a situation in which some idea or pictogram is evoked, floating unbidden into the mind of the analyst in response to the words and music of a given session. Inspired by the writings of the poet, Bion seems to be suggesting that an "irritable reaching after fact" or a practice of "forced recall" shall be relinquished in favor of the disciplined yet fluid state of mind that Keats (1817/1973) referred to as "negative capability."

Bion also seems to be arguing the point that memory that is forced is the past tense of desire, while anticipation is its future tense. Both distract us from the present emotional experience, and this I believe is the crux of the matter if one feels, as I do, that what we hope to achieve is a state of being with the patient in the present so that he can eventually bear to be himself, with himself. So how does this impact our technique in psychoanalysis? Toward answering that question for myself, I was once again put in mind of some of Bion's seemingly peripheral remarks in his paper on "Evidence" (1976/1987) regarding the "publication" of the analyst's emotional experience. In that paper, Bion asks the question: "What are we to say to people who are not psychoanalysts, or have not had psychoanalytic training, or, for that matter, if they have? … to communicate [my emotional experience] to somebody 'not me'" (Bion, 1976, p. 240). Here Bion seems to be asking us to consider our style of interpretation, which needs to be free of cliché or jargon, down to earth, immediate and accessible, especially to the infantile aspects of the patient, and evocative in the here and now in order to facilitate an genuine connection.

I think that Bion's idea of "eschewing memory and desire" implies that when the analyst offers genetic interpretations or even interpretations of the patient's analytic past (in other words, what the analyst has learned about the patient in past sessions or from the patient's own narrative history) she is relying on memory (her own or that of the patient or perhaps even others in the patient's sphere of influence) rather than the analyst's own intuitive observation of the present situation and of the patient who is present in the room. In such instances, the analyst runs the risk of colluding with that part of the patient that strives to conserve the status quo and therefore to impede evolution.

Similarly, if the analyst offers interpretations about what the patient fears will happen or hopes to have happen in the future, the analyst may miss an evolving terror or a longing stimulated by contact with herself, or perhaps even a fleeting experience of satisfaction expressed in the moment: something that is felt to be occurring in the presence of the analyst, rather than what may happen during her future absences. I find that when I can be with the patient while he is experiencing me as either "bad" or "good," then I may have the opportunity to provide him with an experience of a containing object for each of these situations. I also might think—while out of the consulting room—about how my patient and I might work together to foster realistic projective identification; how to best offer myself as a processing plant for unbearable feelings and happenings; and how to further facilitate the patient's introjection of objects that can perform what Bion referred to as the alpha function.

I find that, in order to understand the infantile aspects of my patients, I need to be both willing and able to feel like a baby. Of course, one might think that—since we have all been babies—this experience would be well within our emotional grasp. However, I am frequently reminded of how tempting it can be to use my adult experience and competence, my training and especially my "favorite" theories to avoid feeling the vulnerability and sensitivity of the infant and young child whenever I can. Unfortunately, this may lead to misunderstanding the patient through interpretations that lack contact (on all but an intellectual level) with certain elemental terrors and longings that even a psychoanalyst would rather overlook.

Sometimes it may be far less distressing to address the current situation of the patient's life outside the immediate transference happening, his childhood history or even the dynamics of his internal world. However, in turning my interpretive attention to current events outside the consulting room or towards the historical past, I may be (often accurately) perceived as distancing myself from certain infantile aspects of my patient. In like manner, I may be felt to be altogether abandoning the infant-in-the-patient if I fall into an intellectual discussion with an often precociously adultified patient, about his internal conflicts. As sterile as it may become, I find that this sort of academic engagement is often quite well tolerated by candidates in training.

Additionally, although it can be somewhat disconcerting when a patient does not accept whatever he is given, at such times I might need to consider the possibility that what the patient cannot or will not take in may truly be indigestible for him. I might even need to conceive of a situation in which, in spite of my desires for it to be otherwise, a mouth through which to feed or a stomach in which to hold food has not yet formed in the patient's mentality. At such times I may need to take great pains to detect and to describe this in some way that is meaningful to the patient, while refraining from accusations and explanations that may only serve to heighten the domination of his "rudimentary consciousness."

In other words, I may need to stretch beyond what is "known" in order to encompass what is immediate for the patient at any given moment and to maintain contact, in spite of the distractions, with those elements of the patient that are most in need of my help: those vulnerable, embryonic, fetal, and early infantile aspects that have not yet had the experience of being "conceived" in the mind of another and are not as yet fully formed. Without such an experience, those primordial happenings that have been necessarily foreclosed from awareness will remain unmitigated, unable to be borne in the mind of the patient, which itself has not had sufficient opportunities to settle in, to take root, and develop.

I believe that one key to such development of "mind" is Bion's concept of the "containing function" of the analyst, which needs to be experienced, consistently over a lengthy period of time. Technically speaking, the gradual introjection of (or introjective identification with) the analyst—in the act of receiving, processing, and making meaning of the raw sensory experiences of the patient—may best be achieved through direct, immediate and clear interpretation of the transference as it is experienced from the patient's point of view. I am convinced that contact made in this way offers the patient a sense of being in touch with an emotionally and mentally available and a firm-but-not-rigid bounding presence capable of introjective identification.

When the analyst accurately intuits the patient's "vertex" or point of reference, she may be able to compose what I have come to call an introjective interpretation; that is, one based upon an act of introjective identification. As I have demonstrated in the cases of Hendrick and Anthony, this kind of interpretation often culminates in an experience of "being understood." In contrast to this, when the analyst formulates interpretations based upon her vertex—in other words, her own sense of the patient and of what she believes he is "doing" to her in phantasy through his various defensive maneuvers—this constitutes a projective interpretation wherein the analyst returns that which had been projected into her by the patient. It has occurred to me that this type of interpretation is, in and of itself, an act of projection on the part of the analyst, albeit aimed towards helping the patient to "have understanding" or to "gain insight" into himself. However, the use of this variety of interpretation assumes that the analysand has developed adequate mental space in which to house self-awareness, as well as sufficient ego strength to contend with experiences of separateness. By their very nature, projective interpretations are "weaning" interpretations that require a firmly rooted bonding background.

Arguably, the kind of interpretation that addresses the patient's projections may sometimes be helpful to him, even when the inception of a containing object and a space for thinking is tenuous and rudimentary, if such projections are sincerely perceived and understood by the analyst as a part of the patient's attempt to communicate. In other words, the earliest insight or 'core' insight—like the "good" object at the core of the ego—must be some "good" aspect of the self. This particular subset of "projective interpretation" can further strengthen the positive libidinal tendencies in the patient and may foster his faith in his own inner goodness, which mitigates the potential for envy. Like the "introjective interpretation," this sub-category of the "projective interpretation" may also increase the patient's experience of the analyst's goodness, that is, her capacity to receive and to make sense of his communications. Thus, the patient may begin to take the analyst in as an object capable of understanding in relation to a subject or self that is capable of communicating and being understood.

These modes of interpretation, eventually leading to an experience of "being understood," may also provide an "object lesson" for introjective processes and may eventuate in a positive build-up rather than a negative depletion of the internal world. In other words, along with an experience of being understood, an object capable of tolerance and understanding is established in the patient's psyche through this kind of interpretive work. The installation of such "understanding objects" lays the foundation for even more sophisticated capabilities, such as the aspiration and empathy necessary for the patient to understand himself as well as others.

As this crucial point in mental development is approximated, both the genetic reconstructions and intrapsychic formulations that constitute further subsets of the "projective" variety of interpretation may have a truly productive place in the analysis. At this juncture, they can and will be received (more often than not) with interest and even appreciation. Additionally, once the patient has developed some "presence of mind," these more advanced lines of thinking, stemming from a benign self- and other-consciousness, will likely be brought into play in a non-defensive and heartfelt manner by the patient himself, where previously it may have only been possible to "play" these constellations out in relation to the analyst or to articulate them in a manner that resembles echolalia.

It may be important to clarify here that I am not necessarily describing stages or phases of linear development. Instead, what I am suggesting is that there are cycles that can be detected within a given session or a particular segment of an analysis, related to the working through of certain pathological constellations or states of mind, and leading into the development of the capacity to experience and to think about specific situations as they arise.

In concluding, I will suggest that many of us are drawn to the work of analysis, at least in part, by the desire to do some good. However, paradoxically, this may be the greatest obstacle to actually doing "good analytic work" and therefore the greatest barrier to truly helping the patient. If unbridled, it may prove to be the most obstructive "desire"—in Bion's sense of the word—since our patients may actually need to transform us, in the safety of the transference relationship, into the "bad" object that does harm. In terms of analytic technique, the analyst needs to be able to muster the wherewithal to see, hear, smell, feel, and taste things from the vantage point of the patient. I have found it is of little use to give the patient the impression, in one way or another, that what he made of what I said or did was neither what I intended, nor what I actually did, or said. This tactic almost always misses the point and may even reinforce the patient's sense that his experiences are indeed unbearable.

Our analysands' developmental need to house their "bad" objects and unendurable experiences in us is primary. Within us, these objects and the experiences that have created them, may find an opportunity for rehabilitation and transformation. For example, the experience of the "abandoning object" that we become—during holidays, weekend breaks, silences, and especially in the absence of our understanding in the analytic hour—may have the chance to become an experience of "an abandoning object who takes responsibility for having abandoned the patient" and who, at the same time, is able to keep the patient in mind sufficiently to be able to think about how he might feel about having been abandoned. Most importantly, that same object may also be experienced by the patient as able to bear being "bad," which in itself is "good"! Furthermore, when re-introjected by the patient in this modified form, the "bad" object is not so "bad" at all: it is human, ordinary, with all the ordinary human frailties imaginable, but it is bearable. In this transformed state, the "bad" object (which is now the contained) is enhanced with a "container" (the analytic object), and the patient will be well on his way toward "being" a thinking and feeling individual.

CHAPTER FIVE

Excogitating Bion's *Cogitations*: further implications for technique*

> More than one patient has said that my technique is not Kleinian. I think there is substance in this.
>
> —Bion, 1992, p. 166

In Chapter Four, I have taken up a discussion of three papers by Wilfred Bion that, when considered together, generate significant technical implications for analytic work.[1] Continuing in that same spirit, this communication highlights a few of Bion's more informal musings, posthumously published in *Cogitations* (1992).[2] These particular fragments may each be seen as germane to the theory of psychoanalytic technique. I hope to be able to demonstrate the links between these insights of Bion's in particular and their clinical usefulness, as well as a variety of technical considerations that follow on from each of these. Throughout, I will offer detailed clinical examples in the interest of clarification. Although this paper revolves around some of the work of Bion—arguably one of the most celebrated and original of Klein's

---

*Originally published in (2011) the *Psychoanalytic Quarterly, 80*: 671–698 published by John Wiley & Sons.

analysands—perhaps the epigraph I have chosen to head up this paper may serve as a welcoming gesture to practicing analysts of any psychoanalytic orientation.

By way of disclaimer, it is not my intention to suggest that what is presented in this chapter bears any relationship to what Bion actually meant when he wrote the quoted passages. Rather, the following notes are to be taken as my own thoughts, which have been stimulated by a few of the concerns raised in Bion's enormously thought-provoking book.

Behavior as palimpsest[3]

Addressing the subject of analytic theory, Bion wrote:

> I consider that the behavior of the patient is a palimpsest in which I can detect a number of layers of conduct. Since all those I detect must, by that very fact, be operating, conflicts are bound to occur through the conflicting views obtaining contemporaneous expression. In this way, the conflict that is so important to the patient's sufferings and to theories of dynamic psychology is, according to me, accidental and secondary to two different views of the same situation. (Bion, 1992, p. 166)

In this passage, Bion seems to imply (among other things one might consider) that, much like the writing on a piece of parchment that has been partially or completely erased to make room for another text, a patient's earliest happenings may be virtually erased from consciousness by denial, repression, or splitting and projection, and may then become overlaid by other meaning/experience—paramnesias covering over amnesias, depression underlying mania, untenable anxieties dulled by depression, layers of infantile happenings obscured by pseudomaturity, autistic enclaves hidden beneath the surface of the neurotic personality, and psychotic states encrusted beneath the nonpsychotic. I believe that this reading of Bion is consistent with what Freud (1925) was alluding to in his paper on the "Mystic writing pad."

At the same time on another level, Bion also seems to be arguing that—just as there are conflicting states in the patient, each one competing for expression, attention, and interpretation—similar conflicts may account for many of the controversies between schools of thought in psychoanalysis, each one struggling for expression, attention, and interpretation. Regarding one such controversy, Bion wrote:

> Winnicott says patients need to regress; Melanie Klein says they must not; I say they are regressed, and the regression should be observed and interpreted by the analyst without any need to compel the patient to become totally regressed before he can make the analyst observe and interpret the regression. (Bion, 1992, p. 166, my italics)

Here Bion may be proposing that, whether or not a "facilitating environment" (Winnicott, 1965) is provided, the infantile aspect of the patient does exist and is being expressed, inside or outside the analysis, one way or another, whether or not the analyst wishes to deal with the consequences of that expression. Therefore, it may be that one of the analyst's primary tasks is neither to facilitate that expression nor to inhibit or ignore it, but rather to manage to observe it and interpretively acknowledge it before hyperbole sets in as the patient's way of calling the analyst's attention to the plight of the infant in the adult (or even in the child or adolescent patient).

To illustrate this point, I will quote from a case example brought to Bion for comment during a clinical seminar in Brazil. Although the material reproduced and discussed in this paper is from a case presented to Bion, the comments in this paper are the present author's, not to be confused with Bion's actual remarks on the material, which the reader may wish to review as well (Bion, 1987, pp. 218–220).[4] It will become apparent that I have chosen this case in part because, as the reader will note, the patient himself very directly calls the analyst's attention to the layers of meaning superimposed over other layers of meaning, and because the case illustrates one patient's attempts to "make the analyst observe and interpret" alternative layers of meaning. I believe that the sort of exercise I am engaging in here falls into the category of what Bion called a "psychoanalytic game" (1965, p. 128).[5]

A clinical case presented to Bion

A patient in analysis for five years begins the session, the first of the week, by asking his analyst if he has read a certain psychoanalytic book. "It's a very good book," says the patient. "And I noted several interesting things. It's very good indeed, but I haven't read it all because there are parts I am not interested in. There is a part that describes a duel—this is very interesting indeed because last Saturday I almost didn't go out—I was so tired I had to rest. Do you understand? I had to rest."

In response, the analyst offers an observation that highlights a defense. He says, "You started on one idea, interrupted it, and then went on, telling me about something else."

The patient responds with what appears to be an explanation. He says, "Well, all right. Because I only read the part that interested me, because I noticed that, and because I rested on Saturday. I felt it was important." Perhaps detecting his patient's defensiveness, the analyst says, "I think we are having a duel here, too."

In what appears to be an attempt to get the analyst to notice his experience alongside his defenses, the patient says, "Yes, but it is very difficult, because what is happening is as if there were several situations that are superimposed,"[6] to which the analyst opines, "You feel that if you don't try to tell me what is happening inside you, you will become confused."

After a short period of silence, the patient goes on to say, "When you speak, I feel as if you had left a mark, like Zorro does." Perhaps this statement indicates how the analysand has experienced the analyst's interpretation. At this point, the analyst silently recalls that Zorro is a man who wears a black mask, rides a horse, and leaves the mark of Z engraved with the tip of his sword on the chest of his opponents. As if in self-defense, the analyst exclaims, "Zorro is a man who fights injustice!"

The patient laughs and continues, "Zorro cuts the braces of the sergeant's trousers and leaves the enemy with no clothes. That's why you make me feel irritated." The patient's directness may suggest that he has experienced his analyst as one who, behind the mask of analysis, cuts the defenses (the braces or suspenders) that hold the patient together or that up-hold him, and he is thus left feeling dropped—foolish and irritated. However, in what follows, the analyst appears to feel that it is he who is being made to look the fool, as he reminds the patient that "the person whom Zorro attacks is also a friend of his."

In response, the patient says, "Oh, yes, I quite agree—the sergeant is a fool." The analyst declares, "For you, a friend is a fool. Perhaps that's why you don't show friendly feelings toward me here." Touché!

The patient is silenced—quite possibly a sign that he has given up in despair, feeling unable to connect with, to reach, or to be understood on some vital level.

Discussion

Notice that the patient begins the hour by telling his analyst about a book he is reading. Since this is a book about analysis, one might consider that, on some level, the patient is attempting to communicate his experience of the analyst and of their analytic encounter. Arguably, this may be viewed as a positive development in analysis, as we are assisted to a great extent when the patient finds a way, directly or indirectly, to tell us what he or she thinks of us, which may or may not be a statement of fact about who we are, but is always an indication of who the patient is and of what he experiences at any given point in the hour.

Reportedly, Bion once stated that if a patient comes to analysis, he should be able to learn something about himself (Tustin, 1990a). Perhaps an interpretation addressing what the patient is experiencing with the analyst might enable this criterion to be fulfilled. Additionally, Bion suggested that the fact that an interpretation is given in terms of the relationship with the analyst is not because the analyst is so important (Tustin, 1990a). In other words, if the patient demonstrates anger toward or appreciation for the analyst, this does not necessarily tell us anything about the analyst's character, including whether or not he is benign or malignant (although often it is taken this way). However, such a demonstration nearly always says something about the patient's capacity to experience emotions such as gratitude or hostility—in other words, what the patient is capable of feeling.

In due course, our interpretations may help the patient discover what kind of person he is and what kind of relationship he is able to have with someone who is not himself. Thus, when the patient in this example begins the hour by stating that he is interested in some parts of the book he is reading and not in others, this might be understood as a declaration that he has registered and is reporting only what applies to his own experience in analysis.[7] Along these lines, the patient declares that what is really interesting to him is the part about the duel. At this juncture, one might wonder whether the patient experiences the analysis as a duel—does he experience the analyst as an adversary in that moment?

The patient may only be appearing to change subjects when he says, "This is very interesting indeed because last Saturday I almost didn't go out—I was so tired I had to rest," and he asks if his analyst understands. Among other things, the analyst might be inclined to convey to the patient his appreciation that, at least on one level, the patient is letting him know the following: that in experiencing the interaction between them in the previous week as a duel, the patient may have been left feeling too tired to interact with the world, and thus he may have withdrawn over the weekend; now he believes the analyst may wish to be aware of this.

Alternatively, it may be that the patient is communicating his experience of the analyst (like the book on psychoanalysis) as very good indeed. However, he may not be able to take in all that the analyst offers. Perhaps what the analyst puts forward is too much to digest. Thus, when he is left to sort out his thoughts and feelings on his own, he becomes fatigued and is unable to interact with the world (to go out) over the weekend. This way of thinking about and interpreting the patient's utterances—by taking the transference (Mitrani, 2001)—may open the way for the patient to say something more about his current grievances.[8]

When the patient asks for the analyst's understanding, one might take this as a constructive development. However, the analyst in this example appears to grow impatient and appears to miss this libidinal level of communication. Consequently, when the analyst chooses to point out that the patient is changing subjects, this interpretation is felt as a criticism and the patient becomes defensive, further explaining his attempt to report what has happened to him, how he loses interest and withdraws, and "cannot go out." One might understand this reiteration as itself a demonstration of the patient's inability to "go out," or of his inability to go on when left on his own in that moment in the analytic hour. The patient senses it is important that the analyst know this.

Regrettably, the analyst continues in a way that is experienced by the patient as accusatory, that is perhaps an unwitting duel with the patient in that it points to his defensiveness. It has been my experience that when the anxiety underlying the defense is inadequately addressed, defense analysis tends to incite more defensiveness (Mitrani, 2001). Bion enhanced my understanding of this phenomenon when he refined the Kleinian understanding of the nature of the defensive or pathological organization, introducing his concept of the Superior ego or

Super ego. Bion used these terms interchangeably to denote an internal organization lacking the usual characteristics of Freud's super ego. Bion's Super ego refers to "an envious assertion of moral superiority without any morals ... the resultant of the envious stripping or denudation of all good and is itself destined to continue the process of stripping" (Bion, 1962b, p. 97). This internal constellation is consonant with what Bion called −K[9] and is associated with negative narcissism.[10]

Bion described the situation as follows:

> In −K the breast is felt to remove the good or valuable element in the fear of dying and force the worthless residue back into the infant. The infant who started with a fear of dying ends up by containing a nameless dread ... . The seriousness [of this situation] is best conveyed by saying that the will to live, that is necessary before there can be a fear of dying, is a part of the goodness that the envious breast has removed. (Bion, 1962b, p. 96)

In the case under discussion, the patient may be seen as on guard, convinced that he has to justify himself. He musters up a further attempt to call to the analyst's attention the possibility that his defensiveness is superimposed on what may be viewed as a benign attempt to communicate something of his infantile state of mind—not only over the weekend, but also especially in the present moment. The analyst puts forward his belief that the patient is giving expression to a fear that, if he does not tell the analyst what is on his mind, he (the patient) will become confused.

Although in this instance the analyst interpretively addresses the anxiety as he sees it, he appears to be inferring that communication is itself a defense against confusion, rather than a sign of separateness. When the patient responds by stating, "When you speak, I feel as if you had left a mark," it becomes evident that he has experienced the analyst's response as cutting, persecutory. Aware of the reference to Zorro's wounding signature, the analyst appears to defend himself against what he may experience as the injustice of the patient's complaint. Consequently, the duel goes on.

It seems that the patient attempts, once again, to cause the analyst to become aware that his interpretation has left him feeling "naked and defenseless." Perhaps the patient feels like a fool for having thought the analyst a "good" friend (like the good analytic book). However, once again, rather than taking in the negative transference, the analyst responds by further criticizing the patient for not being sufficiently friendly toward him in the hour. Although this may have been an accurate assessment of the analytic moment, it may also be seen as another example of the sort of intervention that can feed right back into the Superior ego, increasing the patient's defensiveness and even strengthening his protective shell (Tustin, 1990b).[11]

Throughout the hour it might be observed that, with each intervention addressing the patient's defenses, he becomes more and more manic, eventually becoming depressed and apathetic, giving up and retreating, perhaps—in despair of ever being able to interest the analyst in his own experience. I suggest that this situation exemplifies Bion's model of the sequence that follows a failure in maternal containment, expressed in the following lines:

> The infant takes back into itself the sense of impending disaster, which has grown more terrifying through the rejection of the mother and through its own rejection of the feeling of dread. This baby will not feel that it gets back something good, but the evacuation with its badness worse than before. It may continue to cry and to rouse powerful anxiety in the mother. In this way a vicious cycle is created in which matters get worse and worse until the infant cannot stand its own screams any longer. In fact, left to deal with them by itself, it becomes silent and closes within itself a frightening and bad thing, something which it fears may burst out again. In the meantime, it becomes a "good baby," a "good child." (Bion, 1974, p. 84)

Following Bion, both Tustin (1990b) and Steiner (1993) have brought to our attention some of the consequences of this sort of encapsulation of or retreat by the rejected aspects of the self and experience, when these are assumed to be beyond all bearing. I have suggested (Mitrani, 2007) that, in the transference, a built-in assumption of the analyst's vulnerability—for which our patients can nearly always find evidence, especially when we become defensive—may result in the patient's exaggerated fear of our coming in contact with the infant-self that had previously been experienced as a frightening and bad thing, to be kept silently closed off or encapsulated. The need to remain a good baby in order to protect the analyst from becoming overwhelmed often motivates the patient to work overtime to silence both his affectionate and aggressive feelings. Perhaps an example of this constellation might be revealing, this one from my own work with an analysand.

Clinical case: Leonard

Leonard, a quite schizoid man in his forties whose mother had suffered a psychotic breakdown after his birth, had been in analysis with me five days per week for several years. Over time, he had built up, from a more or less consistent experience, a firm conviction regarding my reliable resiliency. This experience had allowed him to relinquish many of his more primitive protections.

Leonard both lived and worked more than an hour's drive from my office. With regularity, he traveled over one of the main East-West arteries through the city to attend his analysis at the end of each day. One Monday, one of the most destructive earthquakes in many years shook the city in the early hours of the morning and caused the collapse of this highway. There were announcements of a curfew to be imposed after dark for the entire Los Angeles area. Around noon, Leonard rang me up to ask if I would be in my office. He wondered if he could safely come to his hour, expressing concern that he might not get through or, at the very least, that he might be delayed in the rerouted traffic.

Ordinarily, I might have confirmed that I would be there for his hour whenever he arrived and would have taken up his doubts and fears during the session. Instead, I said, "Perhaps with the collapse of the road and the security precautions, it may be unadvisable to come ahead." Noticeably taken aback, Leonard replied that he would let me know what he decided later in the day. Indeed, he left me a message just prior to the time he would have left for my office, stating that it sounded like it would be best for him to return home and try again the next day.

On Tuesday, Leonard arrived and began the hour by saying that, with the collapse of the highway, all the streets were packed; there was almost no way to get through. He wondered how we could continue working together until this was repaired: "Maybe it will never be the same, and how can you trust them to rebuild it so it doesn't happen again? I could have fallen off the roadway and been killed. I guess the stress and the weight of everything was too much." Leonard then became very withdrawn, sleeping through much of the hour. I thought it likely that he had taken what I said on the telephone the previous day to be a sign that, like the highway that connected us, I, too, had "collapsed" in the quake under too much stress and strain. Perhaps, whilst feeling that I was protecting myself from his substantial concerns at a time when my own must be just too much to bear, he had withdrawn from contact and given up his approach to me.

In the ensuing hours, we were able to adequately address this expression of mine and his interpretation of it in earnest, taking up his initial call as an attempt at reality testing and an expression of his need for reassurance. Gradually, we repaired the emotional earthquake that my "collapse" had created for Leonard, first in the transference and later in the context of his initial experience of his mother, which had led to the protective encapsulation and arrest of his original spirit, obstructing the path of his mental development.

The process of containing the infantile aspect in the adult patient

As I have previously elucidated (Mitrani, 2001), in Bion's model of container–contained, the mother in a state of reverie first receives and introjects her infant's unbearable and as-yet-unprocessed sensory experiences, which have been projected into her in unconscious fantasy. Second, she struggles to bear the force and affect of these projections upon her mind and body in order to be able to think about and make sense of these, a process that Bion referred to as transformation. Next, having thus transformed her baby's experiences in her own mind, she gradually returns them to him in detoxified and digestible form (as demonstrated through her attitude toward the baby and the way in which she ministers to him when such ministrations may be useful). Bion referred to this last step in the process as publication, which in analysis we commonly refer to as interpretation.

I have proposed that the ability to contain assumes a mother who has flexible boundaries and sufficient mental space to accommodate her own anxieties, as well those acquired in relation to her infant. It also assumes a mother who has a relatively well-developed capacity to bear and to suffer pain, to contemplate, to think, and to convey what she thinks in a way that is meaningful to her infant—a mother who is herself separate, intact, receptive, and who is appropriately giving. A mother who more or less fits the bill, relative to the innate temperament and talents of her baby, will be suitable for introjection as a containing object.

Thus, incrementally over time, the baby's identification with and assimilation of such an object will lead to an increase in his own mental space, the development of his own capacity to make meaning of experience (or what Bion called alpha function), and the evolution of a capacity to think for himself.[12] Bion's use of the term reverie—for the attentive, receptive, introjecting, and experiencing aspect of the container—is also analogous to a function, or the part of the analyst, that is vital to the task of taking the transference (Mitrani, 2001), which is itself a necessary and indispensable step on the way toward the equally necessary and indispensable task of interpreting the transference, particularly in the analysis of primitive mental states.

The complexities of taking the patient's material in the immediate transference, and the consequences of failing to do so are well illustrated in the case of Dr. B and her patient Gaila presented in Chapter Four. Perhaps, in reviewing that vignette, one may consider it to be representative of the conflict between the belief that on the one hand, genetic reconstruction is key and on the other, that transference interpretation is the mutative factor in analytic work (Strachey, 1934). However, might it be that both dimensions of interpretation are necessary to the process of analysis? And if so, how do we gauge what to address and when? What consideration does Bion contribute that might be helpful in determining which of the "conflicting views obtaining contemporaneous expression" (Bion, 1992, p. 166) might warrant attention and interpretation at any given moment? The following model may begin to address such questions.

Meaning and interpretation: a transformative sequence

Focusing on the analytic task of deciding what to interpret, Bion writes: "There is a value, when listening to associations, in making a mental distinction between the meaning of the associations and their interpretation" (Bion, 1992, p. 167). In this passage, I believe that Bion is calling our attention to the distinction between analytic work concerned with intuiting the latent meaning of the content of the patient's associations as distinct from their manifest overlay, and the parallel craft of constructing an interpretation in regard to the most immediate, ongoing, analytic happening.

To illustrate this point, Bion gives this wryly humorous example:

> The patient says, "I went on Hampstead Heath yesterday and did some bird-watching."[13] Taking the meaning first:
> Does he mean he was scrutinizing their sex life?
> Or is it an attempt to describe getting into the hands of the police by behaving in a suspicious way?
> Or does he mean he has at last taken some exercise?
> And so on with other speculations. Then, having decided that point, what is the interpretation?
> In conjunction with the rest of the analysis together with current transference, the preceding associations and the meaning as decided above, you finally produce the interpretation. (Bion, 1992, p. 167)

On one level, we might understand this curious passage as Bion's way of demonstrating and addressing an important technical point: that the analyst's associations to the content of the patient's utterances are merely speculations or imaginative conjectures. He seems to recommend that the analyst's associations be subjected to scrutiny within the context of the current process, titrated and transformed in his mind prior to his formulating the actual interpretation—and all the while the analyst must take into consideration what the patient is likely to be able to use constructively. Subsequently, if the patient has not been able to use the resultant interpretation constructively, the analyst should continue his attempt to understand what was made of the interpretation, in order to restore the creative process through continuing attempts at refining and articulating an evolving understanding of the plight of the patient.[14]

However, what if this transformative sequence does not take place in the analyst's mind? What does the patient do with untransformed or undigested bits of the analyst's process/associations?

Adaptation in perversion[15]

In connection with these questions, I have observed that patients often appear to present material in a manner that may enable them to make use of a given intervention regardless of its veracity or relevance. The patient may do so in one of two ways: either (1) the patient will gain a new experience (a container–contained experience, if you will) leading to the growth of the mind, when the analyst is able to digest/transform/ understand and convey her understanding of what is being communicated and received (Bion's K); or (2) the analyst might deliver more or less undigested/transformed speculations about the patient, missing or misunderstanding the patient's experience in the immediate analytic moment, and in this way the analyst may inadvertently and seamlessly "help" the patient acquire the materials (–K) with which he might successfully buttress a failing defensive organization.

In the second instance, which I call adaptation to perversion, mental and emotional growth remains stultified. However, in a manner of speaking, the patient is compensated with a reinforced means of survival. I will offer an example to illustrate this kind of *folie à deux* from a case presented to me for consultation.

Peter and Dr. C

This material is from a Wednesday hour in a four-days-per-week analysis. Dr. C had cut the previous week short, and Peter had to forego his Thursday session in this week due to a business obligation. Peter and his wife were expecting their first baby in three weeks' time, and much had surfaced relating to Peter's early history, his father's abandonment of him and his mother almost immediately after his birth, and his perception that mother needed him to be the "man of the house."

To begin with, the analyst mentioned that, in contrast to his usual business suit, Peter came to this session in jeans and sandals, appearing much younger than usual. She said that he began the hour by saying he had "lost the thread" of what they had discussed on Tuesday. He thought that he "should have been able to hold onto this thread" in the hours that separated the two sessions. Dr. C was unsure what Peter might be referring to, but was eager to reassure him and said that she thought he "might be in a different place" that morning.

Although Peter agreed that this was possible, he reiterated that he needed to know where they had been on Tuesday; he "needed the consistency." It seems that Peter might have been expressing his inability to hold onto the memory of his analyst in the gap between the hours, demonstrating how his Superior ego (Bion, 1962b) served to carry him through what might otherwise be an insufferable awareness of separateness. Perhaps, while feeling unsure of herself and pressured to reassure her patient, Dr. C missed an opportunity to acknowledge the baby-Peter who held on by a continuous "thread" of persecution when feeling unheld in the analyst's mind. In what appeared to be a transference enactment, Dr. C suggested that Peter had grown up and was therefore in a "different place."

Dr. C told me she had hoped this interpretation might attenuate Peter's self-criticism as well as her own. However, we detected that what followed was Peter's recollection of what they had been discussing: how he "got ahead of himself and could not stay in the moment," and how he tried to "make the future look great" when he actually felt uncertain about where he was at the moment. "I put this pressure on myself to make sure that what I'm feeling or doing now is consistent with whatever I did before," he said.

At this point, Peter's strategy for survival seemed to succeed. In his attempts to hold himself together and gain "consistency" under the pressure of harsh self-criticism, he appeared to be fortified by what he took to be the analyst's desire for him to grow up (i.e., to grow out of his shorts and sandals) and to be the man of the house (i.e., to be in a "different place").

In the material that followed, there was a series of what appeared to be projective transformation[16] in which the baby-Peter (feeling neglected and excluded from care/consideration by the analytic couple in the session) was systematically "relocated" in Peter's wife and the fetus she was carrying, and also in his dog, his work, and even in his future self. In a similar fashion, it also appeared that a negligent or incompetent object, lacking a certain maternal quality, was simultaneously introjectively identified with by the patient, and was split off and projected into his wife.

In response, Dr. C interpreted Peter's desire to evacuate his worries, "to leave them with her so that he could be free to enjoy himself." However, she did not mention why this might be so (i.e., she did not acknowledge the separation anxiety underlying the defense). In consultation, Dr. C and I considered that she might have done well to take up Peter's projections as an expression of the insufferable feeling of abandonment for the baby-Peter.

Dr. C said that the patient went on to speak about the need for a perfect moment: "Everything has to be perfect or the vacation will be flawed, spoiled." He added that his wife was afraid that his obsessional attitude and his perfectionism about the vacation would in and of itself spoil their time together. Indeed, it would seem that his ruminative defenses might likely be employed to protect him from unbearable anxieties about the baby-Peter who was abandoned by the analyst during the session itself, not just during the two disrupted weeks and the upcoming holiday break.

Dr. C reported that she had remained silent while the patient continued on to tell her that he had received a card from his grandmother, who was "frail and old." He realized that he had been neglecting her and felt guilty about this. He was reminded that he had neglected writing to his mother as well. Rather than an increase in his ability to reclaim his own experience/parts of self, this segment might be taken as evidence of further projection of the abandoned and neglected baby-Peter in the session, in the absence of the analyst's understanding.

However, Dr. C interpreted Peter's guilty feeling as related to Peter's leaving her behind to go on holiday, and she suggested that this threatened to spoil his enjoyment. The patient denied this outright. He then recalled a college year that he had spent overseas. He related that, a few months after he had left home, his mother showed up for a visit, disturbing his plans, putting pressure on him "to cede his happiness to her and take care of her needs, to make things perfect for her."

Unable to hear this as a clue to what was happening between them in the present—how Peter heard Dr. C's interpretation (i.e., taking responsibility for his own distress when he was convinced that his analyst/mother required him to "cede his happiness to her")—the analyst took up Peter's resentment toward his actual mother by way of a genetic interpretation.

In response, Peter continued on about having joined the Peace Corps after college and traveling to an undesirable place, one where Mother would not follow. "I had to make a duty out of it so that I wouldn't feel so guilty about leaving her behind." One might hear this as a communication about Peter's response to what he felt to be Dr. C's demands: he went to a place of "peace" where the mother/analyst could not find him, one that was undesirable (the spoiled vacation), albeit devoid of conflict.

Dr. C went on to address Peter's feelings of resentment and guilt toward his mother, and Peter spoke of not being ready for a new baby. "The house is not in order," he said, "and there is so much work to do, both at home and at the office"; he had a "bad feeling" about the upcoming holiday. Nearing the end of the hour, Peter circled back to the guilt about his "frail, neglected grandmother, whose handwriting is getting more and more faint and wobbly," and expressed a wish that she could be that "lion-grandmother" who had been "like a father figure" to him at one time. He said that he dreaded her death more than that of his mother. Indeed, Peter could have been expressing an unconscious need for the analyst to function not as an abandoned mother, but as a lion-grandmother/father, providing some boundary between the mother/analyst and the baby-Peter, and defining each of their roles clearly so that Peter would not prematurely/omnipotently take on the analyst's responsibilities (Klein, 1930).

In this excerpt, one can observe how the patient took in the analyst's speculations about him, thus fortifying his failing defensive organization (characterized by obsessional thinking, displacement, splitting, and projective identification) and furthering his chances for survival (his own and that of the analyst) when faced with separation. However, what was lost in the process was an opportunity for the mental development that results from being known and from knowing one's own mind. It is conceivable that the phenomenon described above, when chronic, may be a factor in interminable analyses, since the pathological defensive organization is reinforced each time the underlying need for that structure is left unmitigated.[17]

The interpretation of projective identification

I will discuss one more technical issue addressed by Bion, this one related to the use of theory. In *Cogitations* he writes:

> Theories are always a matter of some degree of controversy even among psychoanalysts, partly because development of the subject means that there are always some theories that are under trial, partly because there are some theories that, although long accepted, seem to require revision, and partly because the application of theory, perhaps sound in itself, has been defective and so has led to suspicion of the theory. (Bion, 1992, p. 92)

As one example, Klein's theory of projective identification as a defense was refined while under trial by Bion (1967). He suggested that projective identification is a normal, primary means of communication between infant and mother, and as such it plays an essential role in his model of the container and the contained.

However, in some circles this theory is still viewed with suspicion, perhaps not because the theory itself is unsound, but because it is often defectively applied in the clinical situation, when insufficient thought is given to the function of projective identification in Bion's model. I will present a clinical example of what I am describing, as well as the analyst's change of mind and her move to correct her course of interpretation, and then I will further discuss the problems involved in the application of the theory.

Clinical account: Laura and Dr. Z

Laura, a young woman in her second year of five times per week analysis, had missed her Monday hour with Dr. Z following the analyst's three week summer holiday. Additionally, she had arrived for her Tuesday hour some twenty minutes late. In consultation with me, Dr. Z confided that she had felt overly worried when Laura did not turn up for her Monday appointment since she had not even called to cancel. Dr. Z told me that at first she had thought her patient "had forgotten her."

Subsequently, as that day wore on and she still had no word from Laura, Dr. Z became convinced that Laura's absence indicated she had decided to quit the analysis. Of course, this thought stirred up quite a bit of agitation and self-doubt in this young analyst. She attempted to recall the last hour before the break and was distressed to realize that she could not remember anything about it. When the patient did not arrive on time for the Tuesday hour, Dr. Z said she felt certain that she must have done something very wrong, and she spent the time until Laura appeared going through past process notes, trying to discover a clue to the mystery of "Laura's abandonment of her analysis."

When Laura finally arrived, she entered the room smiling and went to the couch as if nothing untoward had occurred. Dr. Z reported that, beginning in the waiting room, she had felt puzzled, anxious, and confused. Laura said, "I really enjoyed my holiday and felt refreshed and ready to go back to work today. Ann [her employer] wasn't happy that I took so much time off, but I just couldn't imagine having to be high functioning with you away. It was better for everyone, even though Ann griped some. And besides, I had the vacation time coming to me."

Dr. Z told me that, because of the nature of her own feelings and the patient's cheery attitude, she had assumed that projective identification was being employed by Laura in order to get rid of her feelings about the break. Thus, she said to the patient, "I believe you were feeling abandoned by me, anxious and persecuted during the break, convinced that you must have done something to turn me away from you. Perhaps you felt yesterday that it would be better if you didn't come to your hour, that it was better for both of us since you were feeling scared, low, and unhappy with me."

After a brief pause, Laura said she was sorry she had missed the Monday hour and explained she had not returned from her holidays until Monday night—but flatly denied feeling low, abandoned, or unhappy. Then, after another brief silence, she reported the following dream:

> I was walking on a rough road with a friend [who had the same first name as the analyst] who was carrying a new baby in her arms. Suddenly she turned to me and thrust the baby at me, and before I knew what was happening, my friend disappeared. When I looked down at the baby, it seemed ugly and dirty, not as it had initially appeared, all pink and pretty in its own mother's arms. I was upset as I realized that I didn't have the equipment needed to care for the baby, and I was frightened and angry that my friend would shirk her duties as a mother.

Upon waking, Laura wondered why her friend had given birth to a baby in the first place. "I don't know what made me think of that dream," she said. "I had it a very long time ago, maybe last Christmas."

Dr. Z spontaneously recalled the past winter break and a similar disconnect that had occurred afterward. Recognizing her misuse of her countertransference and the subsequent error in her understanding, she offered the following to her patient: "I believe that, although the dream is an old one, long forgotten, it could be that you recalled it in this moment because it speaks to your experience of me right now. I wonder if, when I said what I did about your feeling abandoned, low, and angry, it may have seemed that I could not or did not wish to take responsibility for the you who may have been unable to bear the awareness of our separateness over this long break. Maybe it felt that, when I spoke, in that moment I was handing the baby-you over to an older part of you that feels as-yet ill-equipped to contend with such feelings of loss, and I may have left you wondering why I took you on in the first place if I can't bear these feeling myself. Could it be that, although when you first arrived today you felt 'in the pink,' my misunderstanding had the effect of turning your good spirits into a sense of being an ugly and dirty baby that I no longer want anything to do with?"

This brief segment of the exchange between Dr. Z and her patient Laura highlights a frequently occurring problem in the understanding and application of the theory of projective identification as communication, as well as its fruitful resolution. The theory suggests that what is split off from awareness and projected into the analyst in phantasy are the unbearable or untenable aspects of self-other experience. The patient seeks a containing object that is able to process and modify such experience, one who can then return the processed experience to the patient in digestible form. The error in the clinical application of the theory (as illustrated in the first part of this example, and which Dr. Z seems to have eventually noticed, revising her understanding accordingly in the second part) was that the analyst had interpreted Laura's use of projective identification—inferred from the feelings stirred up in her by the patient's mysterious absence—as feelings actually experienced by the patient herself.

It is common for analysts to interpret what the patient is feeling and subsequently they are met with what appears to be resistance to the interpretation. In such cases, further interpretation of the patient's resistance may serve only to perpetuate the error. However, if we refer back to the theory, we find that a consideration of the motive for and effects of projective identification might lead us in quite another direction.

In this example, there is no evidence that the patient felt anything remotely related to what the analyst felt in what is commonly referred to as the countertransference. In other words, if the experience and its concomitant feelings are truly being projected into the analyst in phantasy, and the patient's behavior is providing an atmosphere for evoking these feelings in the analyst, then the patient is not feeling any such thing and, by all rights, will feel misunderstood if the analyst attributes his own feelings to the patient. Being misunderstood often takes shape as an experience of rejection and/or a sense that the mother has disappeared, especially in the infantile transference, wherein the as-yet-underdeveloped, internal containing object is at a loss to contend with the emotional experience being relayed. In this example, the baby-Laura is left feeling unwanted—"ugly and dirty."

To her credit, Dr. Z's non-defensive attention to and thoughtful registration of her patient's reaction to the interpretation—in the form of the dream-as-association—led to a more sincere contact, which furthered the analytic work and afforded Laura the experience of an external object who could take responsibility for her own actions, and who could tolerate her own as well as the patient's experience of loss and uncertainty.

Conclusions

In this Chapter, I have highlighted some of what I believe are universal truths regarding psychoanalytic technique that have been alluded to in Bion's (1992) *Cogitations*, which contain notes that may not have been initially intended for public consumption, but which may contain wisdom of interest to analysts of almost any orientation. For example, there is undeniable value, while listening to a patient's material, in making a distinction between meaning and interpretation. This recommendation is a call for thoughtful discrimination, tact, timing, and taking into consideration to whom one is speaking, which is all part and parcel of the process of transformation in any analysis.

Furthermore, the notion that infantile aspects (as well as infinite other aspects of ordinary human-ness) reside in and are alive-if-buried or encapsulated in each of us seems to be an indisputable-if-inconvenient fact. The position that Bion takes—that these aspects find expression inside or outside the analysis, one way or another, whether or not the analyst encourages them or wishes to deal with the consequences of their expression—seems sound.

I have endeavored to demonstrate some of the consequences that can ensue when the analyst fails to observe the infantile aspects of the patient's personality and experience as they appear in the transference, or when he is unable to interpretively acknowledge these aspects before hyperbole sets in as the patient's way of getting the analyst's attention. I trust that I have been clear in my explication of the transformative sequence that Bion seems to suggest, while accenting the need to discriminate between the meaning and the interpretation of the patient's material.

I have offered my observation that patients may express themselves in such a way that they will be able to utilize the analyst's interventions either for the growth of the mind or (if all else fails) in fortifying their deteriorating defensive organization, depending upon their experience of being either understood or misunderstood. Although the patient may be able to survive in the case of the latter, such fortifications ultimately diminish the possibility for wholesome relationships that can lead to mental and emotional growth. This phenomenon, which I have termed adaptation in perversion, may be one factor accounting for analysis interminable. It is an anti-therapeutic and frequently parasitic process in which the defensive structure is continuously being reinforced while the underlying need for such a structure is left unmitigated.

Throughout, I have also attempted to emphasize, through illustration, the incalculable value of Bion's container–contained model and its pivotal role in promoting psychic growth, and I have addressed one frequently encountered defective application of Bion's extension of Klein's theory of projective identification, which is an essential element in this model. I have also demonstrated how this error in applying what is an otherwise sound theory can lead to stalemate in the analytic work unless and until it is identified by the analyst and worked through by the analytic couple.

Notes

1. These papers were "A theory of thinking" (1962a), "Notes on memory and desire" (1967), and one of his last papers, "Evidence" (1976).
2. Although the inspiration for and focus of this paper is *Cogitations*, others of Bion's works are quoted in order to orient the reader who may be less familiar with the foundations/extensions of these notes published in Bion's earlier/contemporaneous publications.
3. A palimpsest is a manuscript (usually made of papyrus or parchment) on which more than one text has been written, with the earlier writing incompletely erased and still visible. With the passing of time, the faint remains of the former writing that had been washed from parchment or vellum, using milk and oat bran, would reappear sufficiently such that one could make out the text and decipher it.
4. Bion's comments on this case—although also addressing the transference, the unconscious wishes felt toward and communications of experiences of the analyst, as well as the patient's defensive structure—distinctly display his own individual personality, his style of commentary, and his attitudes. Although the nature of my discussion of the case differs from Bion's, it is meant to be complementary to his remarks on the case.
5. Bion considered that what is reported about a given session is but a theory, or what he called a *transformation of a realization*. In other words, it is only one version of what took place between patient and analyst, which may be evaluated in a variety of ways, according to the facets seen by each individual who reviews the material. Bion cautioned that these assumptions about assumptions are merely models and not to be

confused with the actual events that took place. While Bion encouraged us to make as many of these models as possible out of any available material, he reiterated that these models are not substitutes for direct clinical observation or for analysis itself. Such model-making exercises are only preludes to observation and analysis, a "game" intended to develop the analyst's mental muscle.

6. It is of note here that the patient is very direct in calling the analyst's attention to the multiple layers of significance in the material. It is as if the patient, at least unconsciously, recognizes the palimpsest-like quality of his own communications.

7. I believe that this way of thinking about what our patients choose to tell us in a given hour, unconsciously or consciously, is also consistent with Gill's (1979) seminal notions about the transference.

8. Winnicott (1949b) suggests that if the analyst is going to have crude feelings imputed to him, he is best forewarned and so forearmed, for he needs to be able to tolerate being placed in that position. Above all, he must not deny hate that really exists in himself. Hate that is justified in the present setting has to be sorted out and kept in storage, available for eventual interpretation.

9. In Bion's terms, −K stands for the absence of alpha function, that is, a deficiency in the maternal capacity for digesting and making meaning of the infant's communications of his inchoate experiences. In analysis, this may be remedied when the analyst is able to detect an error in his understanding through open-minded listening to the patient's response, and can thus adjust his course of interpretation while acknowledging the patient's role in this benign development.

10. Rosenfeld (1959) noted the following in this regard: "Abraham … discusses the question of severe narcissistic injury or narcissistic disappointments in depression … He stresses not only the feeling of inferiority but of superiority in the melancholic and the inaccessibility of the melancholic patient to any criticism on the part of the analyst of his way of thought. He connects this attitude with a 'purely narcissistic character of the patient's train of thought.' He relates these observations to an over-estimation and under-estimation of the ego in melancholia which he calls 'positive and negative narcissism'" (Rosenfeld, 1959, p. 120).

11. When we analyze the *shell* (Tustin), the *false self* (Winnicott), or the *persona* (Jung), we may miss an opportunity to "touch" the patient. In other words, when we resort to defense analysis as a way of prying open the shell and getting at the heart of the matter, we often further fortify this defensive structure in such a way that we can even be fooled into thinking we have succeeded, when in actuality we have only helped

the patient fortify his coat of armor in ways that comply with our ideals or our preconceived notions and theories.
12. If this description of the mother seems idealized, I refer the reader to Winnicott's (1949a) *ordinary devoted mother* in his model of mental health.
13. *Bird watching* in Great Britain is a slang term that refers to observing women, and often implies some degree of flirtation and even seduction.
14. A military man in World War One, Bion often referred to this process as making *sighting shots*.
15. In this instance, the word *perversion* is used in its broadest sense, referring to the act of changing the inherent purpose or function of something into its opposite. For example, psychoanalysis may be intended as a means of revealing and making the patient's psychic truths more tolerable. However, its opposite may function to strengthen the defenses against these truths and to obscure them through the use of omnipotent fantasy. This adaptation to the environment has been casually referred to as "making lemonade out of lemons."
16. Expanding on Bion's (1965) term, Meltzer (1978, p. 73) considered that these sorts of transformations are inherent in what Klein called the *early transference* based on part-objects, internal objects, splitting, and projective identification.
17. This notion is consistent with Klein's (1961) stipulation that the deepest anxiety situations experienced in the immediacy of the transference need to be interpreted prior to and/or alongside the analysis of defenses against such anxiety situations.

CHAPTER SIX

The past presented: bodily centered protections in puberty and adolescence*

> Past, present and future are often used in psychoanalytic discussion. At best, they can only be suggestions of the need to discriminate qualities, which are being interpreted. The only evidence is that which the analyst can observe for himself at the time while he talks. This fact is obscured by words, which tend to imply that the event or emotion to which he wants to draw attention occurred in 'the past' or in 'the future'. The important thing about the patient's state of mind is that it exists at the time he or she is seeing the analyst.
>
> —Bion, *Memoir of the Future:*
> *The Past Presented*, p. 645

This chapter focuses on the reoccurrence of infantile proto-mental functioning that can be observed in some patients in puberty and in adolescence. I will demonstrate how the infantile tendency to resort to *bodily centered protections* is reactivated at a time

---

*An earlier version of this chapter was published in 2009 as "Bodily centered protections in adolescence: An extension of the work of Frances Tustin." *International Journal of Psychoanalysis*, 88 (5): 1153–1169, published by John Wiley & Sons.

when the enormous internal and external physical and psychological changes brought on in puberty once more threaten the individual with catastrophe.

Additionally, I will illustrate how, when the capacity for adequate mental and emotional development is stultified, sensation and action once again come to the rescue as the young person's way of attenuating nameless dreads associated with the awareness of separateness, added to and resonating with those undigested happenings from earlier developmental periods. I believe that, in analysis, these happenings become the "past presented" in the immediate moment, that is, in the transference. I suggest that a transference-centered therapy may be pivotal in setting previously derailed mental and emotional growth back on track in order to make it less likely that the "past presented" in analysis will be repeated in the future.

Frequently, disturbances observed in adolescents who find their way to analysis seem to correlate with a shift in the balance between the various aspects of the personality. Forward-going development is often threatened when the massive physical and psychic changes beginning with puberty and continuing throughout adolescence, are further complicated by a resurgence of conflicting passions and desires remaining from infancy, which the child has usually been able to keep in check throughout the latency years.

During latency, thought and action are largely controlled by the "non-psychotic" aspect of the personality. However, past anxieties presented once again in puberty provoke a shift in the balance towards the more primitive defenses of what Bion called the "psychotic part of the personality." The problem of the so-called regression to more elemental modes of operation is complicated by the presence of physical and cognitive capacities newly acquired from puberty onward. These capacities—when coupled with the resurgence of the omnipotence of infancy—may create an overwhelming level of persecutory and depressive anxieties.

For example, in the case of promiscuity, intercourse is not a longed-for act of procreation and pleasure. Rather, at the benign end of the spectrum, these are mainly the means of getting inside the other in order to become totally cared for and, at the destructive end, are engaged in order to overpower and demolish the object, all in the service of early infantile wishes that derive from the domain of unconscious fantasy and enter into the realm of possibility when facilitated by the newly acquired capacities of adolescence. These concrete desires create disturbances in those who cannot contain them and profound anxiety about the fate of both the object and the self in young people who may be coping, but who fear that they won't be able to do so in the future.

One way of contending with such insufferable anxieties is through identification with idealized bad objects. Such identifications are at the heart of the pathological-post-pubertal organization. However, although this classical Kleinian model is one I personally find quite useful in my work, Frances Tustin's notions regarding the dimension of auto-generated sensation objects and shapes are also central in my work. I will present a brief review of her findings.

In her paper on "Anorexia Nervosa in an adolescent girl," Tustin wrote about her treatment of Margaret and quotes lyrics from Paul Simon's song "I am a rock": a mighty, impenetrable fortress; a life without need and filled with disdain, and the protection afforded by reading literature in isolation on an island emancipated from the pain of human relationship.

Simon's lyrics poignantly capture both the underlying vulnerabilities and the defenses against the awareness of these vulnerabilities in many adolescent patients. Tustin's seminal discoveries derived mainly from her work with autistic children who found refuge from nameless dreads in a sensation dominated way and she provided an indispensable model for understanding the function and significance of anorexic and bulimic behavior and other problematics found in many children form puberty into adolescence.

Tustin understood that young autistic children, as well as older non-autistic children, engage in activities that produce the *sensation of being "one"* with a never-ending, inexhaustible ever-presence, which provides relief from the conviction that the to and fro of relationship will be exhausting and even deadly for one or both members of the couple. Such expectations of catastrophe seem to coincide with the baby's premature awareness of maternal depression, and familial violence or death that characterize the baby's experience of an absence of mind in the primary environment. In these cases, Tustin found that the baby has made due with Mother's physical presence, relying on sensations of mother's skin, her voice, her smell, taste, and sight to hold him intact when mental containment and emotional contact were critically deficient. However, when these sensations have remained unaccompanied by a reliably affectionate and mindful component, the baby—now overly reliant upon sensorial contact and continuity—experiences great difficulty negotiating the awareness of physical absences.

I would also like to stress the fact that, in puberty, there is yet another layer of physical distance from the parental figures that must begin to be reckoned with. This new stratum seems to be superimposed upon those experienced in earlier childhood experiences of separateness. Adolescent separation experiences are also connected with various societal and peer pressures, as well as the inbuilt, unconscious, psychological taboos that limit physical contact with the parents as the child enters puberty.

In her work on autistic encapsulation Tustin found that, in many neurotic children, development seems to continue normally outside of the autistic encapsulation of certain unmentalized happenings. She pointed out that this pocket of encapsulation gives trouble later on, often beginning in puberty. This "trouble" may take the form of sleep and eating disorders, phobias, psychosomatic disturbances, and some forms of delinquent behavior and acting out. In the case of Tustin's patient Margaret, unconscious conflicts were felt and expressed mainly through her body, with the emphasis on gaining or losing weight. In the transference, Tustin discovered that these gains and losses were *concretely equated* at various times with gaining or losing the affection of the therapist, gaining or losing hope, gaining or losing an hour, weekend breaks and holidays. All in all, she found that *each loss was felt as analogous to the loss of a part of Margaret's bodily self*. Additionally, Margaret was convinced that her gains were made at the expense of the analyst's well-being.

Work with autistic children strongly suggests that this phenomenon is not simply a case of the Talion principle at work in the paranoid-schizoid position, which is central to the metapsychology of Melanie Klein. Something much more primeval seems to be in operation at the core of this experience of growth. In earliest normal infancy (and continuing in unmodified form in those infants who have failed to introject a proper psychic skin or an object capable of mentally containing emotional happenings) undue reliance upon *sensations of bodily continuity with the mother* persists. In these infants, and later on in older individuals, growth and development is *misunderstood* as taking place by acquiring bits of the (m)other, thus diminishing her "thereness."

Psychoanalytic infant observation has found striking support for the notion that this is not a phantasy, but a pre-conception rooted in every baby's normal beginnings. However, this preconception may take a turn for the worse if the growth of the mind and the process of symbol formation are truncated. Infant research continues to fortify the impression that, at first, the neonate experiences the mother's nipple and its own mouth to be "one"—rendered unbroken and uninterrupted by the baby's tongue—just as the umbilical cord had united the mother and baby in utero. In normal infancy, it has been observed that this experience of at-one-ment alternates with "flickering states of awareness of separateness."

With this model as a guide, we can further comprehend the construction of features of the elemental body ego. From the baby's vantage point, mother and baby form two halves of the same body. In health, elemental links are progressively incarnated in the joints of the body through a developmental sequence that begins with the baby feeling that its head is properly joined to its shoulders. Next, at about three months, the baby can succeed in supporting its own head, and some two to three months later it can sit up by itself. Finally, somewhere between ten and fifteen months, arms, hands, legs, and feet are emotionally linked to the trunk, and the baby becomes a toddler who can crawl, stand, and walk. These physical developments coincide with an increasing tolerance for the awareness of both bodily and emotional separateness from the mother.

Proper embodiment results in the child feeling harmonious with his own body. The baby's emotional relationship to his caregiver plays an important role in his ability to assume psychological ownership of his own body. Of course, much is dependent upon the capacity of the mother to remain responsive, to bear the reality of separateness, and to provide adequate psychic boundaries for her baby. In this way, Mother presents an "object lesson" for the baby. However, if these initial challenges are not satisfactorily met by either party, the baby's preliminary conception (or misconception) leads to the awareness of bodily separateness as a threat to his as well as to his mother's "going-on—being." In this state of mind, life is a struggle for continued existence and for the "thing" that insures existence. This model resonates with Winnicott's statement that, at least in the beginning of perinatal life, we cannot speak of a baby without a mother.

A sense of awkwardness or disjointedness ordinarily colors the experience of adolescence in many ways, an experience of both physical and mental development that might be likened to the thrust of opposing tectonic plates in a geophysical event. These developmental earthquakes occur as child and adult strivings in the adolescent clash and overlap, often acquiring the significance of a mental disaster. For example, speaking about her sexual behavior at a party, sixteen-year-old Rhoda said, "It felt like I had lost my head." This seemed to be an expression of Rhoda's concrete sensation of being "dis-located" from her parents and their mindful attentiveness.

Tustin described this dislocation as "A dangerous, fluid state in which the child feels lost on a bodily level, their identity as they knew it slipping away. Changes mean that everything is thrown into the melting pot; [the child] is in a state of flux, which has to be borne if transformations are to occur" (Tustin, 1986b, p. 201). In this fluid state, adhesive identity—heralded by mimicry, echolalia, and the use of both hard and soft sensations—is the means by which the pubescent child may be able to maintain a tenuous sense of "thereness". This protective maneuver in puberty trump projective identification, which cannot be said to operate effectively in individuals who have not been helped to establish a sense of inside and outside along with the proper functioning of an internal containing object.

Here, I would like to present an example of the auto-sensuous maneuvers, which are re-deployed at puberty to restore a sense of oneness when the child feels under pressure to recognize a budding separateness, and the pain and terror that this awareness of separateness precipitates. I thank my colleague Dr. T for allowing me to use his work with a boy on the cusp of puberty to illustrate the use of sensations to ward off a dangerous awareness of separateness.

Dr. T and Taylor

Taylor had initially been referred for treatment subsequent to a diagnosis of autism at the age of two years and five months. He cried inconsolably, could not be held, avoided eye contact, engaged in stereotypical behaviors, was largely incapable of verbal interaction and was unable to attain the level of social development required for a preschool setting. With diligent work, Taylor's analyst was able to contain the child's violent and unbounded overflow of feelings regarding awareness of otherness. Within the first year of analysis, Taylor began to communicate verbally and was increasingly able to respond to the constraints of school, including toilet training, socializing with peers, and attending to teachers and caregivers.

Throughout latency, Taylor gradually became more emotionally related, and his auto-sensuous protections against anxieties regarding intense positive and negative feelings gave way to more cooperative play in the analytic hours as well as with both male and female playmates. However, toward the latter part of latency, although Taylor liked and participated in competitive sports, he threatened to withdraw when he realized that he could not be certain of winning. "Winning" in the analytic situation appeared to have a special significance of being at-one-with Dr. T, while "losing" required an awareness of his separateness from Dr. T, which became increasingly insufferable for Taylor as he began to show outward signs of entering puberty at age ten and a half years of age.

In a session reported from that period in the analysis, the first after a holiday break, Taylor entered the room with a broad smile on his face. He was carrying his iPhone with a look of pride and satisfaction. This was in open defiance of the prohibition against cell phones that was plainly posted on the waiting room door. Taylor stepped into the room and, with an excited voice, described a new NASCAR racing application while proceeding to boot up the device. It was apparent that he had been running the application repeatedly before his arrival to the session and was quite proficient at the game. Taylor then insisted that Dr. T watch closely while he continued to play the game. Dr. T observed that Taylor was becoming noticeably more and more excited.

After a short while, Dr. T said that it seemed to him that Taylor needed Dr. T to be racing right along with him, as if they had never been separated over the holiday break. Immediately, the boy seemed to accelerate in his excitement, racing right past Dr. T. The analyst attempted to address Taylor's need for more and more excitement to cover over the realization that—rather than uniting them as if they had never been apart—the game might be coming between them.

The child seemed to totally ignore this remark as well, continuing to play the game while emitting excited sounds, his eyes and fingers working even more feverishly on the touch screen. Intermittently and with determination, Taylor insisted that Dr. T continue to watch closely. Before long, Dr. T observed that Taylor's remarks shifted. He began to focus his comments on the colors on the touch screen. Gradually the boy grew silent, while continuing to touch the screen and to visually track the cars/colors. Soon Taylor began to produce tiny bubbles of saliva with no apparent awareness. It was the analyst's sense that the child had become ensconced in a auto-sensual state of ocular, tactile, and muscular stimulation that served to obliterate the analyst's words, perhaps creating a sensation that the boy and his analyst existed as "one" in a bubble of Taylor's own making.

One of the essential tasks of the analyst is to receive, metabolize, transform, and address the concrete terrors that plague these patients; to consider the sensation-dominated ways in which they contend with their most elemental terrors, and in doing so, to begin to facilitate the establishment of a process of identification with a feeling and thinking object. I will bring an example of this process from my work with Cathy, an emotionally frozen and physically constricted 18-year-old college freshman, whose parent's seemed to have been less than mindful long before their daughter entered puberty, leaving Cathy more than usually awkward, disjointed, and ill-prepared to face the challenges of adolescence.

In Cathy's case it might be seen that, as a consequence of the therapeutic process, troubling and sometimes life-threatening bodily symptoms could become circumstantially delineated instead of remaining haphazard. Furthermore, work with Cathy suggests that these symptoms can be attenuated and even transformed through a transference-centered analytic process.

Initial consultation with Cathy

Cathy was a tall, gangly but pretty and somewhat exotic-looking brunette. Her mother, an immigrant from a third world country, was characterized as a submissive and insecure woman who "cared more for her roses than her children" and was frequently a major stimulant of shameful feelings for the girl. Father was described as an educated, Anglo-American man, many years older than Mother, who was reported to have cruelly lorded it over his wife and his two daughters.

Cathy initially presented as emotionally frozen and physically constricted. She came to the initial interview and told me that she felt she needed help with what she termed "social and test-anxiety." Cathy also made a point to tell me, more than once, that she had shied away from any contact with her "baby sister" for years because her sister had suffered from depression from early on in puberty. In response to this, I told Cathy that I thought that she might wish me to know how frightened she was of a "depressed-baby" aspect of herself, like her younger sister with whom she avoided contact. I also said that I believed that she might be faintly aware, on some level, that keeping this aspect of herself at a distance might be contributing to her feelings of anxiety about relationships as well as doubts about what she knows and does not know, especially about herself.

Seemingly stunned, Cathy grew silent. Then she looked me straight in the eyes, for the first time in the interview, and said that she wished to begin analysis with me if I had the time. We settled on four days per week, Monday through Thursday, as she said that she felt Fridays were "part of the weekend." I was uncertain at the time whether she feared that I would cut into her weekend, or she into mine.

Over the first year of her analysis, Cathy's growing awareness of her dependency upon me and her longing for closeness with me brought her nearer to feelings of emptiness and loneliness and of having nothing inside during my absences. At first Cathy dealt with these empty feelings by binging on junk food or filling up her schedule, especially letting schoolwork pile up until the weekend, so that she had to work around the clock on Sundays to complete her assignments. This "filling-up" also appeared to serve as an efficient way of warding-off terrifying feelings of falling to pieces, since the weekend binging and her too-busy schedule placed enormous *pressures* on her from within and without, *anxieties accompanied by sensations that seemed to function as a second skin*, in Bick's (1968, 1986) sense of the term.[1]

Her material at the time seemed to express a delusional jealousy toward the baby-she who could depend upon me, as well as toward the young adult-she who was engaged in a creative intercourse with me in the analysis. Additionally, that part of her which felt consistently left out and ignored—having to fend for itself—was so angry that she refused my help when I was available. This refusal functioned to help her to feel physically "mean and tough" rather than soft, helpless, needy, and defenseless.

Separation or abandonment?

In the beginning of the second year of the analysis, I was better able to fine-tune my understanding of Cathy's experience of being left on the weekends and during holiday breaks when she recalled asking mother if she had taken a break from teaching after she was born, to which mother replied that she had merely switched to teaching night courses.

"I just had to get away!" Mother explained. Cathy learned that she had been left nightly, shortly after birth, with a Father who could not tolerate being disturbed, so Mother made certain that Cathy was asleep before leaving and put her in a closet so that her cries could not be heard.

Thus, Cathy often anticipated that I too could not wait to get away from her. She felt that I did not merely leave her at night, on the weekends and on holidays, but that I ran away from her and she was convinced that her cries for help would remain unheard. The latter was evident from her apparent lack of enquiry about how I could be reached in case of emergency and her conviction that I left no one on call for her when I was away on holiday.

Cathy's experience of separation also seemed to be that of being plucked off the breast and discarded, too small to be desired by Mother. This was expressed one Friday hour at the end of one week in the twenty-fourth month of the analysis when she spoke of a flower bed in which flowers were planted by Mother, already tall and mature, while those which did poorly were plucked out and replaced. It seemed that my patient experienced the end of the week as my plucking her out of my flowerbed/couch (not coincidentally my couch is covered in a floral tapestry) and she felt that I discarded her, clear evidence that she was a "loser"; that her neediness and dependency rendered her unsuitable for residence in my flower bed/couch over the weekend, as she was too little to compete with my husband. She could not understand how I would not want to see her grow up, feeling that it was I who both wished for and demanded her instant maturity.

In one dream, I was represented by "Endora the Witch" (a character in a television series). Cathy's associations, to an Hispanic woman at work who did not want her baby girl, lead to our understanding of the witch/mother/analyst as the me Cathy experienced at the end of the "hora" (Spanish for "hour"). When the agony of the breaks became too much to bear, perhaps in identification with the mother who put the baby-her in the closet, Cathy seemed frequently to close herself off in silence for much of the hour, especially before and after breaks. One day, during one such protracted silence, I had the presence of mind to tell her that I believed that she felt me as an intolerant father who has to be protected from the baby's screams by the mother-her in order to safeguard our relationship or perhaps to keep me from becoming angry with her. Cathy immediately began to cry outwardly and audibly for the first time, whereas previously I was unaware that she was tearful until after she rose from the couch or when she infrequently reached for a tissue. On this occasion, she continued to emit an animal-like cry through until the end of the hour. When she sat up she said that she felt "lighter" and thanked me for the first time.

After this piece of work, Cathy reported taking out of storage and giving away some of her old things, which she had been hiding for many years. She also reported that she was losing weight and had not binged on junk food for some time. This I thought corresponded to her efforts to unpack some painful feelings that she had encapsulated, using the analysis as a holding place for these instead, giving up some of the junk food she had been storing up for hard times in her body, and allowing herself to take and to use something fresh from me in its stead.

Shortly after this time, Cathy began to talk about her daily experiences in a new way, categorizing everything as either "good" or "bad", as if she were now sorting out these packed away and stored up experiences into two piles—the bad and the good—which seemed to express a kind of very elemental splitting, which she was now able to effect, rather than an indiscriminate storage of experiences in a muddled-up and locked-away heap.

We also discovered that this primitive sorting and discrimination was occurring as if she were inside some protective bubble, safe from feelings that might overwhelm her. It seemed that this was some very early form of thinking that she could accomplish as we became more able to modify her anxieties about human connection and disconnection.

The beginnings of a capacity to bear otherness

Eventually, Cathy became more able to be aware of others—other patients, my husband, a fellow student who intended to write her term paper on the same topic as Cathy—and it was soon apparent that she felt that I was being torn away from a baby-her by others and that there was not only nothing left for her, but nothing left of her, which was even more devastating.

At this time, I also noticed the way in which my patient was able to create a second skin of "worries" for herself, which would serve to hold her together in my absence or even during my silences. One could feel the growing tension and pressure as she seemed to weave a net of duties and obligations that she pulled tight around herself at the end of each analytic week, tying it up with a knot in her stomach made up of a palpable anticipatory terror that she "would not meet all her deadlines."

In the thirty-fifth month of the analysis, Cathy began to communicate about the ways in which she had been able to preserve certain of her experiences, which she could not mentalize and therefore could neither cope with nor integrate. In one dream, she reported that she was teaching a class on elementary biology to a group of little children. They were visiting a laboratory where insects in various stages of development (from the most elemental to the most mature) were stored in jars, each in its own ecosystem. One little child was about to place the least mature specimen into the jar with the adult.

Cathy said that she had panicked in the dream and rushed to the child shouting, "No, don't! You will disturb the ecosystem!" It seemed that this dream was somehow related to a fear that by exposing me to the needy-baby-she, she would somehow destroy my equilibrium, perhaps even drive me mad.

In subsequent hours she revealed an additional motivation for this "sealing-off" of behavior as a way in which she could protect herself from experiences of loss. Her fear of losing or forgetting what had happened in our sessions compelled her to freeze us in a sort of static way by memorizing the hour. This created a feeling of distance as she was always "being objective" about what *had* gone on between us. It appeared that Cathy's fear was that "we might melt" if there were any immediacy or warmth between us, with one or both of us slipping away into a too faint past. She could not be certain that there would be a future unless she kept us in rigid juxtaposition "like the factors in a mathematical equation."

I was reminded of Tustin's patient Jean (1986a) who, as a thirteen-year-old girl, had been suffering from anorexia nervosa and who returned at the age of twenty-one for additional psychotherapy. Jean felt that she and Mrs. Tustin were like "two jugs pouring water into each other" (Tustin, 1986a, p. 198) and during breaks in the therapy she felt emptied. She felt as if she were a waterfall, falling forever, spilling out of control into a bottomless abyss. Tustin understood that, for Jean, "'spilling' was equated with forgetting" (Tustin, 1986a, p. 199).

Tustin found that during absences, memory traces were felt to be dissolved and (as these memories had not attained a symbolic quality) Jean felt that neither she nor Mrs. Tustin existed: they were no-bodies nowhere. I thought that perhaps for Cathy, like Tustin's Jean, "Forgetting was felt to be lethal" (Tustin, 1986a, p. 199). By keeping herself and me from moving, by memorizing what had once been a lively connection until it was rendered still and could not slip away, Cathy was able to guard against the possible experience of loss, which her progress in the analysis would also lead to.

Paradoxically, Cathy was also just as concerned with keeping us together as she was with keeping us apart. She resented meeting people on the way from the parking area to my consulting room, on the stair, on the street, in the elevator or in the waiting room. These people were concrete markers of the separation between us. Cathy wished for an enclosed conveyor belt from the lot to my room as a smooth, uninterrupted, and continuous contact with me.

It represented quite a developmental move forward for Cathy when she began taking the stairs up the four flights to my office, feeling these to be small, contiguous *links* between us rather than cruel and insurmountable *obstacles* in her way. One day she talked about having noticed an evolution in her experience of the stairs. She said that at first she had been afraid of them, fearing that she would fall. However, she now liked to climb them, as if "they were linking the two of us together."

When she immediately followed this statement by saying that she thought that maybe she was "making a big deal over nothing," I was able to call her attention to a part of her that devalues and belittles her progress. We could see here how frightened she was of changing, as change was equated with separation from the mother-me and how, by keeping us in an unchanging and therefore unthreatening state, she inadvertently had kept herself in a state of helplessness and hopelessness with regard to her own growth and development.

Aloneness and there-ness

Little by little, Cathy was able to have and to be aware of real feelings of aloneness and her need for people, as well as her tendency to withdraw from them for protection. She became steadily more direct in acknowledging her eating disorder, the way in which she used food to bolster a tenuous sense of her own existence. Along with sleeping, eating was also a way in which she filled up the dangerous emptiness inside when she was left all alone.

My patient also came to a painful realization that she sometimes ate so much that her heart pounded and her stomach ached. It seemed to both of us that this aching was preferable to the emptiness and deadness she felt when left alone, and that her pounding heart provided some concrete proof of her survival—proof that her heart was beating, not broken and unable to sustain her life. The sensation of a pounding, aching fullness, which was so uncomfortable and shameful, had been favored over the emptiness and hollowness Cathy felt in the absence of her broken, unwanted self.

Adolescence

Especially well documented in the psychoanalytic literature are the many adolescent disturbances that manifest in a distorted relationship to the body and its functions, exaggerated beyond those considered "normal" for this period of life (e.g., Anderson & Dartington, 1998; Hildebrand, 2001; Laufer & Laufer, 1984; Pestalozzi, 2003.) Additionally, the adolescent's denial of needs and limitations may be expressed in various serious harmful and even life-threatening behaviors, often but not limited to eating disorders, self-mutilation, and substance abuse.

Like many troubled adolescents seen in analysis, Cathy's infantile proto-mental functioning was all she had to deal with the upsurge of needs and the awareness of limitations in her "neither-here-nor-there" state. The dilemma of the "no-longer-child, not-yet-adult" is complicated in those individuals who, as infants, have been unable to locate a presence of mind capable of receiving, digesting, and transforming early experiences and who have been pushed to use their own bodies as containers various "unmentalized happenings" (Mitrani, 1993, 1995, 2001).

The *tendency to resort to bodily centered protections* (that, although self-destructive on the surface, ultimately have survival as their aim) seems often to be reactivated on a grand scale when the enormous internal and external physical and psychological changes brought on in puberty are felt as catastrophic. In the case of my patient Cathy, I have demonstrated how, when the capacity for adequate mental and emotional development is stultified, sensation and action one again come to the rescue as the young adult's way of attenuating the nameless dreads of adolescence, heaped upon and resonating with those happenings from earlier developmental times.

Conclusion

Like the infantile constellations of the paranoid schizoid and depressive positions so frequently addressed in the Kleinian literature, I believe that the constellation of conflicts, anxieties, and defenses of an extremely primitive nature, which I have highlighted in Cathy's case, are frequently encountered in many of our adult analysands as well as in the adolescents we commonly see in analysis.

As analyst's, our appreciation of the elemental terrors inherent in that sense of a tentative bodily existence that, at times, may plague our patients and an attentiveness to the ways in which these patients attempt, at least intermittently, to keep these terrors out of conscious awareness is of paramount importance in nearly every analysis, either of children or adults. An open-minded alertness to and comprehension of various types of auto-sensual maneuvers (e.g., various physical actions, the binging, fasting, and purging of bulimarexia, the various obsessional activities, adhesive object relations (Mitrani, 1994) and isolating encapsulations) as well as a sensitivity to the dimension of the concrete rather than metaphoric nature of our patients' communications may be helpful in our efforts to give them a *sense of being* as well as an *experience of being understood*.

Note

1. Bick proposed the notion of a "psychic skin," similar to Federn's concept of ego boundary in the primitive body-ego and Bion's protomental apparatus. Just as the physical skin holds together, in proper working order, the various internal organs with the fluidic, muscular and bony aspects of the body, Bick suggested that the psychic skin serves to passively bind together the various parts of the nascent self. Bick described this "psychic skin" as a projection of or corresponding to the bodily skin, and she intuited that this internal object was initially dependent upon the introjection of an external object experienced as capable of fulfilling this function. Bick demonstrated that any disturbance in the primal skin function can lead to the development of a "second [or substitute] skin" by which dependence on the object is replaced by a pseudo-independence. Bick's also observed that *the second skin is often patterned after some perceived quality of the primary maternal environment*.

CHAPTER SEVEN

"Trying to Enter The Long Black Branches": some technical extensions for the analysis of autistic states in adults from the work of Frances Tustin*

> Never to enter the sea and notice how the water divides
> With perfect courtesy, to let you in!
> Never to lie down on the grass, as though you were the grass
> *Never to leap in the air as you open your wings over*
> *The dark acorn of your heart!*
> No wonder we hear, in your mournful voice, the complaint
> *That something is missing from your life!*
>
> —Oliver, 1997, p. 61[1]

Introduction

The title of this chapter borrows from a poem by Mary Oliver (1997), which I have quoted in full at the end of this chapter, with the gracious permission of the author and her publisher. The stanza from that same poem, quoted above, seems apposite to many patients who find their way to the analytic couch. These patients leave the impression that they

---

*An earlier version of this paper was published in 2012 in the *International Journal of Psychoanalysis*, 92: 21–42; published by John Wiley & Sons.

are in search of something missing in their lives: perhaps the emotional contact with an elemental quality of self, a certain kind of lived-experience akin to entering a courteous sea, being one with the grass, leaping in air and even opening to the dark acorn of the heart. These missing elements of experience, linked to various unlived and heretofore unheard aspects of self and their "uncontained" (in Bion's sense of the term)[2] perceptions of encounters with the agony and ecstasy of being, often come to inhabit a hidden capsule[3] within many ordinary neurotic, borderline, or psychotic adults (Bion, 1957; S. Klein, 1980; Mitrani, 1992; Rosenfeld, 1985; Steiner, 1993; Tustin, 1986a). This capsule may be shrouded in somatic symptoms, encased in extremes of acting-out, ensconced in therapeutic enactment or overlaid with a verbal message that is, by and large, deceptive in its expression. Nonetheless, as disturbing, misleading and distracting as these protective and decoys may at times be for the analyst hard at work trying to enter "the long black branches of other people's lives" (Oliver, 1997, p. 61)—we frequently discover that their effect upon us (if we can bear to suffer it) is imbued with meaningful-if-encrypted communications, perhaps signaling a point at which that "something missing" might have the opportunity to emerge and to develop.

The implications of the findings of Frances Tustin and this author's technical extensions and applications of those findings to the analytic work within these obscure areas of the lives of "ordinary adults" are the subject of this paper. Throughout, I will demonstrate some of the ways in which Tustin's innovations have and are continuing to open up new possibilities for deepening the analyst's comprehension of those persons in whom unmentalized happenings (Mitrani, 1994) have been silently encapsulated through the use of autosensual maneuvers (Mitrani, 1992). I hope to be able to convey that, although these encapsulations constitute daunting obstacles to emotional and intellectual development, are consequential in both the relational and vocational spheres for many analysands, and present unending challenges for analysts, it is possible to detect and to modify them.[4]

Going forward

Oliver asks, "Who can open the door who does not reach for the latch? Who can travel the miles who does not put one foot in front of the other, all attentive to what presents itself continually? Who will behold the inner chamber who has not observed with admiration, even with rapture, the outer stone?" (1997, p. 61). When the analyst can behold the "inner chamber" without sentimentality, but with an appreciation of both the nature and function of the "outer stone," her own as well as her patient's, she may be able to navigate through a certain range of therapeutic impasse and to tolerate what may at times seem like interminable frustrations when encountering patients' ubiquitous, deeply ingrained and stony autosensual protections. To paraphrase Graham Greene (1929), the category of patient addressed in this paper (not unlike poets and writers) has a splinter of ice in their hearts. Perhaps the analyst's perseverance and her artful and timely delivery of hard-earned and mindful awareness may constitute a warm, therapeutic bath that can enable her to penetrate, to reach and to melt this icy obstruction to development.

By detecting and exploring this dimension of psyche-soma, the analyst may be better equipped to refine her insights, to find new ways in which to articulately decipher the plight of the infant in the adult patient, and *to define her current role in the revival of this predicament in the transference*. A familiarity with the concepts of *autistic objects* (Tustin, 1980) and *autistic shapes* (Tustin, 1984b) is helpful in this effort[5] as is our sensitivity to the existential terrors inherent in both the *pre-mature awareness of two-ness* and the *ecstasy of at-one-ment* (Tustin, 1981). Tustin's emphasis on the role of sensation—as both an integral aspect of primordial terrors and as material for the construction of the protective barrier against the awareness of such terrors—draws attention to the dimension of autosensuality and its centrality to the work within primitive mental states. With these enlightening tools in hand, the analyst may be able to avoid becoming hopelessly lost in this dimension, where shadow and light are occluded from perception and emotional experience. Additionally, the analyst may become more capable of shepherding her analysand out of a mindless island of sameness and into a shared world, where opposites intermingle and attenuate one another, and the "rhythm of safety" (Tustin, 1986a) of the analytic frame, process, and relationship eventually take the place of the virtual "rocking" and "head-banging" of compulsive repetitions, which are sometimes at the root of interminable analyses.

Detecting autistic states in adults

In these individuals, areas of normal development exist, circumventing those *traumatic happenings* of infancy that could not be experienced, but were instead walled-off from both conscious and unconscious awareness (S. Klein, 1980; Tustin, 1986a). Unlike the case of split-off and projected aspects of objects and/or self, or repressed memories of events, it is difficult to locate these encapsulated resources merely by listening for their verbal derivatives, expressed as aspects of self, objects, and perceptions residing in other people in the day-to-day life of the patient or as they might be revealed in dreams. This may be so because, while in an autistic state, projective identification is unavailable as a means of communication (Bion, 1962) and, as with autistic children who cannot play (Tustin, 1988a), these patients rarely dream since, in this domain of the psyche, symbol formation is as yet undeveloped (M. Klein, 1930).

Because encapsulated "happenings" are so well hidden—not just from the analyst but also from the patient himself—we are left to intuit the existence of these "buried treasures" in order to begin to image them, and eventually to be able to explicitly recognize and acknowledge them for and to the patient. This is no mean trick, as it requires the analyst's capacity *to be aware of and to bear the awareness of what is missing*, and to be able to digest that awareness such that it becomes food for thought to be shared with the patient.

Along with our consideration of that which we intuit, a continual and rigorous process of "differential diagnosis"—performed throughout the analytic hour, and derived from a careful and sustained observation and examination of the signs carried on the currents of the immediate transference and countertransference derivatives—is vital in order to insure that the analyst's interventions are usefully geared toward the patient *in that moment*. Accordingly, I will briefly outline some criteria to keep in mind while discriminating autistic states from those more truly object-related states.

Differential diagnosis of autistic states: moment-to-moment

First, while in an object-related state, the patient experiences the analyst either as a part of the mother's body associated with some maternal function, or as an animated, lively whole person who is able to move about at will. In contrast, *the patient in an autistic state does not experience the analyst as a real, animate, lively entity existing in a space of her own, but rather as an inanimate "thing" that is made up, absorbed, exploited, manipulated, or avoided in order to secure a sensation of existence, comfort, safety, and impermeability.*

Second, in an object-related state, some degree of awareness of separateness from the analyst is tolerated to a greater or lesser extent by the patient. In contrast, *in an autistic state, normal "flickering states of awareness of otherness" are unable to be endured*. Consequently, analyst and patient remain largely undifferentiated (from the patient's point of reference) and the resulting contact with the analyst is mainly felt on a sensuous level. In this state, the analyst is not related to, per se, but is "utilized" for the sensations that she engenders upon the surface of the skin, eyes, ears, and/or the mucous membranes of the patient. These sensations serve either to distract the patient's attention away from potentially anxiety producing happenings—providing an illusion of safety, strength, and impermeability—or they may have a numbing or tranquilizing effect, which serves to block out some insufferable awareness.

Third, when the object-related state prevails, anxieties defended against (in unconscious fantasy) are either paranoid-schizoid or depressive in nature: anxieties and defenses well defined by Melanie Klein (1946). In contrast, *those anxieties evaded through auto-sensual or adhesive maneuvers* (Bick, 1968) *in the autistic state are more accurately conceptualized as raw and unmitigated panic equated with the elemental sensations of falling out of control, of discontinuity of being, of nothingness, dissolution, and evaporation, of being a no-body-nowhere,* all terrors delineated in Tustin's work and in the work of Winnicott (1949).

Additionally, while in an object-related state, the individual engages in complex unconscious fantasies (e.g., of splitting, projective identification, and manic denial) to defend against the pain, despair and rage of envy and the awareness of helpless dependence upon the analyst. However, *in the autistic state, the patient employs adhesive equation to block out the painful and life threatening awareness of two-ness and the overwhelming ecstasy of at-one-ment.*

Fourth, in an object-related state, the patient's ego oscillates either between a state of increasing integration and a state of non-defensive regression to unintegration on the one hand, or between a state of integration and a state of defensive disintegration on the other. By comparison, *in an autistic state, ego or self exists and operates predominantly in an unmitigated state of passive primary unintegration* (Meltzer, Bremner, Hoxter, Weddell & Wittenberg, 1975).

Fifth, the nature of "thinking" in the object-related state is either abstract or concrete and may be either realistic or omnipotent in nature. In contrast, *in autistic states there is little actual mentation* (Mitrani, 1994). *What appears to the observer as "thinking" remains on the level of a reflexo-physiological reaction* and "innate forms"[6] (Tustin, 1986a) prevail in the absence of symbolization, unconscious fantasy, and imagination, since transitional space (Winnicott, 1951) is non-existent.

Sixth, the truly object-related individual reacts to separations and losses with either expressions of anxiety, neediness and emotional pain, or with a tight-fisted control of the aforementioned through the use of tyranny and seduction. In contrast, *the individual in an autistic state reacts to the awareness of separateness with either total obliviousness or complete collapse*. Consciousness of dependency in the object-related individual is either experienced as the need for and the act of reliance upon an analyst who is separate from the analysand, or it is defended against through forms of manic denial. *In autistic states, dependency in the analysand assumes the form of a thin and tenacious clinging to the surface of an as-yet-undifferentiated analyst, felt to be part of and contiguous with the analysand*.

Lastly, when defenses against the awareness of *separateness* and loss break down in the object-related state, there is an experience of threat to the patient's sense of omnipotence, culminating in feelings of rejection. In contrast, *when omnipotence fails in the autistic state, this failure is felt as a corporeal collapse, as a dreadful sensation of being ripped-off and thrown away, a bodily feeling of total and irreversible dejection*. It is not an experience of the loss of the analyst or even the presence of the absence (O'Shaughnessy, 1964), as it is in object related states. One autistic child, John, called this the "black hole with the nasty prick" (Tustin, 1972, p. 30). This "black hole" is felt as an awesome force of powerlessness, of defect, of nothingness and of "zero-ness" expressed, not just as a static emptiness, but also as an agonizingly implosive centripetal pull into a void.[7]

Those who have "lingered in the chambers of the sea"

It might be accurate to say that the patients addressed in this paper have "lingered in the chambers of the sea" (T. S. Eliot, 1998, p. 8) for much of their lives. They are unwittingly addicted to their sensation-dominated ways of surviving at the expense of experiences of ordinary human relationship. The frequency with which liquid states are evoked in the clinical material of these patients has been noteworthy (Tustin, 1986). For example one adult patient, Jean, said that she felt like a "waterfall, falling out of control into nothingness" (Tustin, 1986, p. 217) when she was aware of slipping out of the mindful attention of her analyst on holiday breaks.

The experience of freezing in autistic states is a reaction to this terror of falling out of control when a personal sense of existence is still fluid, and when the personality and body are not yet fully differentiated or solidified (Tustin, 1986). In fact, freezing is the way in which a liquid becomes a solid body. However, when our patients freeze up in order to attain a *sensation of solidity*, their icy barrier often impacts others by leaving them cold. Consequently, the occurrence of healing emotional trans-actions is impeded.

In her novel, *The Lovely Bones*, author Alice Sebold's opening words express two different views of the frozen capsule of the autistic state.

> Inside the snow globe on my father's desk. There was a penguin wearing a red-and-white-striped scarf. When I was little my father would pull me into his lap and reach for the snow globe. He would turn it over, letting all the snow collect on the top, then quickly invert it. The two of us watched the snow fall gently around the penguin. The penguin was alone in there, I thought, and I worried for him. When I told my father this, he said, "Don't worry, Susie; he has a nice life. He's trapped in a perfect world." (Sebold, 2002, p. 3)

Like Susie, the analyst may be moved to *feel* the isolation within the perfect world of the icy sphere of autism, while the untrained or emotionally distant observer may see this world as idyllic. We know that without lively human connections, it is not possible for certain vital internal mental and physical structures to develop, and when emotional contact is interrupted, previously developed structures can whither away (Spitz & Wolf, 1946). Without these durable structures, patients can suffer emotional and physical "meltdowns" in the face of life's stressors. In analysis, just as the firm, reliable, resilient, and receptive presence of the analyst is an important factor if these lasting structures are to be established, it is also important that a physical setting with similar qualities be provided.

The setting

To facilitate the emergence of the infantile transference in analysis, an environment of relative safety and security needs to be maintained. Our consulting rooms are equated, in the unconscious, with the maternal body (Klein, 1961). Furthermore, just as the modulation of the ups and downs of the mother's emotional and mental state and her physicality is essential to healthy fetal development and the emergence of the baby from the womb, for adult patients the therapeutic setting and the rhythm and consistency of the work affects development, the ability to attach and to separate healthfully.

In analysis, we aim to and often do penetrate our patients' protective capsules, releasing explosive feelings of violence, overwhelming terrors, unutterable rapture and torrential grief. Thus, it is essential to provide a setting capable of bearing and containing these emotions. For both analyst and analysand, frequent meetings are indispensable. As one patient expressed it, "I'd be crazy to be open and vulnerable when you're only with me once a week!" Perhaps the same can be said for the analyst who is charged with sustaining and transforming all that she has opened herself up to in a given hour.

For both members of the analytic couple, prerequisites of continuity of frame, attention, listening, and interpretation are a necessary complement to the analyst's alert and constrained attention. Within such an ambience, the patient can more readily experience both a listening and speaking object. However, when changes and alterations in the setting or schedule are unavoidable, the analyst is *alert to and mindful of the consequences of such modifications* and the need to be sensitive when listening for and dealing with the patient's reactions, including those experienced/expressed in and the realm of sensation, as might be seen in the following vignettes.

Lucie

Thirty-five-year-old Lucie was vulnerable to the slightest variation in the setting and to any change in my person. Over a weekend prior to the week preceding a long holiday break, I had trimmed my hair. When she saw me on Monday, Lucie appeared grief stricken. Once on the couch her anguish turned to rage and she quickly clammed-up. With time and encouragement, she grudgingly spat out a few telling words: "Your hair! How could you? You didn't even save the cuttings for me."

With this brusque protest, everything came to a screeching halt. Walled off in sullen silence, Lucie turned to face the wall for much of the hour. Absolutely nothing I could say to her served to re-establish contact: it felt that *she had become the wall*. During the silence, I was very aware of my own dread of what would become of her during my absence. I envisioned a very rocky reunion, if indeed she returned to the analysis at all. Then I began to feel that all had come to an end and feared that *I was about to be abandoned*.

Barely overcoming a strong inclination to retreat from her rejection and in light of my fantasies of abandonment and loss, which I took as a sign of how unbearable and permanent our separation had felt to her—not a separation but an amputation, a cut—I told Lucie that I thought she might be communicating the sense that my haircut was a "her-cut." Furthermore, I said that I thought she was letting me know that *she could not bear the feeling* of my thoughtlessly cutting her off along with the soft texture of our contact.

Lucie turned her head slightly in my direction. I thought that this might be a sign that she could now dare to separate from the wall that protected her from the catastrophic awareness of our separateness during the break. Thus, I was encouraged to say, "Perhaps you are also conveying how insufferable is the palpable dread that you and I might never grow back together again, especially when it feels that I cut off those soft and delicate wisps of cooperation that grew in our work together over the term and that I've carelessly thrown it all away."

Lucie opened just a bit and said, "Yes, that's true. And what if there's a crash?" As Lucie's response seemed to let me in on an additional feature of her dilemma, I added, "When I hurt and enrage you so carelessly by cutting you off like that, a terrible collision occurs, with both of us crashing and falling out of control, exploding to bits. So horrifying is this sense of us in pieces, you must turn away from me, gluing yourself to the wall for protection." This last intervention addressed an additional significance in Lucie's turn toward the wall for durable comfort. It seemed to me that when her crashing emotions (provoked by my holiday leave) were felt as potentially threatening ("And what if there's a crash?") to the wholesomeness of our contact, I too was momentarily experienced as "cut" and broken, unreliable and even dangerous, not only when I was absent but when present in that moment as well. Perhaps moments like these, when the analyst can continue to function mindfully and non-defensively in the face of explosive emotions (the patient's as well as her own), the fear of coming apart, falling apart out of control can be attenuated and faith in relationship can be restored.

This moment with Lucie also demonstrates how something that may seem like an image to the analyst from the descriptions the patients articulates, is instead *felt* as "a repertoire of relatively uncoordinated *sensations*, which are sensed rather than imaged" (Tustin, 1986, p. 216). In like manner, what might appear to be fantasies or dreams are more like tactile hallucinations, and the analyst must try to make her own images explicit and present them in a language that may touch the patient in such a state of mind. Another patient, Brad, also suffered from these tactile hallucinations.

Brad

Early in our work together I discovered that Brad felt physically crumpled up and thrown out at the end of the session, equating himself with the paper towel that lay on the pillow of my couch where he rested his head during the hour. He often felt that I peeled him off my body-couch or breast-pillow and that I carelessly threw him away, and he begged me to fold and to save him from time to time (Mitrani, 1992). Otherwise Brad said that he felt he was always "starting from scratch."

I eventually came to realize that the "scratch" my patient referred to was the sensation he experienced on his tender skin. His way of mastering this happening, and thus making it bearable, was to scratch the skin on his arms, legs and face after each session, sometimes until he bled, in order to achieve a renewed sensation of rebirth and "there-ness," to evade an experience of helplessness and vulnerability, and to toughen up against what he felt to be my careless treatment of him.

Audrey

Audrey physically felt the impact of any shifts on my bookshelves, as though my books were parts of me that must be kept in order, always the same. She had memorized their placement, which gave her a sensation of control over me. She could put me in my place and I would stay put. However, each new addition to or subtraction from my library provoked a reaction, much like the stranger anxiety observed in babies in the latter half of the first year of life. With time we could appreciate her indelible sense of Mother's manic-depressive moods swings, which were felt like a mother in pieces, out of control, in fragments and out of sorts: a monster-mother who was unable to hold herself or the baby-Audrey together. This feeling pre-empted the establishment of a sense of comforting familiarity and obstructed the development of a consistent basis for trust in the other, tolerance for change and the evolution of Audrey's self-confidence.

Connie

A similar reaction to variations in light in my room, mainly connected to the varied times I would see her throughout the week. was a source of distress for Connie. She would often brace herself physically by holding onto the doorframe with both hands before entering my room. I learned that this change in the intensity of the light was experienced by my patient as a "dizzying" and "disorienting shock" that, on a sensation level, was felt as a "slap in the face" or as an "earthquake," a harbinger of my "change in mood" or shift in my feeling for her. Connie was able to tell me that these changes were like as a "Tsunami" that threatened to sweep her away.

Such changes in the therapeutic setting may be grist for the analytic mill, and as such can be made meaningful through interpretation. However, the development of "a rhythm of safety" (Tustin, 1986, p. 26) is, in part, established through an experience of constancy in the environment of the consulting room, as well as in the consistent functioning of the analyst as a receptacle for projections and as a reliable source of verbal understanding for the "grist" brought into the therapeutic relationship *by the analysand*. This point brings me to the problem of patients' idiosyncratic use (while in an autistic state) of the reliable setting provided.

The idiosyncratic use of objects

Even though the analyst strives to provide a stable environment within which those in their care may come to feel safe, patients often turn the analyst and the analytic environment upside down, in one way or another. Tustin (1980, 1984b) discovered that autistic children use ordinary objects not in the course of child's play as a mode of communication, but for the sensations that these objects engender on the surface of their skin. Auto-sensuous maneuvers may also become apparent in the way that certain adult analysands use the consulting room, the objects in it—including the couch itself—and the qualities of the analyst. When the analysis is used in these idiosyncratic ways, opportunities for gaining insight into and having experiences from which to learn can be lost. I will present some examples of what I am suggesting from my work with Karen, an outwardly successful professional in her midthirties.

Karen

Throughout the first year of her analysis, no matter if the room were warm or cool, before lying down, Karen would take up the blanket that lay at the foot of the couch. While holding a corner of it in the palm of one hand, the thumb on that same hand was inserted into, sucked, and slid rhythmically in and out of Karen's mouth. The remainder of the blanket was spread out and covered all but Karen's toes, which she wiggled continuously whenever I spoke to her.

So secretive and smooth were Karen's undercover movements, it took many months of careful observation and listening, as well as much attention to my own imagination, before I could make explicit the use that my patient was making of the blanket—to hide a myriad of sensation producing activities. Under cover, Karen constantly caressed her breasts with her free hand or masturbated with her hand in her trouser pocket, activities just barely detectable under wraps from my position in the chair behind the couch.

At the same time, I noticed that Karen's negative feelings toward me were almost never expressed verbally. However, when I was aware of being somewhat off in my understanding of her, it became clear that she would begin to pinch her nipples, scratch her arms, or pick at the skin of her cuticles and tear at her fingernails. Over time and little by little, I was able to speak to Karen about these hidden, self-inflicted wounds as well as the soothing sensations that she could reliably create for herself. We also considered how these each might serve to obliterate any awareness of helplessness, dependency, and the existence of hurtful otherness as well as any real experience of togetherness.

The ecstasy[8] of at-one-ment (Tustin, 1981) can become just as terrifying as the despair evoked by separateness or abandonment. With Karen's unconscious cooperation, I was able to "uncover" the equation of the softness of the blanket with the soft musicality of my voice, further equated with the softness of Karen's own skin and the silent and pleasurable sensations she produced during the hours. My words were rarely taken in for their meaning, but instead were more often felt as harmonious sensations that flowed over Karen's skin and slipped in and out of her ears, not unlike the sensation of her thumb slipping in and out of her mouth in a self-controlled and self-soothing way.

It became apparent that whenever Karen repeated these gestures in the many hours of absence between the sessions and during weekends, she could obliterate the sharp distinctions between separateness and togetherness. Since we were felt to be inseparable, I was neither experienced as a "real person," separate from herself, nor did I exist outside the sensations that I inspired, produced, or provoked for her.

My voice was also equated with Karen's hand and, as she had managed to find an exact duplicate for my blanket and sleuthed out and found the perfume I usually wore, she was also able to reproduce the comforting visual, tactile, and olfactory sensations that she experienced while she was in my physical presence, no matter the place or time of day. Additionally, Karen's thumb—sucked much of the time during the analytic hours and (when no one was watching) between the hours—was *not* a transitional object that functioned to bridge a gap between us during times of felt separation. Instead, the sessions, my voice, and the blanket held in her hand against her face functioned to "re-charge her thumb," so that its utility—as concrete proof of our indivisibility—could retain the power to smooth out the sensations of the jagged and potentially terrifying agony of the separateness, and the equally unbearable ecstasy of our reunions.

Eventually, Karen began to notice that her clever maneuvers had a "short half-life." They clearly failed to sustain her throughout prolonged holiday breaks, when we would be "out of touch" for two or three weeks at a stretch, and with time, these tactics barely sufficed over longer than usual three-day weekends. As we came to appreciate the function of these manipulations and their limited effectiveness, Karen had an important epiphany. "I made you up in my brain!" She said. "You weren't real. But now I realize that, if you aren't real and I lose you, I have no hope of ever finding you again, of remembering you. And if I'm lost and you're inanimate, not real, you won't be able to find me."

It was becoming clear to us that Karen felt the small bits of understanding she was receiving from me as a sign that there was both an inside and an outside, a Dr. M and a Karen, sometimes linked together by tolerable emotional encounters and a growing experience of an "other" who might be willing and able to tolerate and to adapt to her needs, while still remaining a separate individual. These events only became relevant as Karen could begin to bear the awareness that we were two very real people, that we were not "one pretend figment of her brain," but two people who could touch and effect one another on a heartfelt if sometimes disturbing level.

A question of motivation

I'd like to clarify that quite often, although it appears that patients like Karen destructively defy the therapeutic boundaries, it is important to consider that their motives may include, at least in some small part, an attempt to survive. Tustin referred to these wayward[9] patients as suffering from a *miscarriage of motivation*. Rather than attending to the life enhancing possibilities that are available to them, both within themselves and in the outside world, their attention has become fixated upon autochthonous sensation-objects and sensation-shapes that insure survival on the most elemental level. Tustin *would ask patients to abstain from their auto-sensual activities, while at the same time interpreting their intended function alongside the deleterious side-effects of these behaviors as they emerge in the material.*

Certainly, when patients turn the analytic framework upside down, permanent damage can be avoided if we are able to maintain a mindful attitude while being over-thrown. For example, especially in this era of electronic communications (i.e., voicemail, texting, tweeting, and email), patients seek and often do manage to provoke contact with us outside agreed upon hours. In doing so, they challenge the analytic boundaries, perhaps because they have no flexible boundaries of their own. These patients often fall outside the realm of the known and we may need *to be willing and able to fall with them for a time, while maintaining our capacity to right ourselves and them through hard-won and thoughtful interpretative understanding.*

Throughout the process of developing a narrative of shared meaning, enactments of all kinds can be put to good use. Perhaps the experience we gain through free falling with our patients may stimulate us to stretch our imaginations to the fullest. Learning from experience may help us bear *to "know" what we do not know that we know*, to access our faith (Bion, 1970) in the analytic process, in the unconscious and in human relationship. Perhaps by having such experiences, rather than trying to avoid them at all costs, may enable us to reach, to catch, to bear, to better apprehend, and to make known our understanding through our interpretative contributions.

Regarding the treatment of the autistic child, Dick, Melanie Klein wrote,

> In general I do not interpret the material until it has found expression in various representations ... however where a capacity to represent ... is almost entirely lacking, I have been obliged to make ... interpretations on the basis of general knowledge (Klein, 1930, p. 246).

It is this author's belief that our "general knowledge" must include *not just our theories*, but a first-hand and hands-on experience of what it feels like to be physically helpless, dependent and as-yet-unintegrated, stemming from our own experiences in the transference as analysands and from our familiarity, as analysts, with this dimension of the countertransference (Mitrani, 1992, 1993, 1998a, 1999, 2001, 2007a, 2007b). Perhaps one of the most challenging happenings for the analyst in this sphere is related to a specific feature of autistic states, which warrants explication.

The object in the periphery

Tustin linked a particular class of auto-generated sensation-shapes to the well-known observation that autistic children frequently do not look directly into the eyes of others, instead taking in a great deal by peripheral vision. On this topic, she wrote,

> This over-developed fringe awareness means that fringe-shapes are formed which can never be clearly focused and which constantly elude the children. Autistic children show that they are

> constantly tantalized by such elusive, self-generated shapes ... In the end, such shapes are not tranquilizing but tantalizing [and] also impede attachment to the mother, which is fostered by looking at her face, especially at her eyes. As a result of the tantrums of panic and rage that she was not a part of their body that they could take for granted, the children have turned away from the mother and became frightened of her eyes. This separateness had been forced upon their attention before they were ready for it. In Winnicott's terms it "impinged"; they did not find it out in their own time when they were ready for it. This was painful beyond all bearing. They had swerved away from the pain, and from the mother who was the source of it. They stopped looking at her and at other people, attending instead to the fringe shapes they could make by looking out of the corners of their eyes. This brought some sort of order into their bewildering world, but like will-o'-the-wisps, these side-long shapes eventually isolated them in immobilizing bogs, cut off from contact with other human beings. (Tustin, 1986, p. 154)

This variety of soft, blurry, indistinct autistic shape (Tustin, 1984b) initially creates a sensation of at-one-ment with the primary environment. I believe it may be useful to notice that *there exists an analogous phenomenon, commonly encountered in our work with adult patients* in analysis.

For example, many analysts have the experience of speaking to a patient who responds as if the analyst has said nothing. That is, the patient goes right on without reference to the analyst's verbal communication. The sense one gets is that the patient has rolled over, run through or maneuvered around what the analyst has said. Although kept in the periphery of the patient's attention, at times the analyst can detect some faint refraction of her communications, embedded in seemingly unrelated stories that the patient tells about himself in relation to others. Alternatively, the analyst might detect a slight rephrasing of what she has said, presented as though it is the product of the patient's own insight. This situation is quite common and may be the result of a displacement subsequent to some resistance in patients who are neurotically organized and for whom separateness is a narcissistic issue. In the classical Kleinian model, this situation is often taken up as an expression of envy and a sign that the patient is usurping the function the analytic breast, so to speak.

However, the analyst may wish to entertain an additional dimension of significance with regard to this phenomenon: that her intervention has inadvertently forced an *awareness of separateness* upon the patient's attention before he is able to contend with it. As such, the interpretation may constitute an impingement that is painful beyond all bearing. In reaction to this impingement, the patient may swerve away from the pain and from the mother-analyst who is felt to be the source of a *reality that he cannot face head on*. In the countertransference, the analyst can detect this state, as it will often engender in her the feeling that *she does not exist*. It is as if she were invisible or unheard, except for the faint echo of her words in her own solitary mind. At other times, the patient's response may resemble the echolalia of the autistic child. When encountering this phenomenon, the question of motivation is essential for the analyst to consider.

In extreme cases, wherein *the awareness of separateness is an existential issue*, the patient may at first seem relaxed, unperturbed by what the analyst has said, and may simply go on as if untouched. Sometimes there can be varying degrees of weepiness or other bodily signs (e.g., coughing, flatulence, fidgeting) indicating that the analyst has punctured the protective capsule and signaling that a process of *dissolution* (which I will elaborate upon further below) has begun. However, powerful efforts to staunch the flow from the wound of two-ness work rapidly to seal up the protection once again, and such embryonic signs of having been being touched may lead to a "dead end" that is frequently marked by the patient's complaint, registered either directly or obliquely, that he does not feel the analyst to be alive or present.

Ideally, the analyst may be able to convey, both gently and firmly, her sense of the patient's experience. Her understanding needs to address three distinct areas. The first area has to do with acknowledging the pain and dread of separateness "beyond all bearing," provoked by the analyst's intervention. The second concerns the ways in which the patient deadens the insufferable pain and attenuates this nameless dread. Finally, the third area must recognize the ways in which these self-protective maneuvers culminate in the feeling of "being neither here nor there" with an analyst who is either a "no-body" or a tantalizing somebody, out of touch and just out of reach in the periphery of the patient's existence (i.e., the side effect of this protective maneuver.) In time and with patience, a process of working-through may lead to an increasing capacity to tolerate separateness and, in place of the dead-end of therapeutic impasse, the analytic couple may be able to move forward on the road toward emotional and mental development.

The dread of dissolution

In some individuals, *auto-sensual protections against the awareness of unbearable separateness or the turbulence of real emotional closeness* are like the thorny vines surrounding the castle where the Princess Aurora lay protected from the prick of death, or the wall of fire that encircled Brunhilde in Wagner's "Ring." The analyst needs to be courageous, as well as "charming" and imaginative, in order to engage these "sleeping beauties" when faced with the poisonous pricks and the fiery flames of intense emotion. As Tustin once said,

> These patients will break your heart, just as they had once been heartbroken. The therapist can provide an object lesson in bravery and resilience, while suffering life's heart breaks with the aid of human relationship. (Tustin, 1989, personal communication)

Perhaps personal analysis, supervision, and peer consultation could be helpful for managing the heartbreak as well as the primitive dreads that must first be borne by the analyst before the patient can be expected to bear them on his own. Among these dreads, the "dread of dissolution" is predominant.

The term *dissolution* (Tustin, 1986) describes the awesome danger associated with the awareness of otherness in earliest infancy, with the events of psychic and physical changes, and with the emotional havoc engendered by such changes. Changes are often felt, on a primordial level, as a transformation from a solid existence to a liquid state. The terrors of spilling out of control into a bottomless abyss, and even evaporating into nothingness (Mitrani, 1993), threaten to prevail when left uncontained.

When the analyst dares to infiltrate the blockade imposed by auto-sensual protections, she also becomes exposed to these same dangers, especially while "taking the transference" (Mitrani, 2001). This most difficult aspect of our work is an unconscious act governed by unconscious factors in response to emotional happenings actually experienced and suffered by the analyst, to some significant degree. This is essential to what Bion called the maternal function of "reverie": the attentive, actively receptive, introjective, and experiencing aspect of the containing object. Perhaps our capacity to take the transference is never so important as it is with these individuals who have spent much of their lives "wrapped tight," as one patient explained with deep regret.

The patient's history (most convincingly as it unfolds in the transference–countertransference continuum, where we have the chance to learn from experience) approximates the basic constellation underlying pathological auto-sensuality. It is common for Mother's emotional accessibility to be impaired especially while in a narcissistically vulnerable state, such as is often the case during the pre- and post-partum period. The mothers of autistic patients have often been insufficiently supported and are frequently disheartened, depressed or preoccupied by nature or by circumstance around the time of giving birth (Tustin, 1981a). Consequently they temporarily withdraw, recoil, reject, or turn away from their babies on an emotional level, especially when the baby is felt to be a source of potential narcissistic injury.[10]

In cases where a baby is exceptionally sensitive and expressive, its cries may reinforce the mother's sense of being a failure as a mother. If such avoidant behavior on the part of the mother extends beyond the baby's own limited innate capacity to sustain itself, normal projective identification (Bion, 1955)—at first aimed at communicating unbearable states of excitement, pain, or terror in search of reception and transformation—will grow to hyperbolic proportions. Eventually the result is a sealing-off of vital aspects of the infant's nascent self, along with its capacity to perceive emotional happenings. Bion's (1974, p. 84) description of the sequence that follows a failure in maternal containment, quoted in full in Chapter Three, may depict a common precursor to autistic encapsulation.

When we begin to reach some genuine understanding of the specific plight of the infant in the adult patient in analysis, the protective wraps that make up the encapsulation may further loosen their hold and intermittently fall away, gradually allowing ordinary human experience to penetrate (Mitrani, 2006). It is, however, important to keep in mind that the terrors of slipping away into nothingness or bursting open with excitement—provoked especially by absences and reunions—do re-emerge with regularity, followed by the re-deployment of the old, faithful, and familiar protections. This inevitable cycle renders the process of "working through" (Freud, 1914) both painstaking and protracted.

One patient, Julia, was able to help me to get a sense of the seamless quality of the protective fabric within which her infant-self was swaddled. She was put in mind of the film *The Alien* and described how the creature—a monstrous infant—came to the surface, breaking out of the belly of its host, destroying him and threatening those who tried to help. She likened this scene to my efforts to be in touch with what she called her "original self." She was convinced that we would both be destroyed in the process. Indeed, Tustin (1988b, personal communication) said of the autistic barrier, "When this brittle self-sufficiency can no longer be maintained, the situation is devastating for [the patient] because the basic sense of going-on-being is felt to be dependent upon maintaining such a barrier."

I believe that an in-built assumption of the analyst's vulnerability, for which patients frequently find evidence, may be linked with this problematic (Mitrani, 2007b). Such evidence sometimes leads to an exaggerated *fear of the analyst coming in contact with the infant-self* that has been experienced as an alien, "frightening and bad thing," which must be kept silent and closed-off in order to prevent the mother-analyst from becoming overwhelmed. I have written in Chapter Five about one such example of this kind of situation from my work with the patient I called Leonard.

Resistance and collusion: a coincidence of vulnerability analyst and analysand

In concluding, I will put forward one last consideration specifically regarding the countertransference. Since the patients I am referring to, perhaps more so than others, resist interpretations that directly address the infantile transference, they also stimulate the analyst's own resistance to being in contact with states of maximal dependence and vulnerability through this very rejection. At times, this stimulant can be so potent that the analyst may unwittingly collude with the patient by hardening herself, creating her own barriers to emotionality. Noticing the crucial juncture when what the infant-in-the-patient communicates resonates too strongly with what the infant-in-the-analyst has endured, is key. This resonance may evoke a range of reactions rooted in happenings from the analyst's own beginnings, further complicated by those happenings in the early life of the patient as these are communicated unconsciously and often non-verbally.

For example, a patient's material may stir up repressed memories of our own physical injuries or disabilities, psychic trauma and the bodily and mental constraints that we have been subjected to as infants and toddlers. I recall a period with one analysand, whom I call Julia, during which I was faced with a pattern of acting out that required patience for many months. During this period, I was profoundly disturbed by a sense of "nowhere to turn," which was represented in my dreams in such a way that often evoked long-buried memories of having worn leg-braces at nighttime and during naptime to straighten out my feet between the ages of one and three. These braces took the form of oxford-type shoes, separated by a steel bar that constricted my ability to turn over in my crib. I was convinced that these dreams (and other reactions and associations of mine that were consonant with such dreams) somehow held the key to the meaning and significance of Julia's dilemma and that they constituted the essential material from which I might derive an interpretative intervention that could move us forward on the analytic path.

The struggle to tolerate feelings of constriction, defect, despair, and helplessness was worthwhile, as it eventually lead to the uncovering of (as well as the ways and means of teasing-out) the transgenerational roots of one of the major dynamics in the patient's personality structure, which we were gradually able to trace both to the early traumatic beginnings of the patient's mother and her adaptation to that trauma, as well as certain characteristics of the maternal grandmother. Rather than relying on adult experiences, professional competence, training, and most especially theories to circumvent this kind of awkward happening in the countertransference, with determination and faith in the process the analyst may find the mettle with which she might forge those unbidden emotional reactions and physical sensations into useful tools for understanding.

Finally, although some patients may nudge us to attend only to what is occurring outside the room, and frequently try to put us off the trail (e.g., when they tell us, "This is not about you!"), the analyst needs to find a way to remain alive and attentive to the infantile transference and her role in it. To be carried off by current external events or diverted toward an historical past that is *already well-traversed by both members of the analytic couple* may lead to a fortification rather than a relaxation of the patient's autistic barriers. The analyst's open-mindedness to communications from within the dark acorn of the heart, when these momentarily surface, may contribute toward facilitating a wholesome emergence of self.

Have You Ever Tried To Enter The Long Black Branches
By Mary Oliver[11]

Have you ever tried to enter the long black branches
of other lives—
tried to imagine what the crisp fringes, full of honey,
hanging from the branches of the young locust trees, in early morning,
feel like?
Do you think this world was only an entertainment for you?
Never to enter the sea and notice how the water divides
with perfect courtesy, to let you in!
Never to lie down on the grass, as though you were the grass!
Never to leap to the air as you open your wings over
the dark acorn of your heart!
No wonder we hear, in your mournful voice, the complaint
that something is missing from your life!
Who can open the door who does not reach for the latch?
Who can travel the miles who does not put one foot
in front of the other, all attentive to what presents itself
continually?
Who will behold the inner chamber who has not observed
with admiration, even with rapture, the outer stone?
Well, there is time left—
fields everywhere invite you into them.
And who will care, who will chide you if you wander away
from wherever you are, to look for your soul?
Quickly, then, get up, put on your coat, leave your desk!
To put one's foot into the door of the grass, which is
the mystery, which is death as well as life, and
not be afraid!

To set one's foot in the door of death, and be overcome
with amazement!
To sit down in front of the weeds, and imagine
god the ten-fingered, sailing out of his house of straw,
nodding this way and that way, to the flowers of the
present hour,
to the song falling out of the mockingbird's pink mouth,
to the tippets of the honeysuckle, that have opened
in the night
To sit down, like a weed among weeds, and rustle in the wind!
Listen, are you breathing just a little, and calling it a life?
While the soul, after all, is only a window,
and the opening of the window no more difficult
than the wakening from a little sleep.
Only last week I went out among the thorns and said
to the wild roses:
deny me not,
but suffer my devotion.
Then, all afternoon, I sat among them. Maybe
I even heard a curl or tow of music, damp and rouge red,
hurrying from their stubby buds, from their delicate watery bodies.
For how long will you continue to listen to those dark shouters,
caution and prudence?
Fall in! Fall in!
A woman standing in the weeds.
A small boat flounders in the deep waves, and what's coming next
is coming with its own heave and grace.
Meanwhile, once in a while, I have chanced, among the quick things,
upon the immutable.
What more could one ask?
And I would touch the faces of the daisies,
and I would bow down to think about it.
That was then, which hasn't ended yet.
Now the sun begins to swing down. Under the peach-light,
I cross the fields and the dunes; I follow the ocean's edge.
I climb, I backtrack.
I float.
I ramble my way home.

Notes

1. "Have You Ever Tried to Enter the Long Black Branches," from *West Wind: Poems and Prose Poems* by Mary Oliver. Copyright © 1997 by Mary Oliver. Reprinted by permission of Houghton Mifflin Harcourt Publishing Company. All rights reserved.
2. When the object is unable or unwilling to receive, to make sense of and to reflect the baby's own internal state, or when the object projects her own internal state onto the infant, intentional states will not be *symbolically bound* and the developmental basis of the self-structure will be absent (Fonagy & Target, 1996). The weakness of such a self-image leaves the child with affective and perceptual happenings that remain nameless, confusing, and frightening, what Bion considered to be unmetabolized or uncontained (Bion, 1962) and what this author has termed "unmentalized" (Mitrani, 1994).
3. Sidney Klein first described patients who, despite the appearance of progress in the analysis, remain untouched in some essential way due to encapsulating forces that cut them off from the analyst as well as from the rest of the personality. Klein posited that walled off in these cystic areas are intense and unbearable fears of "pain, and of death, disintegration or breakdown" (S. Klein, 1980, p. 400) related to unmentalized experiences of separateness of early infancy. He suggested that such phenomena "are strikingly similar to those observed in so-called autistic children" (ibid). Compellingly, novelist Patrick Süskind (1986) writes of this encapsulation phenomenon in the extreme. He describes his protagonist Grenouille, born of an overly preoccupied, deprived, and unsupported mother. His means of survival is compared to that of a tick "For which life has nothing better to offer than perpetual hibernation ... which by rolling its blue-grey body up into a ball offers the least possible surface to the world; which by making its skin smooth [and] dense, emits nothing ... makes itself extra small and inconspicuous [so] that no one will see it and step on it. The lonely tick, which, wrapped up in itself, huddles in its tree, blind deaf and dumb and simply sniffs ... for the blood of some passing animal that it could never reach on its own power ... the tick, stubborn, sullen and loathsome, huddles there and lives and waits ... for that most improbable of chances ... and only then does it abandon caution and drop and scratch and bore and bite into that alien flesh ... The young Grenouille was such a tick ... encapsulated in himself [he] waited for better times" (Süskind, 1986, p. 25).
4. All clinical material concerns patients who, after the initial evaluation sitting up in a chair, were engaged in four or five time per week analysis reclining on a couch utilized for that purpose only.

5. Tustin distinguishes *autistic objects* from ordinary objects (inanimate or animate) in that the former are *not related to as objects*, but rather *used for the tactile sensations which they engender* upon the surface of the skin of the subject. Autistic objects differ from "transitional objects" (Winnicott, 1958), which are a combination of "me" and "not me" that constitute a bridge that links the two together during physical absence, while autistic objects are barriers to the awareness of "not me" and as such is an impediment to growth and development. *Autistic shapes* are differentiated from objective shapes (such as a square or a circle), in that they are idiosyncratic, endogenous swirls of sensation produced upon the surface of the skin or internally with the aid of bodily substances or objects. These distinctions, first based upon observations with autistic children, are now widely extended to include numerous other behaviors observable in adults and children with an enclave of autism, which may be conceived of as sensation-dominated delusions. The key word here is "sensation." Such sensations either serve to distract one's attention away from insufferable happenings, providing an illusion of safety, strength, and impermeability, or they may have a numbing or tranquilizing effect upon the individual, which blocks out some terrifying awareness.
6. Tustin defines these as "flexible, sensuous moulds into which, at an elemental level of psychic development, experience is cast, and which are modified by the experience so cast. When an innate form seems to coincide with a correspondence in the outside world, the child has the illusion that everything is synonymous and continuous with his own body stuff" (Tustin, 1986a, p. 85).
7. Due to the limitations of scope of this paper, I have not addressed in depth the differential diagnosis between dissociative and autistic states, a topic that deserves a paper of its own. Suffice to say that, although both states are related to trauma, *the dissociative state can be included in the object-related category. It may be expressed* in amnesia (forgetting) or fugue and dissociative/multiple personality disorders (in which the split off or repressed aspect(s) of self can be given life/expression, at least temporarily). In contrast, the encapsulation common to autistic states constitutes a virtual isolation chamber in which the unmentalized traumatic perception (as well as what Meltzer and Bion described as the associated aspect of the dismantled perceptual apparatus) is hermetically sealed off from future development, expression or memory. Such relatively advanced defenses as splitting and projection, repression, denial, and displacement are not relevant in the autistic state. As such, traumatic events can neither be remembered nor forgotten. Additionally, the traumatized aspect of the personality

cannot be lived (in the ordinary sense of the word) either tentatively or alternatively.

8. Dr. Theodore Mitrani pointed out that the word "ecstasy" comes from the Greek term *ex stasis*. So it appears that, in ancient times, the Greeks knew something about the de-stabilizing effect of experiences of joy, beauty, and love, which may become overwhelming to the baby when left unmet and uncontained by the mother (J. Mitrani, 1998b).

9. In a scholarly paper drawing the work of clinicians from several orientations, American analyst Ruth Stein (2005) discussed patients who were seen as engaged in non-sexual perverse relationships with their analysts whom they approach as inanimate things, manipulated in service of creating physical sensations that camouflage hatred and paranoia. She coins the term "false love" to characterize the nature of relatedness that may appear affectionate, but which circumvents affect.

10. In the interest of clarification, although Tustin often stated that Bettleheim's (1967) notion of "the empty fortress" was an apt way of describing the autistic protection, she explicitly disagreed with his characterization of the mothers of autistic children when she wrote, "I have a great deal of sympathy for these mothers. In my view, Kanner started a regrettable fashion in seeing them as being 'cold and intellectual'. Ever since he said this, phrases such as 'refrigerator mothers' have been bandied about to describe them. I do not subscribe to this view" (Tustin, 1986a, p. 61). Consistent with Tustin's attitude, perhaps it is essential to take into consideration the possibility of either a failure in the environment, a failure of constitution, and/or a combination of both: what I have referred to as a "coincidence of vulnerability" in the infant–mother couple (Mitrani, 2003).

11. "Have You Ever Tried to Enter the Long Black Branches," from *West Wind: Poems and Prose Poems* by Mary Oliver. Copyright © 1997 by Mary Oliver. Reprinted by permission of Houghton Mifflin Harcourt Publishing Company. All rights reserved.

CHAPTER EIGHT

Minding the gap between neuroscientific and psychoanalytic understanding of autism*

> Perhaps one day in the future, a bridge between clinical and psychoanalytic observations and neuro-scientific findings regarding autistic states will be discovered. I would like to believe that I might contribute to building that bridge in some small way.
>
> —Tustin, 1994a, *personal communication*

This chapter follows my own personal pilgrimage through decades of learning. Sometimes what I was learning had, at the time, no apparent connection with where I wished to go in terms of my desire to become an analyst. Perhaps this process is analogous to what we as analysts come to appreciate: that sometimes the most seemingly insignificant and tangential finding may become key to a greater understanding of our patients as well as ourselves. In this chapter, I will demonstrate how the findings of one group of neuroscientists in Parma, Italy regarding a special class of brain cells called "mirror

---

*"Minding the gap between neuroscientific and psychoanalytic understanding of autism" by Judith Mitrani, published in *Journal of Child Psychotherapy*, 36 (3): 240–258 (2010), published by Taylor & Francis Group, www.tandfonline.com

neurons," and the work of researchers at the University of California in San Diego have been applied to the problem of autism and how I believe these might intersect with Frances Tustin's discoveries about the nature, function, and meaning of psychogenic autism in children and even autistic states in neurotic adults.

Included in my considerations are the results of some by now well-known studies conducted by a group of biologists at the University of California at Berkeley in the 1960s on the effects of "enriched" versus "deprived" environments upon the development of the brain, and a study of autistic children diagnosed as brain damaged and treated psychoanalytically at the Pediatric Neuro-Psychiatric Institute of the University of Rome in the 1980s. The chapter concludes with a more coherent picture of various dimensions of autistic phenomenon and points toward new areas for discussion and study.

Introduction

By the end of her life, Frances Tustin had made a vital contribution to the psychoanalytic understanding of the development of autistic states in children and adults, and had formulated guidelines for their psychoanalytic treatment based upon that understanding. A tireless advocate for these children and their parents, her thoughts expressly reached into a future toward a time when discoveries in neuroscience might cross paths with her own, leading to more effective handling of this tragic disorder, one that reportedly affects one out of 150 children and their families.

Inspired by Tustin's dedication and indebted to her ideas, over the years, I have closely considered the complex puzzle of autism, and the individual contributions made by experimental psychology, psychoanalysis and more recently, neuroscience to furthering its understanding. Here, I endeavor to elaborate some of this understanding, concluding with a multidimensional sketch of autism, pointing the way toward some areas for further discussion and future study and serving to mind the gap between psychoanalysis and neuroscience.

Neurobiological studies

While majoring in psychobiology at The University of California in Los Angeles, I was introduced to experiments conducted at Berkeley's biology laboratories (Rosenzweig, Krech, Bennett & Diamond, 1962). Perhaps impelled by a sociopolitical climate in which animal rights activists were lobbying for a more humane treatment of laboratory animals, these researchers used rats selected for genetic uniformity to ensure that the results of their experiments were not due to genetic differences. Once weaned from their mothers, the animals were raised in one of three environmental conditions.

One set of rats was placed in a deprived environment, isolated in a dark and quiet room, but with as much access to food and water as the other rats. A second set of rats was confined in a minimal social condition, housed three to a cage within the peopled environment of the lab. The third group lived in the rodent's equivalent of a summer camp: twelve to a cage, in an enriched environment where they played daily with toys and mazes and were frequently handled by the scientists.

The Berkeley team discovered that rats raised in the "enriched" environment, with toys and social interaction, were not only smarter than rats raised in impoverished conditions of social isolation and sensory deprivation, but the improvement in performance also correlated with a significantly larger cerebral cortex (Bennett, Diamond, Krech & Rosenzweig, 1964). This is the area of the brain that determines intelligence, personality, and motor function and is involved in the interpretation of sensory impulses, and therefore the capacity to plan and to organize.

After ruling out competing theories, the researchers concluded that a combination of intellectual and social stimulation was necessary for the cortical gains observed in their rats. Additionally, further research showed that such cortical growth also occurs in adult rats placed in an enriched environment. Further studies at the University of Illinois (Volkmar & Greenough, 1972) suggested that enriched environments also enhance the brain's ability to process information. They found that the increase in cortical weight was accompanied by an increase in the number of dendritic branches. These are the tendrils that receive communications from other neurons, especially in layer IV of the cortex, an area important to communication between the brain's relay station, the thalamus, and the cortex.

In addition, Greenough (1988) found that rats originally reared in a deprived environment, if placed in an enriched environment, also develop larger brains with more neural connections and their performance improves on subsequent testing. These findings suggested that previously stultified brain development might be set back on track through environmental improvements.

Going further, Greenough, Black and Wallace (1987) demonstrated that in humans, one critical component of an enriched environment is that it induces learning. In other words, researchers found that true "learning from experience" (Bion, 1962), and not just rote exercise, has a dramatic influence on the physical structure of the brain. Although the exact relationship between these changes in physical structure and intellect remained unclear to them, their experiments provided evidence of actual links between physical makeup and abstract qualities of intelligence and creativity. These studies also suggested and reinforced the sense that all aspects of the mind—from memory, to dreams, to emotions—have physical correlates and that sensory deprivation and constricted "experience" may result in atrophy of the physical structure as well as the function of the brain.

When I first read about these research projects, I wondered if they also contained implications for the ways in which certain kinds of psychotherapies work to set physiological as well as psychic and emotional development back on course in human beings. But what sort of psychotherapy and what varieties of constricted development might this model apply to?

The work of Frances Tustin

In the early 1980s I was introduced to the work of Frances Tustin, who had been trained at the Tavistock Centre and at Great Ormond Street Hospital in London where she treated autistic and psychotic children in psychoanalysis. Tustin's keen capacity for observation, her third ear for listening to a child's unconscious process, and her finely honed insight as well as eyesight, enabled her to identify the possible forces that moved these children to do the things they did and would not do.

Tustin (1981) came to understand that the "impressive caesura of birth," originally referred to by Freud, might include the shock of the premature awareness of bodily separateness experienced by the infant. "Premature" is meant here in the sense that it has occurred before the infant has developed the capacity to sufficiently differentiate his feelings, emotions, and anxieties from his bodily sensations, while, at the same time, he has yet to separate himself fully from his mother. This shock appears to give rise to certain existential dreads of being "gone" or of having lost an essential bodily bit, for example the nipple on the breast, initially experienced as part of the baby's mouth; or the joints that connect his body parts, originally experienced as the mother's arms; or, in some cases, the entire half of the baby's body, originally experienced as the mother (Haag, 1985). Tustin (1981b) noticed that, in health, in spite of the impressive caesura of birth, there is a gradual transition from the sensations associated with being inside the womb to being outside of it. The tactile sensations of being in a "watery medium" are carried over into the child's earliest experience of the post-natal environment.

She observed that under "good-enough" circumstances, if the awareness of separateness threatens to overwhelm the infant, he may attempt to communicate his primal terrors to an ordinarily attentive mother. Perhaps, owing to the mother's ability to empathize with the plight of her particular baby, she modifies his ordeal by filtering it through her own previously digested experience of the ups and downs of being and living. She is able to attenuate her baby's fears by communicating with and lending her confidence to him through the many ways in which she cares for him.

Tustin thought that, when these events go well-enough, the commonsensical, empathic yet individual qualities of the post-natal womb of the mother's mind foster psychological integrations in the neonate. This is similar to the healthy physical womb of the mother's body promoting bodily integration in the fetus. However, some babies are more vulnerable than others and more difficult to care for. Sometimes these more touchy infants are serendipitously coupled with mothers who have themselves been insufficiently helped to negotiate their own feelings of separateness in infancy. When these feelings are rekindled in the perinatal period of motherhood, they may constitute a source of stress and preoccupation for that mother, and when a mother is preoccupied, either by circumstance or character, or when feelings of inadequacy, loneliness, and depression prevail, the job of mothering can become further complicated with the extremely difficult task of caring for an atypical infant.

If Mother is unable to feel, to think about and to sort out these feelings for herself, she may not have nor be able to convey a sense of being able to hold, to catch, to sooth, to bond with, to separate from, and to preserve her infant's entirety. So the question arises, what is a mother to do? Tustin (1994b) observed that such well-meaning mothers often instinctively compensate for this deficit by becoming physically over-protective. However, paradoxically, their loving focus on the physical dimension of mothering may contribute to a state of what Tustin called "dual unity" or "adhesive unity," wherein the emphasis is on a sensation of being, rather than the sense of well-being. This overemphasis upon tactile contact leaves the baby extremely vulnerable in times of Mother's bodily absence. Thus, in her last paper, Tustin clarified that, in her view, psychogenic autism is:

> A protective reaction that develops to deal with the stress associated with a traumatic disruption of an abnormal, perpetuated state of adhesive unity with the mother—autism being a reaction that is specific to trauma. It is a two-stage illness. First, there is a perpetuation of dual unity, and then the traumatic disruption of this and the stress that it arouses. (Tustin, 1994b, p. 14)

It is vitally important to note that Tustin (1972) fully acknowledged the role of the innate disposition and sensitivities of each baby, which includes possible neurological abnormalities. She repeatedly stressed that the absence of neurological problems in the autistic children she treated meant only that these problems were undetectable by the diagnostic methods then available. In contrast to Kanner's (1943) "refrigerator mothers," Tustin observed that the mothers of these hypersensitive children are more often than not quite loving mothers who do their best to relate to an unresponsive child while struggling to survive themselves. These mothers inspired compassion and therapeutic ambition in her. However, she suggested that the mother's preoccupation with survival may interfere with the establishment of what Winnicott (1956, 1960a) called "normal primary maternal preoccupation" with what the more-than-ordinarily-vulnerable baby is going through and his needs and desires as separate and distinct from her own.

It is my observation that such feelings of insecurity are more common in new mothers than we like to think, as many are increasingly geographically or emotionally cut-off from the close and affectionate support of their families. Additionally, sometimes their husbands are themselves preoccupied, for example with their own insecurity about the prospect of becoming a father or the pressures of providing for an expanding family. Thus the fathers may be unavailable to lend emotional support to the neonatal couple: support that is both necessary for healthy bonding and for timely separation between infant and mother.

I believe it may be possible that these unavoidable environmental conditions, increasingly prevalent in our modern culture, may be at least one factor contributing to the frightening increase in the incidence of autism in the past three decades.

Tustin (1990a) suggested that, under optimal conditions, mother and baby match each other's rhythms, gestures, vocalizations, or actions. They are both complete and similar-if-separate from birth. Under these conditions, normal developmental imitation gradually evolves into a process of introjective identification. This means that there exists a relationship that is complementary and reciprocal, rather than competitive or parasitic. However, when the overly sensitive and inadequately prepared infant experiences (what is for him) too great a gap between himself and a now suddenly separate mother, he may protectively and perhaps reflexively withdraw into his own disconnected sensual experiences. In this instance, imitation is of a fusional nature, and adhesive rather than introjective identification prevails as the sensual experiences that had once linked mother and infant become autosensual and are therefore increasingly cut-off from experiences of human contact and from relationship.

In reporting the experience of her patient John, Tustin (1972) wrote that, when he emerged from his autistic shell, he was able to tell her of the sudden wrenching away of the nipple from the mouth of which it was originally felt to be a part. This event had been perceived by John as a sensation of the "black hole with the nasty prick" (Tustin, 1990a, p. 78). Tustin noted that this sort of "happening" is one version of the "nameless dread" (Bion, 1962a) of premature twoness: premature in that the infant has yet to be adequately helped to tolerate such situations.

Jean described the nature of the terror she endured during the breaks in analysis. She felt that she and her analyst were "two jugs pouring water into each other, only Jean's jug had a hole in it and the water spilled out of her" (Tustin, 1986, p. 198). Jean also said that she felt, "deep down, as if she were a waterfall, falling forever out of control into a bottomless abyss, into nothingness" (Tustin, 1986, p. 198). Jean emphasized that it was the "feeling of being out of control, as much as the falling, that was unbearable" (ibid) as she felt that she was losing herself.

Tustin was able to speak to Jean about her waterfall feelings being "deep down," in that they came from the very beginnings of life when her body was felt, not just as fluid, but as composed of fluids that could be spilled out and lost. Thus, the baby-Jean was in danger of losing all sense of having a body, of existing. Worse than the fear of dying, where at least her body would be left behind, Jean's fear was one of complete annihilation: "She would be a no-body, a non-entity" (Tustin, 1986, p. 198). Such fears of being gone were heard repeatedly in the communications of Tustin's patients, as well as in those child cases for which she was consulted. This sense of catastrophe seems highly significant: instead of normally timed differentiation and integration, explosive disintegration or paralyzed unintegration prevails. It is important to note that it is the awareness of this state that has to be avoided by the child in the interest of psychic survival. So what is a baby to do?

Tustin discovered that infants like John and Jean rally extraordinary, auto-generated protections in an effort to block out the awareness of the gap between self and other. Her theory of autistic objects (Tustin, 1980) and autistic shapes (Tustin, 1984b) addresses these autosensual tactics and makes more comprehensible the myriad idiosyncratic and often covert activities engaged in by the autistic child: activities that function to enclose them in an impenetrable world apart from our own.

Tustin (1990a) noticed how autosensual maneuvers—for example repetitive movements, echolalia, and retention of feces or urine—serve to create a protective exoskeleton, made up of sensation-dominated delusions that block out both the insufferable awareness of two-ness and the overwhelming ecstasy of at-one-ment. This happens when such awareness threatens the baby's developing sense of personal continuity and integrity. Here, Tustin observed that these delusions are the "thing-in-itself," not to be confused with more sophisticated mental representations like metaphors.

With the elaboration of her models of autistic objects (1980) and autistic shapes (1984), Tustin developed a coherent picture of autism that complements current observations from both behavioral and neurobiological disciplines. She distinguished autistic objects from ordinary inanimate or animate objects, in that autistic objects are not related to as objects in the ordinary sense. Instead they are used for the tactile sensations that they produce.

For instance, Tustin observed that autistic children use toys, not in the course of child's-play as a mode of expression, or in therapy for communicating their experience, but for the sensations that these objects engender upon the surface of the skin. A toy car might be turned upside down and the wheels spun for hours, creating a sensation for the child of being fused with the wheels going round and round. Thus, he is able to gain a sensation of going round and round forever without the shock of beginnings or endings: a sensation of timelessness and immortality. Or when held tightly in the palm of the hand, the car becomes a source of comfort, as the child can feel himself to actually be that hard durable "thing."

Moreover, the idiosyncratic shape produced in the palm of the child's hand by the object can afford him an additional soothing sensation. As this shape is idiosyncratic, it belongs to him and him alone and thus cannot be taken away. To be clear, Tustin differentiated autistic shapes from objective shapes—such as a square or a circle—in that these are eccentric, endogenous impressions or swirls of sensation, produced upon the surface of the skin or upon the internal surfaces of the body with the aid of bodily substances, like feces, urine or spit, malleable materials like clay, or impressible objects like the toy car.

Of course, the flaw in this survival strategy is that, although the child may tentatively gain a sensation of invulnerability or safety by fusing with these inanimate objects and often use people in this way as well, they cease to develop their own sense of growing or a growing sense of being truly lively, animate, flesh and blood creatures. Instead they come to feel, as one patient of mine put it in retrospect, "Like an inanimate thing in a world of the dead."

It is essential to notice that the key word in Tustin's psychology is "sensation." The sensations provided by the autistic use of objects and the creation of autistic shapes may not only be tactile, but may be visual, auditory, olfactory, or gustatory sensations as well, all perceived as tactile in nature, perhaps through an abnormally sustained capacity for what Stern (1985) called amodal perception.[1] We only need to recall expressions such as, "his eyes were glued onto me" or "he was lost in the music" or "the smell of perfume captivated him" to get the gist of the all-enveloping tactile sensations derived from various perceptual modalities. These sensations, by rights of their denial of physical distance, either function to distract attention away from feelings of indefensible anxiety—by providing an illusion of safety, strength, and impermeability—or they may have a numbing or tranquilizing effect on the individual. This serves to protect him from such dreaded sensations of bodily catastrophe as falling forever, liquefying, spilling, evaporating, burning, or freezing. Unfortunately, in their extreme form and when used to excess, the child becomes addicted to this mode of perceived bodily and psychic survival.

Tustin (1990a) underscored the fact that the protective shell of autism constitutes a barrier to the potentially healing effects of human relationships and what Bion (1962b) called "learning from experience." Fortunately, this self-protective encapsulation gradually becomes less necessary as the child, in the course of intensive analytic psychotherapy, begins to develop what another of Tustin's patients called the "rhythm of safety" (Tustin, 1986, p. 268). This is a mind–body state in which sensory experiences and individual bodily rhythms become re-associated with a relational, cooperatively founded tempo involving self and other. In this kind of treatment, the consistency of time and place, along with the firm and benign attitude and empathically founded understanding of the therapist, can provide a mental and emotional as well as physical ambient cadence that securely enfolds the child in relationship. This then gradually replaces the reliance on auto-generated sensations that had previously helped the child to "get a grip on himself."

This said, might it be that on a neuro-physiological level the autistic child's auto-sensuous maneuvers might function by actually inhibiting the workings of various areas of the brain. Is it possible that a vicious cycle is created whereby learning from experience—most especially the experience of and with others—becomes increasingly truncated, resulting in the stultification of neural as well as emotional and mental development? If so, this stultification may, in turn, further interfere with learning, leading to the eventual atrophy of various regions of the brain. In other words, if what the infant perceives is too much to bear, might it be that what Meltzer (1975)[2] referred to as a dismantling of the apparatus of perception not only occurs in unconscious fantasy, but also has a counterpart in physical reality? It may be possible to consider this situation as connected with what neurologists refer to as "brain damage" or even retardation in autistic children.

Certainly we know that autistic infants are often mistakenly thought to be deaf. Thus, if autosensual maneuvers are effective in blocking out some unbearable awareness, might it be said that the infant creates and lives within a deprived environment. This is reminiscent of the context that functions in much the same way as the dark, isolated cages in the Berkeley experiments, where physical provisions were adequate for survival, while mental and emotional supplies were deficient for growth of the mind. I am reminded here of Klein's (1930) observation of her autistic patient Dick who retreated into the dark, empty, mummy's body, when he could not bear the feelings engendered by his premature empathy for and identification with the mother. Perhaps some light might be shed upon these questions as we consider the next piece of my puzzle.

The Rome studies

Through my personal association with Tustin, I became aware of the work of Gianotti and de Astis (1978, 1989), two psychoanalytic psychiatrists treating autistic children and conducting research at the Pediatric Neuro-psychiatric Institute of the University of Rome. Their studies involved the intensive, psychoanalytically informed psychotherapy with thirty-nine psychotic and autistic children, additionally diagnosed as having significant neuropathy, a factor frequently thought to be causal in autism.

As is still often the case, the consequences of such a diagnosis by medical experts might rule out any possibility of normal psychic or intellectual development in these children, and consequently psychoanalysis would be contra-indicated. However, De Astis and Gianotti had followed Tustin's work, and that of Donald Meltzer and his group (1975), who were all psychotherapeutically treating autism, oftentimes with noteworthy success. Thus, they resolved to proceed with an analytic protocol.

Much to the surprise of the organicists at the University of Rome, after these children had been engaged in an intensive psychoanalytic process for up to five years, neuropathy was absent in follow-up brain studies. These findings in the test children corresponded to a marked improvement in their cognitive and emotional functioning. Tustin, who consulted on these cases and who conducted seminars in Rome for the therapists, opined, "To the superficial observer, the type of autism that mainly originates from psychological disturbances can look virtually the same as that which originates from gross organic [brain] damage" (Tustin, 1990a, p. 10).

In light of the Rome results, I became convinced that psychoanalysis was the kind of therapy that could set physiological as well as psychic development back on track in certain children who have been afflicted with pervasively constricting developmental disorders.

Mirror neurons

At the University of Parma in Italy, a group of neuroscientists (Rizzolatti, Fadiga, Gallese et al., 1996) serendipitously stumbled into a particular line of research. They were working with monkeys as subjects, testing neurons that fired whenever a monkey would grab for a peanut. They assumed that the neurons that fired were motor neurons. However, one day a scientist grabbed a peanut and the monkey's cells fired as well. The monkey had not moved, but the human had. This suggested that the cells under study "equated seeing something with doing something." The head of the experimental team, Dr. Rizzolatti, thought it significant that the cells involved with motor planning for the monkey also responded to the movements of others, even the movements of a member of another species.

These neurons eventually came to be known as "mirror neurons," because it appeared that the brain can mirror the movements it visually perceives. This unanticipated discovery stimulated these and other scientists to conduct more experiments. Soon it became clear that mirror neurons exist in human beings as well as in monkeys (Iacoboni et al., 1999). Further data suggested that mirror neuron systems are fully developed in human infants (Falck-Ytter, Gredebäck & von Hofsten, 2006) and that these systems help humans to make sense of others' actions. It is of note that this outcome is consistent with findings from psychoanalytic prenatal and infant observations that demonstrate the baby's capacity to make rudimentary meaning out of his perceptions right from the moment of birth, and even before that in utero (Brazelton & Cramer, 1990; Levin & Trevarthen, 2000; Mancia, 1981; Piontelli, 1987).

We know that humans learn by observation and imitation. We humans are both moved by and can move with others in our imagination. It also appears that the rich body of knowledge that we acquire in this way can be applied to the task of comprehending the world. The Parma group posited that these mirror neurons might be the neurological means of translating what we observe so that we are able to connect with and share the world.

Many different functions for mirror neuron systems have since been suggested. Some studies link mirror neurons to understanding goals and intentions. For example, since mirror neurons are found in the inferior parietal lobe (the region of the brain recognized as an association cortex, which integrates sensory information and codes the same act in a different way according to the final goal or context of the action) these are thought to be the neural basis for predicting another individual's subsequent actions and inferring intentionality.

Mirror neurons have also been linked to empathy, because certain brain regions (in particular the anterior insula and inferior frontal cortex) are active when a person experiences an emotion and also when they see another person demonstrate an emotion. Most recently, researchers at the University of Parma demonstrated that people who are more empathic have stronger activations both in the mirror system for action and the mirror system for emotion, providing direct support for the idea that mirror systems are linked to empathy (Ramachandran & Oberman, 2006).

Mirror neurons have also been found in the inferior frontal cortex, close to Broca's area, which is the language center of the brain. This finding also suggests that human language may have evolved in association with a system where gesture is linked to performance and to understanding implemented by mirror neurons. Mirror neurons are also thought to have the potential to provide a mechanism for action-understanding, imitation-learning, and the simulation of other people's behaviors. As we have discovered, babies understand language long before they can speak a word.

The mirror system seems also to be involved in the way that we tap into and harness our abilities and put them to use in the world. People are uncommonly adept at watching and translating what they see. Perhaps that is why sports fans tense with the action of the game, grimace and jump up and down; when you know the game, then your neurons are firing as if you're playing the game. Iacoboni (1999)—at The University of California at Los Angeles (UCLA)—suggests that mirror neurons link us to other people's feelings as well as to their actions. He found that the part of the brain that is working when someone "makes a face" is the same part that is activated when they see a face. He pointed out that, when we look at faces, we feel more or less comfortable depending on whether the expression on the face is positive or negative, happy or sad, friendly or angry. He also found that normally, when we imitate faces, there is an even greater neural response. Thus, it appears that by sending messages to the limbic or emotional system in our brains, mirror neurons help us tune into each other's feelings, and Iacoboni (1999) suggests that this is the essence of empathy.

Iacoboni is convinced that there is a unifying mechanism that allows people to actually connect at an elemental level. He seems to be suggesting that there are neurons in our brains whose job it is to enable us to experientially live in other people's minds, and even to live in other people's bodies. In other words, we have the capacity to identify with others. As psychoanalysts, this comes as no surprise. After all, identification is at the heart of what we call countertransference, which so helpfully informs us of the subtle, non-verbal or infra-verbal communications coming from a patient. As analysts, it is our job to "read" other people's minds. Here I am not suggesting that we use telepathy in our work. Rather, we can and do unconsciously adopt others' points of view. We call this introjective identification, and it appears that, in health, all human beings do this. Thus, the question arises: if mirror neurons help us to connect emotionally, then what about people who have trouble connecting? For example, autistic children have difficulty with normal developmental imitation, with empathy, with communicative language and with using and comprehending metaphors.

Etiology and other features of autism

Given the increase in the diagnosis of autistic spectrum disorders, interest in its etiology has also attracted research by neuroscientists. Ramachandran and Oberman (2006) at UCSD designed a particular experiment. They recorded the mu waves in the brains of test children using an EEG while they opened and closed their hands, and while they looked at a movie of somebody else opening and closing their hands. For most children, these brainwaves are suppressed, whether they are performing or observing this action. But for children with autism, the mu wave suppression that takes place when they are "doing" does not occur when they are watching someone else's action, or even when they are imitating another's action. This finding suggests that autism might have something to do with what Ramachandran and Oberman (2006) call "broken mirror" neurons. It is also in harmony with Tustin's observation that what appears on the surface to be normal developmental imitation of another in the autistic child, is really a state of imitative fusion (Gaddini, 1969) that actually serves to block out the awareness of otherness.

According to Ramachandran and Oberman (2006), it is a given that healthy human beings are intensely social creatures, inventing shared ways to connect, like games, handshakes, dances, language, and storytelling. He concluded that deep down in our cells, we are normally built to be together. However (and this is key), unlike any other system in our bodies—for example the digestive system, motor system, and visual system—there would be very little point in having a mirror system if one lived in isolation; no point in having a mirror system if one did not want or could not bear to interact or relate to other people.

I believe that, if Tustin was right in thinking that children at risk of autism cannot bear to be aware of otherness and therefore cannot tolerate true interaction with others, and if their idiosyncratic, auto-sensuous behaviors function to block out any awareness of otherness, it may be that the broken, deficient or dysfunctional mirror systems are the result of these addictive behaviors that distract attention away from the perception of otherness. If so, is it possible that their subsequent prolonged engagement in auto-sensuousness actually functions by shutting down the mirror systems in the brain? Could it also be that these behaviors, and the subsequent shutting down of mirror systems, enclose the autistic child in an isolated and insulated state, akin to the deprived environment described in the Berkeley rat studies? Might it even be conceivable that these mirror systems were at one time turned on, and that relating to a depressed or preoccupied mother, even for a relatively brief time, is just unbearable for some children?

Arguably, in health, human beings are able to effortlessly understand each other's actions and intentions because an action performed by one person activates the neural pathways responsible for performing the same action in the brain of another person. On a visceral level, the observer seems to "understand" what the actor is doing, because a mirror mechanism affords him an experience in his mind that approximates the experience of the actor. Although scientists say that they do not know which genetic and environmental risk factors can inhibit the development of mirror neurons or alter their function, many research groups are now actively pursuing this hypothesis because it predicts symptoms that are unique to autistic spectrum disorders.

For example, mirror neurons have been embraced by simulation theorists who talk about "theory of mind" (Baron-Cohen, Leslie & Frith, 1985), which refers to our ability to infer another person's mental state and their beliefs and desires from their experiences or behavior. According to simulation theory, a theory of mind is available to us when we subconsciously put ourselves in the shoes of the person. We are observing and accounting for relevant differences; we imagine what we would desire and believe in the same scenario. In short, we identify. Thus, in some circles, mirror neurons are thought to be the mechanism by which we "simulate" others in order to better understand them. Therefore, the discovery of mirror neurons has been taken by some as a validation of simulation theory.

Another finding from this research, connected to the phenomenon of empathy, is that stronger EEG responses related to mirror neuron systems have been recorded in women as compared to men. To my way of thinking, this hypothesis is consistent with the idea that women tend to be more empathic, that the mirror neuron system is related to empathy, and that weak responses in the mirror neuron system could be linked to a so-called masculine mind and to autism, which is diagnosed to a far greater extent in male than in female children (Baron-Cohen, 2003).

These results cause me to wonder if women (biologically destined to be mothers) might ordinarily be endowed by nature with a greater capacity for empathy? This would surely be adaptive for the species since, as we analysts know, empathy is the basic communicative link between mothers and infants (Bion, 1962a). Perhaps we might contemplate what impact the use of labor inducing and anesthetic drugs have upon what Winnicott (1956b) called "primary maternal preoccupation," an empathic state of heightened and exclusive sensitivity in the mother towards her infant, upon which his existence depends.

Additionally, might a deficiency in a mother's capacity for empathy (relative to the needs of a particularly sensitive newborn) leave her baby both under-stimulated and frustrated in his attempts to engage with her? Could it be that some infants, while initially lacking an active response from the mother relative to their individual needs, reflexively shutdown their mirror systems? Perhaps this is the case when the operation of such systems would be experienced as painfully unnecessary when human social connection is felt to be thwarted, unsatisfying, and even traumatic. This state of affairs might be analogous to findings in the field of linguistics (Fauconnier, 1985) that demonstrate that, up until six months of age, all babies are more or less able to perceive all allophonic contrasts of the world's languages, no matter where they are born. However, the requisite phonemes for most languages "drop out" of the baby's babbling repertoire if he doesn't hear these sounds in his environment during a certain critical period. Perhaps these two situations are examples of a "use it or lose it" tendency in the human organism.

Furthermore, on the subject of empathy and language, the University of California at San Diego (UCSD Group) discovered that people with autism exhibit reduced mirror neuron activity in a part of the brain's pre-motor cortex, perhaps explaining their inability to assess the intentions of others. They have also found evidence that the dysfunction of mirror neurons in the insula and anterior cingulate cortex are linked to related symptoms such as the absence of empathy. Moreover, deficits in the angular gyrus may result in language deficits, both known to be connected with autism. This causes me to speculate that, if the mirror systems are shut off or broken and the neural activity that would ordinarily allow a child to understand intentionality is absent, it could be that when the autistic child's auto-sensuous behaviors are interrupted, he could suddenly find himself in an incomprehensible and therefore frightening world where seemingly ordinary events are experienced as extraordinary. Might it be that the tantrums seen in the autistic child are signs that this interruption has occurred? Is it possible that new or extraordinary happenings are instinctively anticipated as so very threatening to the survival of the child who has had little practice in contending with them, that these happenings are massively blocked out of awareness and thus might appear (to the observer) to go unnoticed by the autistic child?

In addition to explaining the primary signs of autism, Ramachandran and Oberman (2006) opine that mirror neuron theory can also account for some of the less well-known symptoms of autism. For instance, researchers know that children with autism have problems interpreting proverbs and metaphors. For example, when they instructed one of their subjects to "get a grip on himself," the child took the message concretely and started grabbing at his own body.

We know that understanding metaphor requires the ability to extract a common denominator from superficially dissimilar entities. For example, take the bouba/kiki effect, discovered by German-American psychologist Wolfgang Köhler (1929). In a replication of this study by Ramachandran and Hubbard (2001), two crudely drawn shapes (one jagged and one curvy) were shown to a group of subjects. The subjects were asked, "Which of these shapes is bouba and which is kiki?"

And no matter what language the subject spoke, ninety-eight percent designated the curvy shape as "bouba" and identified the jagged one as 'kiki,' suggesting that the human brain is somehow able to tease out abstract properties from shapes and sounds that are shared, not idiosyncratic. These researchers believe that this type of "cross-domain mapping" is analogous to metaphor, and must involve neural circuits similar to those in the mirror neuron system. Consistent with this hypothesis, autistic children perform poorly on the bouba/kiki test, as do non-autistic subjects with damage to the angular gyrus, which is at the crux of the visual, auditory, and tactile centers of the brain and is another site where mirror neurons have been detected.

I would suggest that one way of understanding this phenomenon may be derived from Tustin's observation that, for the autistic child, words are not ordinarily used for communication. Rather these are used idiosyncratically as "shape producing objects" (Tustin, 1984b) or as "hard autistic objects" (Tustin, 1980). Tustin found that the tactile sensations of tongue in mouth, made by the utterance of certain words that are specific to a given child, provide a calming or soothing sensation for the child. Words can produce sensations of filling the mouth perceived as a black hole, thus blocking out the insufferable awareness of otherness and loss felt as a "nasty prick."

Additionally, Tustin observed that jagged edges can sometimes be a relieving sight to the autistic child, who may actually feel himself to be the hard edges that he sees and therefore is reassured of his "thereness" and durability, while rounded shapes can be felt to provide a tactile sensation of soothing softness, of timelessness and continuity. Tustin highlights the need to take into consideration the idiosyncratic and concrete nature of the autistic child's world. For example, when her patient David (1972) had emerged from his shell, he was able to tell her that he had felt that the words "Tustin" and "Austin" were the same (the latter referring to a little toy "Austin Martin" car that he gripped in his hand as a hard autistic object). These words felt the same on his tongue and lips, and the sensation was the same when the sight of them met his eyes or the sound of them filled his ears. This use of words does not allow for shared meaning, nor does it allow for meaningful discrimination. For the autistic child, words are frequently an agglomeration and agglutination of tactile shapes and objects that function to block out the awareness of difference and similarity between two lively entities. This is in contrast to an acknowledgement of and an attempt to communicate with other human beings, since in order for connections to be made, separateness must first be tolerated.

Diagnosis and treatment

When all of the above issues are taken into consideration, the crucial question arises: if autistic children suffer from "broken mirrors," can they be repaired? Researchers believe that the discovery of mirror neuron deficiencies in autism may open up new approaches to diagnosing and treating the disorder. For example, Ramachandran and Oberman (2006) propose that pediatricians might use the lack of mu-wave suppression (or perhaps the failure to mimic a mother sticking out her tongue) as a tool to diagnose children with autism in early infancy so that therapy can begin as quickly as possible. It would also be fascinating to investigate the possibility that a similar test of the post-partum mothers might identify those who, while preoccupied and taken-up with their own predicament, may unwittingly employ certain obsessional activities that can result in a shutdown of their own mirror systems. This in turn would render them temporarily lacking in empathy and might be further tuned-out to the emotional experience of their infants. In such cases, perhaps the support provided by infant observers (and other engaged in identifying and intervening with mothers and infants at risk of difficulties in bonding and attachment) who lend their own empathic understanding to the nursing couple at these crucial junctures might be able to assist in mediating the mirror-neuron systems of both mother and baby. Such work is being done in parts of Australia (Salo, 2007) and Europe (e.g., the work of Haag (1985), Houzel (1996), Lechevalier-Haim (2003) in France, Maiello (1995, 1997) in Italy and Rhode (2007) in England). These "early interventions" may serve to lessen the downward spiral of mutual disappointment that can be a contributory factor in the development of autistic spectrum disorders.

Ramachandran and Oberman (2006) suggest that "salience landscape theory" can explain other symptoms of autism, for example repetitive motions such as rocking to and fro, avoidance of eye contact, hypersensitivity, and aversion to certain sounds. These are all symptoms that cannot be explained by the mirror neuron hypothesis. They point out that when perceptions—for example, sights, sounds, and smells—are processed by sensory areas in the brain, information is relayed to the amygdala, which acts as a portal to the emotion-regulating limbic system. Using input from an individual's stored knowledge, the amygdala determines how the person should respond emotionally—for example, with fear at the sight of a mad dog or indifference when confronted with trivia. Messages then cascade from the amygdala to the rest of the limbic system and eventually reach the autonomic nervous system, which prepares the body for action. So if a person is faced with a mad dog, his heart rate will rise and his body will sweat to dissipate the heat from muscular exertion. Autonomic arousal, in turn, will feed back into the brain, amplifying the emotional response. Over time, the amygdala creates what they call a "salience landscape."

Autistic children are thought to have a distorted "salience landscape," perhaps because of altered connections between the cortical areas that process sensory input and the amygdala, or between the limbic structures and the frontal lobes that regulate subsequent behavior. As a consequence of these abnormal connections, any trivial event or object might set off an extreme emotional storm in the child. This hypothesis is thought to offer an explanation as to why autistic children avoid eye contact and other novel sensations that might trigger an insufferable upheaval of emotions.

Salience landscape theorists believe that such distorted perceptions of emotional significance might explain why many autistic children become preoccupied with trifles such as train schedules, while expressing no interest at all in things that most children find salient (Ramachandran & Oberman, 2006). The UCSD Group found support for this hypothesis when they monitored autonomic responses in autistic children, by measuring the increase in skin conductance related to perspiration. In contrast with control subjects, they found that children with autism have a higher level of autonomic arousal, and although they become agitated, when exposed to trivial objects and events, they often ignore stimuli that trigger expected responses in the control group (Ramachandran & Oberman, 2006).

However, another question arises: how could a child's salience landscape become so distorted? The UCSD researchers found that nearly one third of autistic children have had temporal lobe epilepsy in infancy, related to repeated random volleys of nerve impulses traversing the limbic system. They conjecture that these seizures eventually scramble the connections between the visual cortex and the amygdala, indiscriminately enhancing some links while diminishing others. They also recognize that both environmental and genetic causes could apply here as well. Such findings on autonomic responses are thought to provide an explanation for the clinical observation that high fever sometimes temporarily alleviates the symptoms of autism (Ramachandran & Oberman, 2006). Since they know that the autonomic nervous system is involved in controlling body temperature, and because fever and the emotional upheavals of autism appear to be regulated by the same neural pathways, these researchers suspect that fever can mitigate emotion.

Initially, upon reading their hypothesis, I was reminded of Tustin's observation that "autistic children seem to have an immunity to common childhood illnesses, and that when they begin to emerge from the autistic shell, they not only suffer from emotional meltdowns, but also loosen their immunity to the ordinary fevers, colds, influenza, mumps, measles and chicken pox of childhood" (Tustin, 1990a, p. 140). She observed that psychosomatic disturbances appear when the protective shell of the autism is lifted. So, might this be another way to find meaning in the UCSD data?

Salience landscape theory appears also to provide an explanation for the repetitive motions and headbanging seen in children with autism. These researchers realize that self-stimulation somehow dampens the child's autonomic storms. Furthermore, because studies found that self-stimulation not only has a calming effect, but also leads to a measurable reduction in skin conductance in autistic children, they have proceeded to work on a possible symptomatic therapy for autism. This involves a portable device that could monitor an autistic child's skin conductance, detect autonomic arousal, and turn on another device—called a squeeze vest—that provides comforting pressure by gently tightening around the child's body (Ramachandran & Oberman, 2006).

However, if we take into consideration Tustin's theory of autism, might it be understood that the proposed squeeze-vest may function as a "second skin" (Bick, 1968, 1986), to supplement the failing autosensual maneuvers that thee autistic child employs. Thus might it be that the sensation of being held together is reinstated when the sense of being held together in the empathic understanding of another is insufficient? Although not as simple or as cost efficient as a squeeze-vest, could it be that empathic human understanding might offer both a symptomatic relief and, gradually lead to the development of an internalized mental structure that holds both body and mind together in times of stress?

UCSD's two-theory explanation for the symptoms of autism—mirror neuron dysfunction and distorted "salience landscape"—are seen as complimentary and these researchers believe it is possible that the same event that distorts a child's "salience landscape" also shuts down the mirror neuron systems. Alternatively, the altered limbic connections are thought to be a side effect of the same "event"—whether genetic or environmental—that triggers dysfunctions in the mirror neuron system. However, all agree that the ultimate cause of autism remains to be discovered.

Putting it all together: discussion and tentative conclusions

In concluding, I will summarize by pulling together my puzzle and I will end with some further questions for study and research. The reader should bear in mind that my aim throughout has been to suggest some cooperative links between Tustin's psychoanalytic explorations of the subjective experience of autism on the one hand, and on the other, some hypotheses advanced by neuro-scientific researchers. Inevitably, these links must remain speculative. They cannot at this stage address the finer details, such as the existence of different sub-groups within the autistic spectrum that have been outlined by Tustin (1972), by Alvarez and Reid (1999) and by psychiatrists such as Wing (1996).

Arguably, Rizzolatti's (1996) discovery of mirror neuron systems sheds light on the neurological areas involved in autism and specifically on the issue of empathy. Through continuing research based on their findings, Ramachandran and Oberman (2006) at UCSD and others have been able to identify a possible connection between the dysfunction of these systems and some of the symptoms observed in autism. However, I want to underscore that it is explicitly stated in all of these studies that scientists have yet to identify which genetic and/or environmental factors actually lead to the development and functioning of mirror neuron systems and which of these factors may prevent their development or impede their functioning. The same applies to factors that can lead to a distorted "salience landscape" or those that aid in the development of one that is relevant and true.

Since the possibility that an individual's mirror neurons may be dormant or suppressed (rather than altogether lost or irreparably broken) is clearly considered by all of these researchers, the question remains as to what if any therapeutic process might possibly revive or restore this neural capacity and its related mental and emotional functioning? What therapeutic process might mitigate the distortions in the experiences of the child to create a more helpful and accurate salience landscape?

Perhaps psychoanalysis, with its penchant for the discovery of the meaning of things, can offer a new and illuminating map of the landscape that other disciplines have been exploring. Tustin viewed many autistic children as intrinsically bright and sensitive, although autism can appear to correlate with significant intellectual impairments. Might hypersensitive children come into the world genetically endowed with well-functioning mirror systems, but lacking the capacity to process or contain resulting emotions by which they then can feel flooded? In such instances, it could be said that the infant—by rights of his precocious capacity to perceive his mother's insecurities, to empathize with her—becomes flooded with his own as well as her undigested infantile terrors of separateness? If this is so, what is a baby to do?

Tustin suggests that that the baby may take over the mother's function of holding and containing his bodily essences, as-yet-undifferentiated from their mental and emotional counterparts, through autochthonous activities that afford him a sensation of being safely held together within a second skin. But when auto-sensuousness replaces mental and emotional activity, keeping out unwanted or insufferable stimulation and happenings, the baby may become enclosed in an impoverished environment.

Could this result in stultification of cortical development and truncation of neural connections, furthering isolation? This situation could be considered as a virtual Möbius strip, where neural systems needed for interaction with the environment are disabled, and the interaction with the environment necessary for further neural development becomes increasingly lacking.

The Möbius strip is an excellent model for the world that the autistic child attempts to maintain, as described in the popular limerick often associated with this design:

> A mathematician confided
> That a Möbius strip is one-sided,
> And you'll get quite a laugh,
> If you cut one in half,
> For it stays in one piece when divided.[3]

Indeed, Tustin underscores the autistic child's aversion to the awareness of two-ness and the effect he can have upon his environment while avoiding this reality. For example, the parents and caretakers, who feel compelled to repeat what they say to the child many times, just in order to get his attention, may reinforce echolalia. Thus, they are forced to emulate the child's autistic ways. So Tustin warns, "If as therapists, we unduly collude with the child's use of words as objects, we risk leaving him in the grip of his pathology, with no possibility for developing genuine relationships characterized by effort and co-operation" (Tustin, 1980, p. 32).

Tustin also described how:

> Mother and child become autistic objects for each other; [living] in a sensation-dominated cocoon in which they fit each other predictably and perfectly. They become each other's ecstasy. Some autistic children come into therapy with a history of such an idyllic infancy. But the benefits from such an infancy are spurious. (Tustin, 1981a, p. 119)

Often children seem to be developing normally, until such time as an event, such as the birth of a sibling, abruptly interrupts this blissful state of affairs. She points out that, "A beneficial feature of the bearable lack of fit of the 'good-enough mother' is that it provides a space in which chance happenings can occur. Such chance happenings are agents for transformation and change" (Tustin, 1981a, p. 119). I would add that these are opportunities for learning from experience in contrast with rote memorization and repetition. You will recall that the Berkeley scientists found that opportunities for learning from experiences were a necessary component of an enriched environment essential for cortical development, especially neural connectivity.

Tustin cautioned that:

> The mother and baby who become entrancing autistic objects for each other and fit each other perfectly, prevent the possibility of such a space. This means that the child's mental development is massively stunted and goes awry, because agents of change are shut out. (Tustin, 1981a, p. 119)

Tustin thought that the father could be one such agent, playing an important role in supporting the nursing couple through the trials and tribulations aroused by the lack of a perfect fit, and the realization that they cannot absolutely control one another. An absent, passive, or too malleable father is easily used as yet another autistic object. However, father's interested and firmly supportive presence can serve as a bounding third party that holds mother and infant together in ever growing and changing experiences. He can facilitate a safe and sound separateness that may be tolerable. The therapist may be able to function in this way as well, to mitigate, through empathic understanding, the "black hole experience" that has necessitated the rigid defensive maneuvers that have isolated him from life's experience.

The Rome studies (Giannotti & De Astis, 1978, 1989) attest to the possibility that neural as well as emotional and mental development that has been thwarted, stagnated, and distorted on all scales and measures can be stimulated and supported through psychoanalytic therapy. This can provide a firm, empathic (rather than entangling or collusive) experience that serves to open the child's mind to the riches available in his environment, freeing him from his caged isolation.

Notes

1. The innate general capacity of the infant to take information received in one sensory modality and to somehow translate it into another sensory modality.
2. Meltzer defines dismantling as the most primitive working of obsessional mechanisms. Unlike the splitting processes described by Melanie Klein that make use of the sadistic drives, dismantling (which is reversible at any time) relies on a relaxation of the function of attention.
3. I found this on a website: http://academics.smcvt.edu/twhiteford/Math/Student%20Projects/Peters.htm which is titled: Math Cabinet of Curiosity By Peter Garrecht. The limerick's author is cited as anonymous. Accessed 20 June 2014.

CHAPTER NINE

Surviving unthinkable trauma: dissociation, delusion, and hallucination in *Life of Pi*

> All living things contain a measure of madness that moves them in strange, sometimes inexplicable ways. This madness can be saving; it is part and parcel of the ability to adapt. Without it, no species would survive.
>
> —Martel, *Life of Pi*, 2001, pp. 44–45[1]

Introduction

In the previous chapters, I've written about trauma occurring in infants who have not yet achieved a tangible sense of being held securely in the womb of mother's mind that coincides with the physical sensation of being held safely in her arms. It is widely known that the most primitive forms of anxiety are often indistinguishable from physiological sensations (Bick, 1968) and, as such, might produce what Bion (1967) called "nameless dreads." These dreads threaten a sense of "going-on-being" (Winnicott, 1965) as well as the "rhythm of safety" (Tustin, 1987) necessary for the development of a self that is able to tolerate traumatic experiences in later life. When left unmitigated in early life, the awareness of such dreads (or even the capacity for that awareness) may be felt as a deadly toxin that must be expelled or withdrawn from.

I have also suggested that, with the onset of puberty, the return of many of these primitive anxieties, previously held at bay by a barrier of latency, provokes a shift in the balance towards the more radical defenses employed by what Bion (1957) called the "psychotic part of the personality." This shift often occurs even in normal adolescent development. However, when traumatic happenings occur during adolescence, the ascendance of the "psychotic part of the personality" may reach extremes (Mitrani, 2007a). In such instances, extensive *dissociation, delusion, and hallucination* may be recruited in service of physical as well as psychic survival. It is to the illustration of these phenomena that I devote this chapter: an illustration derived not from clinical data, but from a work of art, in this case a contemporary film based upon a popular novel.

Methodology

The practice of using fictional characters to illustrate and exemplify clinical ideas follows a rich tradition from the inception of psychoanalysis. For example, in 1907 Freud utilized the analysis of a work of fiction, examining the protagonist Norbert Hanold in Jensen's *Gradiva* (1903). In that paper, Freud made an analogy between the burial and excavation of Pompeii and the expulsion and re-emergence of Hanold's emotional experiences, all while developing a suitable case for his argument that dreams and delusions are mental events imbued with meaning.

Yet another memorable use of an *imaginary patient* can be found in Melanie Klein's (1955) seminal paper "On identification," where she employed the character Fabian Especel in Julian Green's *If I Were You* (1947) to highlight the "ins" and "outs" of projective identification, as well as its destructive side effects.

Of course, the existence of these and other remarkable contributions does not, *ipso facto*, justify the substitution of fictional characters for flesh and blood analysands. However, there are times when one finds that confidentiality cannot be maintained if a lengthy and detailed case history is used to illuminate a given theory. At the same time, there are theoretical discussions, such as the one I am about to embark upon, which seem to beg for illustrations of such extended length and detail.

Those readers familiar with my paper (Mitrani, 1995) on Patrick Suskind's (1986) novel *Perfume*, and its fictional character Jean—Baptiste Grenouille, may agree that the use of such characters may be merited, not only in the interest of maintaining the privacy of our patients, but also because *the magnification of the artist's imagination serves to draw attention to those subtle features that might otherwise escape our notice*. Additionally, just as extraordinary pathology can draw our attention to more normal neurotic conditions, perhaps extraordinary-if-ficticious tramatic events may throw light on the consequences of more ordinary traumatic events in the lives of our patients. It has also been said that certain artists, having "turned away from external reality … know more about internal, psychical reality and can reveal a number of things to us that would otherwise be inaccessible to us" (Freud, 1933, pp. 58–59).

I strongly believe that director Ang Lee's (2012) film-rendition of Yann Martel's novel *Life of Pi* (2001), as adapted by screenwriter David Magee, can be taken as a fable that expresses some basic truths about human struggles for both physical and psychic survival in the face of unbearable, traumatic happenings and the role of the unconscious in this regard.

It is a working assumption of psychoanalysis that *nothing in the life of the mind is random*. After all, the mind is an elaborate associative network, with mental events linked to one another in meaningful and complex ways. Within certain broad parameters, all mental activity follows the logic of this associative network.

Although I am appreciative of the numerous other ways in which Ang Lee's film might be interpreted, this chapter will address only those aspects that create a compelling representation of *the survival function of the defensive triumvirate of dissociation, delusion and hallucination*. Throughout this Chapter, I will do my best to describe the images that were so beautifully rendered in the film and that lend credibility to my interpretations.

Background

As background for the film's credits, the viewer is given a glimpse of the lush botanical gardens and exotic zoo, situated in mid-twentieth century Pondicherry, known as the French Riviera of India. The music, introduced during this interval, and reprised throughout the film, is known as Pi's lullabye: unmistakenly East Indian in romantic tone and melody and delicately embroidered with the strains of a French accordion. It is said that Ang Lee's vision for this song was that it would convey the sense that "A child sleeps, not because he is sleepy, but because he feels safe." It becomes clear in the lyrics of the lullaby that Pi's mother transmits to her child a sense of well-being, confidence, and at-one-ment with nature as she urges him to "sleep humming" while she conveys a sense of safety, faith in and at-one-ment with nature. She sings him to sleep describing him as a peacock, a tiger and the courage of the tiger; she calls him the eyelid and the dream within that eyelid, as well as a sweet lotus flower and its nectar.

Pi's story is told by way of a conversation that takes place between a middle aged Pi, now living in French Canada, and a French Canadian novelist who has come from India to hear what was described as "a story that will make you believe in God" (Martel, 2001, p. 108). Although theologians and spiritualists have no doubt weighed in on this point, I will consider the ways in which *Pi's story increases our belief in the wonders of the unconscious mind.*

Life of Pi

In 1954, Santosh Patel—a modern, rational, atheist businessman—established a zoo in the town's botanical gardens. Gita, a Hindu botanist, worked in the gardens and the two met, married, and had their son Ravi one year later. Piscine was born, two years after Ravi with the aid of a herpatologist who happened to be paying a visit to the zoo in order to attend to an ailing monitor lizard. After the birth, Gita and her infant son were both healthy, but the lizard was trampled by a frightened Casuary. As such, from the moment of his birth, the sacrifice of another was linked to Piscine's survival.

At the age of five, Gita introduced Pi to the Hindu god Krishna, preserver and sustainer of the universe. Lying in bed with her young son, Gita told him the story of how Yashoda once accused her baby Krishna of eating dirt. When little Krishna denied having eaten dirt, his mother demaded that he open his mouth. Krishna obeyed and, to her amazement, Yashoda saw the entire universe stretching out before her. In a comic book, Pi sees the image of all that the baby Krishna carries inside himself, what his mother sees when she looks into his wide-open mouth—all the stars and the planets, all the yesterdays, todays, and tomorrows—the universe unfolding in all its wonderous and awesome detail. For Pi, Krishna was a superhero, as was the god Vishnu, the supreme soul and the source of all things. We are told that Vishnu sleeps, floating on the shoreless cosmic ocean, and we are the stuff of his dreaming.

Although Santosh warns his sons not to be fooled by the stories and pretty lights, Pi's interest in God persists nonetheless and does not stop at Hinduism. On holiday in the mountains, Ravi dares twelve-year-old Pi to go into the church and drink the holy water. Pi rises to the challenge and drinks from the font in the chapel. But as he turns to look up at the stations of the cross, the priest enters the sanctuary and calls out to him, "You must be thirsty!" He brings him a cup of water and explains that one can't understand God in all his perfection, but one can understand God's son and his suffering as one would a brother's. That night, Pi thanks Vishnu for introducing him to Christ and he prays to the statue of that Hindu God, which lies prone next to the his bed.

Pi continues to struggle with questions about the sacrifice of Jesus, and eventually is inspired to be baptized. He also discovers Islam, with "Salah" its ritual of purification by water. Water has surely played a significant role in the life of Pi, even in even in his naming. The story is told that Father's best friend Francis—also known as uncle Mamaji—was an expert swimmer who traveled the world collecting swimming pools like others collect souvenirs. He raved to Santosh that "Piscine Molitar," a public pool in Paris, was the most beautiful in the world, with "water so clean and clear you could have used it to make your morning coffee" (Martel, 2001, p. 12). Impressed by the story, Father named his youngest Piscine Molitar Patel. It is also noteworthy that this "uncle" was responsible for teaching Pi an essential survival lesson: that a mouthful of water may not kill, but panic will.

Predictably, at the dawn of puberty Piscine becomes an object of ridicule, teased mercilessly by his peers for his name; No pissing on the playground they'd chant. However, at the age of twelve, he finds a clever way to regain his dignity. He begins the school year by introducing himself as Pi—the sixteenth letter of the Greek alphabet connoting an irrational and infinite number, representing the relationship between the circumference and the diameter of any circle. This number is rounded off to 3.14—Pi. In this way he transforms himself from an object of scorn and derision into something of a school legend, as his classmates and teachers applaud his ability to fill the blackboards with Pi written out from memory as far as space will allow.

Around this same time, Pi decides to "meet" the zoo's new tiger—Richard Parker. He calls to the tiger and offers a piece of raw meat, which he holds in his hand through the bars of the cage. He tell the tiger that the meat is for him and the tiger approaches slowly, with head up and ears forward, his jaws and lips slack as he slowly begins to accept the meat. However, all of a sudden the boy is yanked away by his father, whose shouts startle both boy and beast, with the latter running away in terror.

Santosh scolds Pi, accusing him of anthropomorphizing. Pi pleads his case: that he can see in the eyes of animals that they too have souls. But Santosh insists that what the boy sees is the reflection of his own emotions and nothing more. To illustrate this point, he commands a worker to bring a live goat, which he ties to the bars. Gita pleads that Pi is just a boy, fearful that Pi will be scarred for life by what she realizes her husband is about to do. But Father forces Pi to watch as the tiger returns, this time couching, ears laid back, stalking and abruptly pouncing on his prey: ruthlessly dragging it off to his lair.

Afterward, Pi feels that his world has lost its enchantment. School is filled with facts, fractions, and French: words and patterns that go on and on, just like his irrational nickname. Soon we see Pi at the age of sixteen, grappling with existential dreads, searching for something that might bring meaning back into his life.

He has been engaged to play the drums for a dance class, and afterward follows the lead dancer, Anandi, asking her about the meaning of her hand gestures in the dance. She explains that they indicate that a lotus flower is hiding in the forest. This encounter is touching for both young people and they become inseparable thereafter.

Unfortunately, at this tender time in his life, Pi's father once again catches him off guard, leaving him bewildered. One night at the dinner table, Father announces that the family must leave the zoo, emigrate to Canada, and sell the animals there in order to obtain a price that might enable them to start a new life. Pi grapples with the loss of the only home and way of life he has known, as well as the heart-wrenching loss of his precious Anandi. He remembers every moment of their last day together, but sadly cannot recall ever having said goodbye.

Aboard the Japanese freighter, which is to transport his family and all of the zoo animals to Canada, Pi encounters the cruelty of the world and the demands for compromise that exist outside his once sheltered environment. A cruel French chef mocks and belittles his vegetarian Mother, and Father nearly come to fisticuffs with the Frenchman. An amiable Budhist sailor suggests that, on the ship, gravy is taste—not meat—but the family remains stoic and eats only steamed rice.

Beyond the port of Manila, above the Marianna Trench, a mighty thunderstorm wakes Pi from his slumber belowdeck. Pi climbs topside and, as if to defy the Gods, he shouts at the lightening, dancing, running, and laughing maniacally, flailing his arms and nearly falling overboard. When he overhears shouts and screams from the bridge of the ship, Pi begins to come to his senses. As huge waves inundates the bow of the freighter, he's put in touch with the reality of the life-threatening nature of the tempest. He races toward the hatch and climbs below to warn his family. However, finding their cabins completely under water, he struggles to return topdeck where animals and crew are scrambling in chaos.

Thus far, we have Pi's history, up until the ship begins to go down, as he is pushed into a lifeboat just before its release into the storm-tossed waters. Beyond this point, although the film's narrative stretches our imagination in the extreme, the cinematic story is told in such strikingly vivid detail, that our *disbelief becomes suspended, as in a dream*.

Pi's tale of survival

Terrified and at the mercy of nature, Pi finds himself in the lifeboat with only a helpless, wounded Zebra that has jumped overboard from the deck of the freighter, landing hard in the stern. Pi looks on as the ship founders and sinks, all the while calling for his lost father and mother and his brother Ravi. As the lifeboat is carried farther and farther away from the sinking ship on turbulent seas, Pi tosses out and reels in a life preserver, hoping that it might be carrying a loved one. Instead, he sees Richard Parker, the Bengal tiger, clinging to it for dear life. In spite of his efforts to fight off the tiger with an oar, a large wave washes the big cat aboard.

Alarmed at the prospect of being in the same boat as this aggressive beast, Pi jumps overboard, descending into the depths of the raging waters. Pi lingers in shock for a a long moment, staring at the submerged ship. Unexpectedly, he struggles to the surface, hanging onto the pole at the stem of the small boat. As the storm subsides, the tiger Richard Parker is no longer in sight. Instead, a hyena emerges from under the tarp at the bow of the lifeboat. Pi tries to fend off this vicious scavenger with the oar, just as the mother orangutan "Orange Juice" approaches, floating on a bunch of bananas. The hyena disappears under the tarp, but as the day turns to night, it re-emerges to attack the injured zebra while Pi and Orange Juice scream helplessly in outrage.

In the morning, Pi discovers supplies: life jackets, a survival guide, sea rations, a whistle, and more oars and life preservers that he fashions together into a life raft, utilizing the net from the bananas. Suddenly, the hyena appears again to ravage the lifeless zebra. Orange Juice courageously strikes him down. However, unexpectedly the hyena recovers, attacking and killing Orange Juice. As the boy's fury is provoked by this monstrous turn of events, we witness a *transformation in Pi*, whose image is suddenly eclipsed by the roaring tiger, Richard Parker, charging out from underneath the tarp and attacking and killing the scavenger. Quickly a terrified Pi casts the life raft overboard and dives into the water.

In the next scene, Pi is alone on the life raft, tethered by a long rope at a safe distance from the boat that carries Richard Parker. Pi fortifies the structure of his floating retreat and pulls himself cautiously toward the bow of the boat to retrieve the emergency rations left behind just under the tip of the tarp. Pausing to drink and to take nourishment while loading cans of fresh water and baked wheat bisquits into the life raft, Pi is once again confronted by the tiger, just as Pi discovers yet a sixth refugee from the sunken freighter: a rat, which he captures and tosses to the tiger. Using this moment of diversion, Pi dives onto his raft and paddles away to a safe distance from the powerful force of unbound natural aggression.

As the day turns into night and the sun rises once more, we see Pi on calm seas in his life raft, linked to but safely separated from the ferocious cat in the boat. From time to time, Pi pulls himself back to the boat on his raft, momentarily facing Richard Parker who is peeking out from his hide under the tarp, only to push off again as he is repelled by what he sees in the eyes of the tiger. Pi consults the charts that show the ocean's currents, longitudes, latitudes, and depths. But there are no such lines, no lines anywhere as he looks out on an endless ocean with no landmarks to guide him.

Of all those tactics recommended in the survival manual, telling stories and not losing hope have meaning to Pi. He discovers a sea anchor and finds that the use of this device can diminish or increase the impact of the currents and waves on the rocking movement of the boat. He decides that if he cannot make Richard Parker his friend—if he cannot tame him—perhaps he can train him.

Using his whistle to reinforce associations for the tiger, he rigs the anchor to stabilize his raft. He attaches a set of lines to each end of the boat to enable him to turn it parallel to the waves to make the big cat seasick. He can also diminish the animal's discomfort by using the opposing line to turn the boat into the waves. He accompanies each orientation with the change in pitch and volume of his whistle. After some time, Pi attempts to rejoin the tiger on the boat in order to test the effectiveness of this conditioning and to assert his dominance. Standing defiantly on the tarp with Richard Parker seasick in the stern, Pi shouts and gestures to indicate his territory while urinating on the tarp. However, in response, the seasick Tiger struggles to his feet, turns his back to the boy, and urinates with great force right into Pi's face. So much for Pi's attempt to set boundaries for coexistance with Richard Parker!

However, not easily defeated, Pi takes a new approach: training with rewards. He brings a bucket of fresh water collected in his solar still to Richard Parker, who drinks as Pi softly blows his whistle. Fearing that the tiger's last meal will be an emaciated vegetarian boy, Pi returns to his raft to decide how to provide food for the carnivore.

A small eco-system has formed beneath Pi's raft and tries fishing for the cat's dinner, at first unsuccesssfully, using some of his biscuits as bait. Watching the scene, the tiger drools and licks his lips, as the boy makes a plea for patience. Suddenly, Richard Parker leaps into the water, as if determined to catch his own fish. Failing this, the tiger turns and heads toward the raft, provoking a petrified Pi to drag it and himself aboard the boat, stranding Richard Parker in the water, where he just barely hangs onto the side of the boat throughout the night. By dawn, Pi has fashioned a ladder of sorts, which he casts overboard to enable the now exhausted animal to climb back into the boat. As the tiger does so, Pi pushes his life raft overboard and swims out to this floating asylum.

In the morning, Pi takes inventory of his rations and loads them all onto the raft for safekeeping. He turns to the task of catching one of the huge Dorado that swim beneath his raft. Snaring the fish in his banana net, partially draped below the raft, Pi wrestles it aboard and beats it mercilessly with the back of his axe. As the fish dies, his brilliant blue, gold, and green colors fade to grey. He weeps in sorrow and with remorse, bringing his hands together in prayer to thank the God Vishnu for coming to him in the shape of a fish and saving their lives. He hurls the large fish into the boat with a thud and blows a soft whistle to tell the tiger that supper has been served.

That night, a full moon shines and the water is illuminated with irridscent plankton. Fish swim in all directions, when suddenly a cone of rushing energy presses upward toward the surface. It's an enormous humpback whale, wrapped in the phosphorscent organisms, mouth gaping, fifty feet in length, thrusting up into the air. As it plunges back into the water, the leviathan overturns the life raft, submerging all of Pi's sea rations and scattering the cans of fresh water over the ocean's surface.

The next day, Pi scratches his thirty-eighth mark in the hull of the lifeboat with his knife. He realizes that hunger changes everthing you know about yourself. As fish swim just beneath his raft, he looks across to the lifeboat where his gaff lies hooked into the tarp at the bow of the boat. He crawls onto the tarp to release the gaff, just as Richard Parker pops his head out from under the tarp. As Pi braces for the tiger's attack, he is struck across the face by a flying fish. The blow is so strong that it sends him lurching backward onto the tarp as the slender blue-grey winged fish flops beside him.

Richard Parker rises up on his haunches, jaws agape. Pi grabs the fish and tosses it to the hungry cat, when all at once, a whole school of flying fish descend upon them like a swarm of locusts. They are pushed through the ocean by a hoard of Tuna in a feeding frenzy, and the water boils with life and death. Richard Parker joins in the kill, leaping blocking and batting down as many as he can, while Pi yelps with anguish—beaten and battered repeatedly by countless, airborn, piscene creatures. A large yellow-fin tuna lands hard onto the center bench, falling into the middle of the boat between boy and cat. Pi gaffs the fish, pulling it up on the tarp and waves his boathook while shouting menacingly at Richard Parker, who turns his attention to the smaller fish in the bottom of the boat.

Having achieved a tentative position of dominance, Pi tears into the huge tuna with his knife and consumes meat for the first time in his life. Afterward, he realizes that the nature of his relationship with Richard Parker must be settled once and for all. His strength and resolve, replenished by the first real nurishment he's had since the shipwreck, Pi begins to resume the cat's training, positively reinforcing his commands with chunks of tuna, his voice, his whistle, and the tap of his harpoon.

While resting under a canopy he's arranged for himself on his raft, glancing across at the tiger lounging in the stern of the lifeboat, Pi uses his knife to sharpen his pencil and writes in the margins of the survival manual that doubles as a diary. He had never thought that a piece of shade could bring him so much pleasure, or that a bucket, a knife, a pencil could become his greatest treasures. He realized that knowing Richard Parker was there brought him peace. Pi was struck as he realized that the tiger has as little experience of the real world as he himself did. They had both been raised in a zoo by one and the same master, Pi's father. It seemed as if nothing else remained for the two of them of their past with the exception each other. Without Richard Parker Pi believed that he would have already died. Pi's fear of the cat had kept him alert and tending to Richard Parker's needs had surely given the boy's life purpose.

Months pass and Pi has grown gaunt, eyes wild from exhaustion and endless solitude. His hair has grown long, his olive-caramel skin turned cocoa brown and his clothing has become threadbare and nearly transparent. For some time, Pi stretches out on the tarp in the bow, watching Richard Parker looking out over the portside. He asks the cat what he sees. Looking for the answer, Pi rolls onto his belly, head over the side of the boat, assuming the same position as the tiger. For the first time, Pi sees the world through the tiger's eyes: the sea life, the dead past and out into the universe. Pi's feral hair and eyes look almost as much like an animal's as the tiger with whom, until now, he has been unwilling to identify.

In daylight, Pi writes that words are all he has left to hold onto. Everything's mixed up, fragmented. He can't tell daydreams from nightdreams or nightdreams from reality. As his tiny stub of a pencil runs out of lead, Pi becomes aware of the rumble of thunder, as clouds rise up over the horizon and blacken the heavens. They dwarf the small vessel within a matter of moments.

Pi tries to stow his gear in the storage compartments of the boat, wrapping his manual in its plastic bag for protection. However, the storm front sweeps across the lifeboat with tremendous force, knocking Pi off his feet into the water as the book flies away into the storm. He struggles to climb back aboard the swamped little vessel, shouting like a lunatic to his God and beckoning Richard Parker to come out from beneath his sheltering tarp to join in a celebration. A spell of mania possesses Pi, just as it had on that fateful night when another storm that sunk the

184   PSYCHOANALYTIC TECHNIQUE AND THEORY

freighter. He frenetically unfastens the tarp, exposing the terror stricken tiger, while the life raft is ripped from its teather. As Pi watches helplessly while it dissappears in a violent sea, he regains his grip on the reality of the danger he is in. Richard Parker is drowning!

Pi tries to batton down the tarp that had been the Tiger's salvation, but the two are tossed together in the swamped boat as if in a washing machine. The sense of defenselessness, like the storm, is a powerful and unrelenting force. However, days after the gale subsides, Pi awakens under cloud-covered skies. He sees Richard Parker lying on the sideboard of the lifeboat, emaciated and limp. He sits next to the big cat, pulling the animal's heavy head into his lap. He admits to the tiger that they are dying.

In the next scene it is daytime, but which day is not clear. Pi lies on the tarp with the sun on his face, appearing to awake from a deep sleep. He opens his eyes to find that his boat has nestled itself into the shore's edge of a strange island, not covered with sand, but with a thickly webbed mass of tubular seaweed and the canopies of large trees, their profusion of leaves burning colorfully with an unreal intensity. Richard Parker is no longer on the boat.

Pi disembarks, secures his vessel, and crawls out to taste the plantlife. Soon he's grabbing handfulls of vegitation, eating as fast as he can. Satiated, he climbs further up the ridge into the trees, which appear as if growing out of the seaweed, as if they are one single organism. Pi hears sounds of life: a sea of meerkats surrounding countless, small, perfectly rounded ponds filled with fresh water. He parts the sea of docile animals and slips into one of the ponds.

Emerging refreshed, Pi observes Richard Parker, far away in the distance, alive and well and feasting in a sea of meerkats. As the sun begins to set, Pi rigs his fishnet between the branches of a high tree, a hammock in which to sleep the night. All at once, he catches sight of herds of meerkats, running with the sound of elephants stampeding away from the ponds, scurrying up into the trees. He hears a roar and watches as Richard Parker runs to the boat for safety.

In the middle of the night, Pi awakens bathed in a green irridescent glow. Below him, the once clear, calm pools of fresh water appeared as glowing, roiling pits of acid filled with dead and dying fish. As Richard Parker looks toward the shore from his post in the lifeboat, one gets a glimpse of the island at night from a distance. Pi reaches for a piece of fruit hanging from the tree and discovers that, within this fruit that appears to open like a lotus flower in his hands, there is a human tooth. He realizes that the island is carnivorous: that the life it gives by day, it takes away by night. Slowly Pi came to understand what it all means: years ago someone had found himself on the island. Like Pi, he thought he could stay there forever. But with only meerkats for company, he was unbearably lonely. Eventually he died, leaving behind only a tooth. Pi realized how his life would end if he stayed. He had to leave or die trying.

At daybreak, Pi collected up as much seaweed as he could carry in the lifeboat and captured as many meerkats as he could confine in the storage compartments for the tiger. He couldn't leave without him, it would have meant killing him. He called out to the tiger, who appeared out of the forest and lept aboard the lifeboat, and they pushed off from land to find their destiny.

Many days later, Pi pulled his boat ashore in Mexico. He was so weak, he feared that in shallow water, so close to deliverance he would drown. He dragged himself up on the sand and felt two eyes smiling at him. Richard Parker disembarked, stretched his legs, and wandered along the beach toward the jungle. Pi was sure that he would look back—ears pined close to his head—growling. Pi hoped that the tiger would end their relationship with some ceremony. But instead Richard Parker just stared ahead. After some time, a member of Pi's own species found him and marshalled a group of natives to carry him to safety. Pi wept because of the way in which the tiger and he had parted.

Another Life of Pi

Investigators from the Japanese shipping company interviewed Pi while he recovered in the Mexican hospital. He was the sole survior of the shipwreck. Finding his story too incredible to bring back to their superiors, they asked for one that would be more believable. What Pi gave them was a story without animals or mystical islands: it was a story of unthinkable tragedy. In this version of Pi's life, the zebra was the happy Buddhist sailor who had jumped into the lifeboat and had badly broken his leg, the hyena was the cruel French cook who killed the sailor and ate his flesh, and who eventually murdered Pi's Mother (the orangutan), throwing her overboard to be eaten by sharks; and Pi was the tiger who killed the cook and disappeared into the jungles of

186   PSYCHOANALYTIC TECHNIQUE AND THEORY

Mexico. The undisputable facts were that Pi had lost his family and had surely suffered, no matter which story they chose.

Discussion

In his film, Ang Lee leaves the viewer with a final image, one we can't help but wish we could believe in: a happy boy braving the seas in a small boat alone with a tiger. But the tragedy, as told *en face* by a young teen in a hospital bed—depicting cruelty, torture, canabalism, cold-blooded murder, revenge, terror, hardship, madness, and unimaginable aloneness—is so unadorned, down-to-earth and filled with emotion that it cannot be easily dismissed.

Which version of the story the viewer "chooses" depends on the extent of one's capacity to identify with a truly wretched victim or our need to idealize a colorful hero. The novelist in the story—like the Japanese shipping investagators—represents the latter, while as analysts we may be equipped to endure the former.

So how do we make sense of the story most would prefer to believe? What is the role of *dissociation, delusion, and hallucination* in preserving Pi's life? Do these three protective elements constitute the "madness that is part and parcel of Pi's ability to adapt"? And if this be so, how does the unconscious mind function to serve up the necessary psychic provisions for this extraordinary survival strategy? Is it possible to start with each event and trace the multiple associations linked to its transformation? Perhaps these otherwise fantastic productions make sense when the larger unconscious associative network is made explicit.

The creation of a delusion

First discussed in his "psychopathlogy of everyday life" and beautifully illustrated in his paper on the relationship between dreams and delusions in Jensen's *Gradiva*, Freud writes the following:

> Dreams and delusions arise from the same source—from what is repressed. Dreams are … the physiological delusions of normal people. Before what is repressed has become strong enough to break through into waking life as a *delusion*, it may have achieved a first success … in the form of a dream with persisting effects. For during sleep, there is a *relaxation* in the strength of the resistance with

which the dominant psychical forces oppose what is repressed. It is this relaxation that makes the formation of dreams possible, and that is why dreams give us our best access to a knowledge of the unconscious part of the mind—except that, as a rule, with the re-establishment of the psychical [investment in] waking life, the dream once more takes flight, and the ground that had been won by the unconscious is evacuated once again, resulting in delusion. (Freud, 1907, p. 61)

Reading Freud, one can't help but be reminded of Lee's vision for Pi's Lullaby. In "the more favorable conditions" of earliest childhood, perhaps Pi's sheltered environment, his purity and innocence expedited his capacity to dream, which was surely facilitated by Gita's spiritual outlook on the world: one that nurtured Pi's faith in his own inate goodness. We watch Pi as a young boy beginning to develop into both the courageous tiger and the tender lotus blossom of Mother's lullaby.

Perhaps Mother's past, as present in her faith, formed the foundations of Pi's optimism and curiosity as well as his active, aggressive, and ingenious way of defending himself from pain, for example in the instance of the creation of his nickname. Alongside Mother's Hinduism, Christianity provided Pi's model for generosity and self sacrifice, and his Muslim faith reinforced his link to the purifying qualities of water. Mamaji also instilled in Pi a fearlessness toward and mastery of water, teaching him to swim and underscoring an essential bit of wisdom: a mouthful of water will not kill you, but panic will.

In both the scene where brother Ravi dares Pi to drink the holy water and in the scene where Pi demonstrates his willingness to confront the priest in order to quench his "thirst" for understanding, young Pi reveals his ability and willingness *to mindfully take up challenges and to respectfully question authority with an earnest desire to discover himself*. This seems to signal the beginnings of a binding together of Pi's personality at the dawn of puberty, and the process of integration of his native healthy aggression with his fluid, libidinal sensitivities.

Unfortunately, Father's "lesson" with the tiger creates a rent in young Pi's sense of self: one that leaves the boy in a state of conflict. This rent mirrors Santosh's own scars, left over from his polio and his subsequent loss of faith. Thus, the growing network of Pi's inner forces begins to unravel before he can attain a stable, adult personality structure. From this point onward, Pi begins to doubt and disown both his intuitive sense of and his trust in nature, as his tenderness and aggressivity—tentatively bound together in early adolescence—are wrenched apart in that stunning scenes of "Father's lesson." Recall that in the first encounter, the Tiger's ferocity is initially tempered by Pi's benign intent. The tiger's whole body language is telling: it is powerful yet contained. However, after the wrenching away that frightens both boy and tiger, just a moment before their point of contact, we witness Richard Parker's aggression return unbound. In contrast to Pi's attempt to get to know Richard Parker, we watch as the tiger is baited with Father's ill-intent. He crouches, premeditatedly hunting his prey and pouncing with raw, unbridled, and instinctual brutality. No longer is nourishment offered as validation that this animal has a soul, but instead it becomes tied to Father's rational proof that the soul does not exist.

It is significant that Father's admonishment emphasizes that what Pi sees in the tiger's eyes is *only a reflection* of the boy's own emotions: that *what Pi sees is a projection, not an accurate perception*. From this moment on, against a background of a life changing, sociopolitical upheaval, Pi at sixteen feels as if drained of an elemental aspect of himself. Pi reads Camus' *Stranger* and other existentialists. His premature awareness of two-ness is conspicuous and we can apprehend how relevant for him is Camus' statement: that Hell is the other. Pi's existential crisis has been ushered in by Father's violent introduction of this notion of *antagonistic otherness*, before Pi has developed the capacity to bear it. Father inadvertently wrenched Pi away from his childhood illusion of at-one-ment with nature and what was surely the beginning of a growing harmony within himself.

Pi was also yanked away from his first love, Anandi, when Father announced the family's move to Canada. From this point on, Pi shifts from bewilderment at the dinner table in India to shock and dismay at the inhumanity he witnessed in the galley of the freighter. His reaction to the thunderstorm—a classic manic triumph and subsequent near-suicidal recklessness—signals the emergence of what we might call "the psychotic part" of Pi's personality (Bion, 1957). Pi cracks, just like the lightening; splitting becomes the primary line of defense against an oncoming and overwhelming depression and anxiety, brought on by the reality of his separatness from his family trapped below the rushing waters. Such omnipotent protections may also have enabled Pi to surge upward toward survival in the face of sheer terror. Amidst the chaos on deck, Pi is hurled into a lifeboat that drops like a stone into the storm-tossed sea as the freighter begins to founder. This image marks the point of Pi's insufferable trauma, the point at which he begins to seriously *dissociate,* and the juncture at which his delusional system takes shape.

In his paper on "Neurosis and psychosis," Freud describes delusions as patches "applied over the place where a rent had appeared in the ego's relation to the external world" (Freud, 1924/1981, p. 215). In psychoses, one attempts to solve conflicts with reality, not by altering feelings, as one does in neurosis, but by withdrawing from or "disavowing" reality and replacing it with fantasies that are treated as realities. A careful examination of the chaotic scene before Pi jumps ship reveals to observers (but not to Pi) a nearly seemless, yet confused and confusing replacement of the human beings—who enter or are about to enter the lifeboat along with Pi—by their fantasied animal counterparts. It almost appears as if an error has been made by the film's editor; we watch as a zebra jumps into the boat from above, and we hear, but do not see, a hyenna yelping. However, the 'editor' is actually Pi's unconscious mind, in which the dissociative splits in his reality are spliced together with elements of fantasy.

Heaved out to sea by gigantic waves, away from the ship that carries his family and the animals amongst whom he had been reared, Pi is pulled farther away from reality. Frantically, he casts a life preserver into the turbulent waters, only to find that he has inadvertently rescued Richard Parker. At this moment, perhaps Pi nearly becomes reunited with the tiger-within, his earlier disowned aggression that carries his will and capacity to survive. This may be what provokes a terrified Pi to dive off the lifeboat, as the tiger climbs onboard. Underwater, surrounded by sharks and suspended by the current, Pi gazes at the sunken ship. It's as if he's struggling with a wish to reunite with his dead and dying loved ones and his past, although in the end he swims to the surface and clings to life in the present.

Surviving these losses entails the transformation of Pi's dreamlife into a unwavering and stable delusional system that aquires an unshakable conviction in waking life, not because of what is a protective falsehood in the delusion, but rather because of the grains of truth concealed within it. These grains of truth are derived from Pi's unconscious registry of memories and experiences that predate the traumatic event. Thus, the Buddhist sailor with the broken leg appears as the Zebra that jumps ship; the malicious French cook morphs into a mocking, vicious hyena; Gita, becomes the mother Orangatan; and *Pi lives as the formidable Richard Parker.*

Lee deftly leaves a trail of clues to the unconscious links between Pi and the tiger in various images and interactions. First, in Pi's mother's lullaby, Pi is *a tiger and the courage of the tiger.* When Pi is caught drinking the holy water in the church, the Catholic Priest exclaims, "You must be Thirsty!" Is it only a coincidence that we are told the story in which Thirsty was the tiger's name before his identity was confused with that of his captor—the hunter Richard Parker—during his aquisition by the Zoo? Furthermore, there is the crucial lesson where Pi's Father insists that what his son sees in the eyes of the tiger are merely the boy's projection of aspects of his self.

One notices the marked similarity between the comic-book image of Krishna's mouth containing the whole universe and the images that Pi sees through the eyes of the tiger on the lifeboat. On film, these images are remarkably similar. Other heart-rending clues to the links between boy and tiger are hinted at in dialogue. For example, in the aftermath of the storm that nearly drowns them both, mixing them together as if in a washing machine, Pi cries, "We are dying, Richard Parker." It is of note that, on more that one occasion, Pi declares that he could not have survived without the terrible one who kept him alive, this alongside Pi's ambiguous declaration that he couldn't leave the island without Richard Parker because it would have meant killing him. Finally, on the beach in Mexico, as Pi is carried off to safety, he despairs of the unceremonious loss of Richard Parker, without any goodbyes, this reminiscent of his inability to recall saying goodbye to Anandi upon departing India.

The creation of an hallucination

As regards the floating carnivorous island, one questions its miraculous appearance, just as Pi and Richard Parker are on brink of death, when the storm wrenches away Pi's life-sustaining raft: that floating eco system filled with food and water. This threat of imminent death may have precipitated the collapse of *Pi's life-preserving delusion of being both teathered to and safely separated from Richard Parker.* As earlier stated, the sense of conviction in ones delusional system derives, not so much from what is false, but from the grains of truth in the delusion. So when the delusional system begins to fail and unconsciousness is not an option for the preservation of life, what next? Perhaps there is much evidence that this island, which we are told was never seen again, constituted *the next tactic in Pi's life-saving strategy: the formation of an hallucination.*

Hallucinations are auto-sensual, vivid, substantial, and located in objective external space. They appear in wakefulness and are often linked to deprivation, illness, or injury. Hallucinations are distinguished from dreams, which don't involve wakefulness; from illusions, which involve distorted or misinterpreted-yet reality-based perceptions; from imagery, which does not mimic real perceptions, but are instead under voluntary control; and from delusions that constitute a disavowal of reality, which is replaced instead with fantasies that are treated as concrete realities.

The hallucination is wish-fulfilling and its specifics are drawn from the unconscious. We can actually track aspects of memory that reside in Pi's unconscious, as well as the needfull wishes emanating from it. First, consider the image of Pi as a small child thanking the staue of the god Vishnu. This image of Vishnu lying prone and the shape and look of the island—as seen from afar through the eyes of Richard Parker on the lifeboat at night—eerily coincide with each other in the film: Vishnu sleeps, floating on the shoreless cosmic ocean, and we are the stuff of his dreaming.

Additionally, Pi describes the island as a floating eco system, nearly the same words used to describe the life raft that had been taken by the storm. The island is a source of food and safety for both boy and tiger. It is made up of seaweed, with small round lakes of fresh water and broad canopied trees that sustain Pi safely at night, not unlike the network of oars, life jackets and netting out of which Pi constructed the life raft with its canopy of shade, stocked with small cans of fresh water and vegetarian sea rations.

It is also significant that Richard Parker is not visable when Pi first reaches the island, which is instead inhabited by countless meerkats. I can't help but wonder if these small, harmless vegan creatures were hallucinated by Pi for a number of unconscious reasons. Most convincing is the possibility that the name "meerkat" may be an unconscious pun: a play on words that uses one expression to allude to another, a homophone or word that sounds the same as another, spelled differently and with a different meaning. If so, it may be that Pi has hallucinated an island populated by "mere" cats, in the sense that—as an

192   PSYCHOANALYTIC TECHNIQUE AND THEORY

adjective—the word "mere" means meager, measly, plain, simple, and ordinary. These linguistic aspects may be essential, unconscious components of Pi's wishful retreat from the extraordinary Richard Parker/his own complex inner-tiger.

Might Pi have known that the name "meerkat" was coined by sailors from the Dutch East India Company? This word, in the noun form, means "lake cat" and derives from the Sanscrit "monkey." Of course, Sanskrit is the Indian liturgical language of Hinduism as well as the literary language of Buddhism. The meerkat is also known as the "sun angel," protecting villages from the "moon devil" or the werewolf known to attack *lone tribesmen*. This unconscious trail may well also link with memories Pi had of his father feeding tranquilizers-filled bananas to the monkeys on the ship; with Pi's Hindu mother who appeared in his delusion as the Orangatan floating to the lifeboat on a sack of bananas; to the "happy Buddhist sailor" and even to the memory of the harsh French cook who angrily yelled at Pi's father, "You feed monkeys."

Finally, what are we to make of the island as it turns toxic by night? I suggest that Pi's elaborate hallucination begins to break down as he slumbers and perhaps dreams in safety, high in the trees surrounded by "mere" cats. After some time, Pi awakens, and indeed, as he reaches out for what appears to be a ripe fruit that opens like a lotus flower in his hands, he begins to become truly aware of the danger he is in, perhaps for the first time since the ship wreck. As evidence, compare Anandi's Lotus flower dance gestures with the lotus-fruit opening on that fateful night on the island. With his discovery of the tooth embedded in the *lotus flower hidden in the forest*, could it be that Pi begins to realize that he is in danger of encasing and fossifying his own will to live life? In this moment of recognition, has Pi begun to repossess his life force? One recalls the scene where Pi waits for Richard Parker to jump onboard the lifeboat, prior to his final attempt to return to the world or die trying. Perhaps this is the point where Pi begins to re-own his own healthy aggresivity, facing the impossibility of living without it? Is this the point where he begins to fight his way back to and even to tolerate the reality he has previously withdrawn from: a reality with all the horrors of loss and regret, as revealed in the second story of what happened in the Marianna Trench and beyond?

Like the novelist in the film, some may choose the conclusion drawn by the Japanese investigators and written in the shipping company's final report: as improbable and fantastic as the story of the animals and the island seem to them, they opt for this tale when the truth of the loss and lonliness bourn by Pi are truly unthinkable. In the cinematic finale, Ang Lee offers a somewhat realistic if bittersweet ending: the adult Pi is married with two children and a cat. One wonders, has this "end" been made possible by the mind's capacity to protect and defend life in the face of tragedy and the gradual suffering and working-through of a multiplicity of losses, owing to Pi's growing ability for mindful maturity? Still other questions and interpretations may bring additional significances to *Life of Pi*.

Note

1. Excerpt from LIFE OF PI by Yann Martel. Copyright @ 2001 Yann Martel. Reprinted by permission of Knopf Canada and Houghton Mifflin Harcourt Publishing Company. All rights reserved.

REFERENCES

Alvarez, A., & Reid, S. (1999). *Autism and Personality*. London: Routledge.
Anderson, R. (2005). Adolescence and the body ego: The reencountering of primitive mental functioning in adolescent development. Unpublished paper presented for the Annual Melanie Klein Lectureship, Psychoanalytic Center of California, Los Angeles.
Anderson, R., & Dartington, A. (1998). *Facing It Out*. New York: Routledge.
Balint, E. (1968). The mirror and the receiver. In: E. Balint, *Before I was I* (pp. 56–62). London: Free Association Books, 1994.
Baron-Cohen, S. (2003). *The Essential Difference: The Truth about the Male and Female Brain*. New York: Basic Books.
Baron-Cohen, S., Leslie, A. & Frith, U. (1985). Does the autistic child have a "theory of mind"? *Cognition, 21*: 37–46.
Bennett, E. L., Diamond, M. C., Krech, D., & Rosenzweig, M. R. (1964). Chemical and anatomical plasticity of brain. *Science, 146*: 610–619.
Bick, E. (1968). The experience of the skin in early object-relations. *International Journal of Psycho-Analysis, 49*: 484–486.
Bick, E. (1986). Further considerations on the function of the skin in early object relations. *British Journal of Psychotherapy, 2* (4): 292–301.
Bion, W. R. (1957). Differentiation of the psychotic from the non-psychotic part of the personality. *International Journal of Psycho-Analysis, 38*: 266–275.

Bion, W. R. (1959). Attacks on linking. *International Journal of Psycho-Analysis, 40*: 308–315.

Bion, W. R. (1962a). The psycho-analytic study of thinking. *International Journal of Psycho-Analysis, 43*: 306–310.

Bion, W. R. (1962b). *Learning from Experience*. London: Karnac.

Bion, W. R. (1965). Transformations. In: *Seven Servants*. New York: Jason Aronson.

Bion, W. R. (1967/1988). Notes on memory and desire. In: E. Spillius (Ed.), *Melanie Klein Today: Vol. II.* (pp. 17–21). London: Routledge.

Bion, W. R. (1970). *Attention and Interpretation*. London: Tavistock Publications.

Bion, W. R. (1974). *Brazilian Lectures, I. Sao Paulo 1973*. Rio: Imago Editora.

Bion, W. R. (1976). Evidence. In: F. Bion (Ed.), *Clinical Seminars and Four Papers* (pp. 239–246). Abingdon: Fleetwood Press.

Bion, W. R. (1979). Making the best of a bad job. In: F. Bion (Ed.), *Clinical Seminars And Four Papers* (pp. 247–257). Abingdon: Fleetwood Press.

Bion, W. R. (1992). *Cogitations*. London: Karnac.

Brazelton, B., & Cramer, B. (1990). *The Earliest Relationship*. Cambridge: Perseus.

Camus, A. (1946). *The Stranger*. (M. Ward, Trans). New York: Knopf.

Chesterton, G. K. (2009). *St. Thomas Aquinas*. New York: Dover Publications.

Decety, J., & Chaminade, T. (2003). When the self represents the other: a new cognitive neuroscience view on psychological identification. *Consciousness & Cognition, 12*: 577–596.

Eliot, T. S. (1998). *The Love Song of J. Alfred Prufrock*. London: Penguin.

Fairbairn, W. R. D. (1952). *Psychoanalytic Studies of the Personality*. London: Hogarth Press.

Falck-Ytter, T., Gredebäck, G. & von Hofsten, C. (2006). Infants predict other people's action goals. *Nature Neuroscience, 9*: 878–879.

Fauconnier, G. (1985). *Mental Spaces*. Cambridge, MA: MIT Press.

Federn, P. (1952). *Ego Psychology and the Psychoses*. New York: Basic Books.

Ferenczi, S. (1933). Confusion of tongues between adults and the child. In: *Final Contributions to the Problems and Methods of Psycho-Analysis, 1955* (pp. 156–167). London: Maresfield Reprints, 1988.

Fonagy, P., & Target, M. (1996). Playing with reality: I. Theory of mind and the normal development of psychic reality. *International Journal of Psycho-Analysis, 77*: 217–233.

Freud, S. (1901). Fragment of an analysis of a case of hysteria. In: *Standard Edition of The Complete Works of Sigmund Freud, 7*, (pp. 7–124). London: Hogarth Press.

Freud, S. (1907). Delusions and dreams in Jensen's Gradiva. In: *Standard Edition of The Complete Works of Sigmund Freud*, 9, (pp. 7–94). London: Hogarth Press.

Freud, S. (1912). The dynamics of transference. *Standard Edition of The Complete Works of Sigmund Freud*, 12, (pp. 99–108). London: Hogarth Press.

Freud, S. (1914). Remembering, repeating and working-through (Further recommendations on the technique of psycho-analysis II). In: *Standard Edition of The Complete Works of Sigmund Freud*, 12, (pp. 145–156). London: Hogarth Press.

Freud, S. (1924). The loss of reality in neurosis and psychosis. In: *Standard Edition of The Complete Works of Sigmund Freud*, 19 (pp. 182–187). London: Hogarth Press.

Freud, S. (1925). A note upon the "Mystic writing-pad." In: *Standard Edition of The Complete Works of Sigmund Freud*, 19 (pp. 225–232) London: Hogarth Press.

Fuller, P. (1980). *Art and Psychoanalysis*. New York: Writers and Readers.

Gaddini, E. (1969). On imitation. *International Journal of Psycho-Analysis, 50*: 475–484.

Giannotti, A., & de Astis, G. (1978). *Early infantile autism: considerations regarding its psychopathology and the psychotherapeutic process*. Paper presented at the eighth National Congress of the Italian Society of Infantile Neuropsychiatry, Florence.

Giannotti, A., & de Astis, G. (1989). *Il Diseguale*. Rome: Borla.

Gill, M. (1979). The analysis of the transference. *JAPA, 27*: 263–288.

Greene, G. (1929). *The Man Within*. London: Heinemann.

Greenough, W. T. (1988). The turned-on brain: developmental and adult responses to the demands of information storage. In: *From Message to Mind: Directions in Developmental Neurobiology* (pp. 288–302). Sunderland, MA: Sinauer Associates.

Greenough, W. T., Black, J. E., & Wallace, C. S. (1987). Experience and brain development. *Child Development, 58*: 539–559.

Haag, G. (1985). La mere et la bebe dans les deux moities du corps. *Neuropsychiatrie de l'Enfance, 33*: 107–114.

Haag, G. (1990). Le dessin prefiguratif de l'enfant, quel niveau de representation? *Journal de la psychanalyse de l'enfant, 8*: 19–29.

Hildebrand, P. (2001). Prospero's paper. *International Journal of Psycho-Analysis, 82*: 6.

Hinshelwood, R. D. (1989). *The Dictionary of Kleinian Thought*. London: Free Association Books.

Houzel, D. (1996). The family envelope and what happens when it is torn. *International Journal Psycho-Analysis, 77*: 901–912.

Iacoboni, M., Woods, R. P., Brass, M., Bekkering, H., Mazziotta, J. C., & Rizzolatti, G. (1999). Cortical mechanisms of human imitation. *Science, 286, 5449*: 2526–2528.

James, M. (1960). Premature ego development: some observations on disturbances in the first three months of life. *International Journal of Psycho-Analysis, 41*: 288–294.

Jensen, W. (1903). *Gradiva*. Berlin: Verlag.

Joseph, B. (1984/1989). E. Spillius & M. Feldman (Eds.), *Psychic Equilibrium and Psychic Change*. London: Routledge.

Joseph, B. (1992). Psychic change: Some perspectives. *International Journal Psycho-Analysis, 73*: 237–243.

Kanner, L. (1943). Autistic disturbances of affective contact. *Nervous Child, 2*: 217–250.

Keats, J. (1817). From a letter to George and Thomas Keats, 21 December 1817. In: J. Paul Hunter (Ed.), *The Norton Introduction to Literature: Poetry* (pp. 477–478). New York: W. W. Norton & Co, 1973.

Klein, M. (1930). The importance of symbol-formation in the development of the ego. *International Journal of Psycho-Analysis, 11*: 24–39.

Klein, M. (1935). Contribution to the psychogenesis of manic depressive states. *International Journal of Psycho-Analysis, 16*: 145–174.

Klein, M. (1946). Notes on some schizoid mechanisms. *International Journal of Psycho-Analysis, 27*: 99–110.

Klein, M. (1952). On observing the behavior of young infants. In: *Envy and Gratitude and Other Works 1946–1963* (pp. 94–121). London: Hogarth Press.

Klein, M. (1955). On identification. In: *Envy and Gratitude and Other Works 1946–1963*, (pp. 141–175). New York: Free Press edition, 1975.

Klein, M. (1957). Envy and gratitude. In: *Envy and Gratitude and Other Works* (pp. 176–235). New York: Free Press edition, 1975.

Klein, M. (1961). *Narrative of a Child Analysis. The Conduct of the Psychoanalysis of Children as Seen in the Treatment of a Ten-Year-Old Boy*. New York: Basic Books.

Klein, M. (1963). On the sense of loneliness. In: *Envy and Gratitude and Other Works 1946–1963* (pp. 300–313). New York: Free Press edition, 1975.

Klein, S. (1980). Autistic phenomena in neurotic patients. *International Journal of Psycho-Analysis, 61* (3): 395–401.

Kohler, W. (1929). *Gestalt Psychology*. New York: Liveright.

Kohut, H. (1971). *Analysis of the Self*. New York: IUP.

Lacan, J. (1949). Le stade du mirior. In: *Ecrits* (pp. 93–100). Paris: Editions du Seuil, 1966.

Laufer, M., & Laufer, E. (1984). *Adolescence and Developmental Breakdown*. London: Karnac.
Lechevalier-Haim, B. (2003). Long-term mother–infant psychoanalytic psychotherapy in a case of infantile autism with anomalies of the cerebellum. Paper presented at the seventh Annual Frances Tustin Memorial Lecture, Los Angeles.
LeDoux, J. E. (2002). *Synaptic Self: How Our Brains Become Who We Are*. London: Pan MacMillan.
Lee, A. (2012). *Life of Pi*. Los Angeles: Twentieth Century Fox Films. (Screenplay by D. Magee based on the novel by Y. Martel).
Levin, F. M., & Trevarthen, C. (2000). Subtle is the lord: the relationship between consciousness, the unconscious, and the executive control network (ECN) of the brain. *Annual of Psychoanalysis, 28*: 105–125.
Maiello, S. (1995). The sound object: a hypothesis about prenatal auditory experience and memory. *Journal of Child Psychotherapy, 21* (1): 23–41.
Maiello, S. (1997). Prenatal trauma and autism. Paper presented at the first annual Frances Tustin Memorial Lecture, Los Angeles.
Mancia, M. (1981). On the beginning of mental life in the foetus. *International Journal of Psycho-Analysis, 62*: 351–357.
Martel, Y. (2001). *Life of Pi*. Canada: Knopf.
Martin, J. (1960). Pre-mature ego development. *International Journal of Psycho-Analysis, 41*: 288–294.
Meltzer, D. (1975). Adhesive identification. *Contemporary Psychoanalysis, 11* (3): 289–310.
Meltzer, D. (1978). *The Kleinian Development, Part III*. Perthshire: Clunie Press.
Meltzer, D., Bremner, J., Hoxter, S., Weddell, D., & Wittenberg, I. (1975). *Explorations in Autism*. Perthshire: Clunie Press.
Milner, M. (1952). Aspects of symbolism in comprehension of the not-self. *International Journal of Psycho-Analysis, 33*: 181–194.
Mitrani, J. L. (1992). On the survival function of autistic maneuvers in adult patients. *International Journal of Psycho-Analysis, 73* (2): 549–560.
Mitrani, J. L. (1993). Deficiency and envy: some factors impacting the analytic mind from listening to interpretation. *International Journal of Psycho-Analysis, 74* (4): 689–704.
Mitrani, J. L. (1994). Unintegration, adhesive identification, and the psychic skin: variations on some themes by Esther Bick. *Melanie Klein and Object Relations, 11* (2): 65–88.
Mitrani, J. L. (1995). Toward an understanding of unmentalized experience. *Psychoanal. Q., 64*: 68–112.

Mitrani, J. L. (1996). *A Framework for the Imaginary: Clinical Explorations in Primitive States of Being*. Northvale, NJ: Jason Aronson.

Mitrani, J. L. (1998a). Never before and never again: the compulsion to repeat, the fear of breakdown and the defensive organization. *International Journal of Psycho-Analysis, 79*: 301–316.

Mitrani, J. L. (1998b). Unbearable ecstasy, reverence and awe, and the perpetuation of an "aesthetic conflict." *Psychoanalytic Quarterly, 67*: 102–127.

Mitrani, J. L. (1999). The case of the flying Dutchman and the search for the containing object. *International Journal of Psycho-Analysis, 80* (1): 47–71.

Mitrani, J. L. (2000). *Ordinary People and Extra-Ordinary Protections: A Post-Kleinian Approach to the Treatment of Primitive Mental States*. London: Brunner/Routledge.

Mitrani, J. L. (2001). "Taking the transference": notes on some technical implications in three papers by Bion. *International Journal of Psycho-Analysis, 82* (6): 1085–1104.

Mitrani, J. L. (2003). Notes on some transferencial effects of the holocaust: unmentalized experience and coincidence of vulnerability in the therapeutic couple. *Israel Psychoanalytic Journal, 1* (1): 71–88.

Mitrani, J. L. (2006). Quelques implications du concept Kleinian de développement premature du moi. *Journal de la psychanalyse de l'enfant, 38*: 189–218.

Mitrani, J. L. (2007a). Bodily centered protections in adolescence: an extension of the work of Frances Tustin. *International Journal of Psycho-Analysis, 88*: 1153–1169.

Mitrani, J. L. (2007b). Some technical implications of Klein's concept of "premature ego Development". *International Journal of Psycho-Analysis, 88*: 825–842.

Oliver, M. (1997). Have you ever tried to enter the long black branches. In: M. Oliver, *West Wind: Poems and Prose Poems* (pp. 61–63). New York: Houghton Mifflin.

O'Shaughnessy, E. (1964). The absent object. *Journal of Child Psychotherapy, 1* (2): 34–43.

O'Shaughnessy, E. (1981). A clinical study of a defensive organisation. *International Journal of Psycho-Analysis, 62*: 359–369.

Pestalozzi, J. (2003). The symbolic and concrete: Psychotic adolescents in psychoanalytic psychotherapy. *International Journal of Psycho-Analysis, 84* (3): 733–753.

Piontelli, A. (1987). Infant observation from before birth. *International Journal of Psycho-Analysis, 68*: 453–463.

Ramachandran, V. S., & Hubbard, E. M. (2001b). Synaesthesia: A window into perception, thought and language. *Journal of Consciousness Studies, 8* (12): 3–34.
Ramachandran, V. S., & Oberman, L. M. (2006). Broken mirrors: a theory of autism. *Scientific American*, 63–69.
Rhode, M. (2007). Helping toddlers to communicate: infant observation as an early intervention. In: S. Acquarone, (Ed.), *Signs of Autism in Infants: Detection and Early Intervention* (pp. 193–212). London: Karnac.
Rizzolatti, G., Fadiga, L., Gallese, V., & Fogassi, L. (1996). Premotor cortex and the recognition of motor actions. *Cognitive Brain Research, 3*: 131–141.
Rosenfeld, H. (1959). An investigation into the psycho-analytic theory of depression. *International Journal of Psycho-Analysis, 40*: 105–129.
Rosenfeld, H. (1985). Psychosomatic symptoms and latent psychotic states. *Yearbook of Psychoanalysis and Psychotherapy, 1*: 381–398.
Rosenzweig, M. R., Krech, D., Bennett, E. L., & Diamond, M. C. (1962). Effects of environmental complexity and training on brain chemistry and anatomy: A replication and extension. *Journal of Comparative and Physiological Psychology, 55*: 429–437.
Roth, P. (1994). Being true to a false object: a view of identification. *Psychoanalytic Inquiry, 14* (3): 393–405.
Salo, F. T. (2007). Recognizing the infant as subject in infant–parent psychotherapy. *International Journal Psycho-Analysis, 88*: 961–979.
Schore, A. N. (2003). *Affect Dysregulation and Disorders of the Self*. New York: Norton.
Schore, A. N. (2006). Personal communication. Los Angeles, CA.
Sebold, A. (2002). *The Lovely Bones*. New York: Little Brown.
Shakespeare, W. (2008). *The Tragedy of Romeo and Juliet*. Newburyport, MA: Focus Publishing/R. Pullins Company. (First published 1594).
Spitz, R. A., & Wolf, K. M. (1946). Anaclitic depression. *The Psychoanalytic Study of the Child, 2*: 313–342.
Stein, R. (2005). Why perversion? "false love" and the perverse pact. *International Journal of Psycho-Analytic, 86* (3): 775–799.
Steiner, J. (1982). Perverse relationships between parts of the self. *International Journal of Psycho-Analysis, 63*: 241–251.
Steiner, J. (1987). The interplay between pathological organizations and the paranoid-schizoid and depressive positions. *International Journal of Psycho-Analysis, 68*: 69–80.
Steiner, J. (1990). Pathological organizations as obstacle to mourning. *International Journal of Psycho-Analysis, 71*: 87–94.

Steiner, J. (1993). *Psychic Retreats: Pathological Organisations of the Personality in Psychotic, Neurotic and Borderline Patients*. London: Routledge.

Steiner, J. (1994). Patient-centered and analyst-centered interpretations: some implications of containment and countertransference. *Psychoanalytic Inquiry*, 14: 406–422.

Stern, D. N. (1985). *The Interpersonal World of the Infant: A View from Psychoanalysis and Developmental Psychology*. New York: Basic Books.

Strachey, J. (1934). The nature of the therapeutic action of psycho-analysis. *International Journal of Psycho-Analysis*, 15: 127–159.

Süskind, P. (1986). *Perfume: the Story of a Murderer*. New York: Alfred Knopf and Pocket Books.

Symington, J. (1985). The survival function of primitive omnipotence. *International Journal of Psycho-Analysis*, 66: 481–488.

Tustin, A. (1984). Personal communication. Amersham, England.

Tustin, F. (1972). *Autism and Childhood Psychosis*. London: Hogarth Press.

Tustin, F. (1980). Autistic objects. *International Review Psycho-Analysis*, 7: 27–38.

Tustin, F. (1981a). Psychological birth and psychological catastrophe. In: J. Grotstein (Ed.), *Do I Dare Disturb the Universe?* (pp. 181–196). London: Karnac.

Tustin, F. (1981b). *Autistic States in Children*. London/Boston: Routledge and Kegan Paul.

Tustin, F. (1983). Thoughts on autism with special reference to a paper by Melanie Klein. *Journal of Child Psychotherapy*, 9: 119–132.

Tustin, F. (1984a). The growth of understanding. *Journal of Child Psychotherapy*, 10 (2): 137–149.

Tustin, F. (1984b). Autistic shapes. *International Review of Psycho-Analysis*, 11, (3): 279–290.

Tustin, F. (1986a). *Autistic Barriers in Neurotic Patients*. London: Karnac.

Tustin, F. (1986b). Spilling and dissolving. In: *Autistic Barriers In Neurotic Patients* (pp. 197–214). London: Karnac.

Tustin, F. (1987). Personal communication. Amersham, England.

Tustin, F. (1988a). Psychotherapy with children who cannot play. *International Review Psycho-Analysis*, 15: 93–106.

Tustin, F. (1988b). Personal communication. Amersham, England.

Tustin, F. (1989). Personal communication. Amersham, England.

Tustin, F. (1990a). *The Protective Shell in Children and Adults*. London: Karnac.

Tustin, F. (1990b). Personal communication. Amersham, England.

Tustin, F. (1991). Revised understanding of psychogenic autism. *International Journal of Psycho-Analysis*, 72 (4): 585–592.

Tustin, F. (1992). *Autistic States in Children*. London: Routledge. (Revised edition, first published in 1981).
Tustin, F. (1994a). Personal communication. Amersham, England.
Tustin, F. (1994b). The perpetuation of an error. *Journal of Child Psychotherapy, 20*: 4–23.
Volkmar, F. R., & Greenough, W. T. (1972). Rearing complexity affects branching of dendrites in the visual cortex of the rat. *Science, 176*: 1445–1447.
Wilkinson, M. (2006a). *Coming Into Mind: The Mind-Brain Relationship A Jungian Clinical Perspective*. London: Routledge.
Wilkinson, M. (2006b). Personal communication. London, England.
Wilkinson, M. (2007). Jung and neuroscience: the making of mind. In: A. Casement (Ed.), Who owns Jung? London: Karnac.
Wing, L. (1996). *The Autistic Spectrum: A Guide for Parents and Professionals*. London: Constable.
Winnicott, D. W. (1945). Primitive emotional development. In: *Collected Papers: Through Pediatrics to Psycho-analysis* (pp. 145–156). New York: Basic Books, 1958.
Winnicott, D. W. (1949a). Mind and its relation to the psyche-soma. In: *Collected Papers: Through Pediatrics to Psycho-analysis* (pp. 243–254) New York: Basic Books, 1958.
Winnicott, D. W. (1949b). Hate in the counter-transference. *International Journal Psycho-analysis, 30*: 69–74.
Winnicott, D. W. (1951). Transitional objects and transitional phenomenon. In: *Collected Papers. Through Pediatrics to Psychoanalysis* (pp. 229–243). New York: Basic Books.
Winnicott, D. W. (1956a). On transference. *International Journal Psycho-Analysis, 37*: 386–388.
Winnicott, D. W. (1956b). Primary maternal preoccupation. In: *Collected Papers: Through Paediatrics to Psycho-analysis* (pp. 300–305). New York: Basic Books.
Winnicott, D. W. (1958). Reparation in respect to mother's organized defense against depression. In: *Collected Papers: Through Pediatrics to Psychoanalysis* (pp. 91–96). New York: Basic Books.
Winnicott, D. W. (1960a). The theory of the parent–infant relationship. In: *The Maturational Process and the Facilitating Environment* (pp. 37–55). London and New York: Hogarth and International Universities Press.
Winnicott, D. W. (1960b). Ego distortion in terms of true and false self. In: *The Maturational Process and the Facilitating Environment* (pp. 140–152). New York: International Universities Press, 1965.

Winnicott, D. W. (1962). Ego integration in child development. In: *Maturational Processes and the Facilitating Environment* (pp. 56–63). New York: International Universities Press, 1965.

Winnicott, D. W. (1967). Mirror-role of mother and family development. In: *Playing and Reality* (pp. 111–118). London: Tavistock Publications, 1985.

Zetzel, E. R. (1956). Current concepts of transference. *International Journal of Psycho-Analysis, 37*: 369–375.

INDEX

abandonment 113
adaptation in perversion 92–93
adhesive unity 152
adolescence 118
Alvarez, A. 168
Anderson, R. 118
"Anorexia Nervosa in an adolescent girl" (Tustin) 107
authoritative statements 19–32
   job description and 21
   Kleinian, definition of 23–31
   overview 19–21
   self psychology and 21–23
autism, neuroscientific and psychoanalytic understanding of 147–151
   etiology and features of 160–165
   introduction 147
   neurobiological studies 147–148
autistic detection 124
autistic encapsulation 108
autistic shell 50, 153, 167
autistic stages, differential diagnosis of 124–126

bad objects 79
Balint, E. 44
Baron-Cohen, S. 161–162
behavior as palimpsest 82–83
Bennett, E. L. 149
Berkeley's biology laboratories 148–149
Bick, E. 12, 43, 50, 57, 113, 119, 125, 167, 173
Bion, W. R. xvi–xvii, 1–2, 20, 23, 31–32, 34, 37–40, 43–44, 53, 59–62, 67–69, 72–76, 79, 81–88, 90–93, 96–97, 100–101, 105–106, 119, 122, 124, 135, 139, 144–145, 150, 153, 156, 162, 173–174, 188
   clinical case presented to 83–85

205

model of container–contained 38–39
Black, J. E. 150
Brazelton, B. 158
Brazilian Lectures (Bion) 38
Bremner, J. 126

Camus, A. 188
case studies
  Alex 21–31
    "Charlie horses" 24
    definition of "Kleinian" by 23–31
    "Kleinian mother" 24
    off balance or in grip 25–27
    on self psychology 21–23
    pigeonhole 29–31
    "pissing contest" 27–29
    unbearably afraid 22
  Anthony 3–6
  Audrey 130–131
  Brad 130
  Carla 40–44
    aesthetic emotion 43
    ecstasy of oneness 42
    "empathic attunement" 44
    mother of 42–43
    perception of 43
    positive feelings by 41
    self-conscious 40
    transformation in 41
  Cathy 112–119
    aloneness and there-ness 117–118
    and otherness 115–117
    consultation with 112–113
    "Endora the Witch" 114
  Chloe 48–50
  Connie 131
  Cora 6–7
    and fear 66
    Dr. A and 63–69
    expression of need 63
    patient's material 6, 63
  Dick 34–35, 37–38
  Gaila, Dr. B and 69–73
  Hendrick 45–47
    "glory holes" 46
    impermeable countenance 45
    mother's "sickness" 47
    "unemployable" 45
  Julia 140–141
  Karen 132–134
  Laura, Dr. Z and 97–100
  Leonard 89–90
  Lilly 7–13
    as "smart baby" 10
    delusional jealousy 12
    dream 9–10
    "empty feeling" 11
    feelings of being held 11–12
    feelings of rage 10–11
    hopelessness in 8
    hostile behavior 10
    interpretation of need and fear 8–13
    relationship with sister 8
    transference 10
  Lucie 128–130
  Marc 14–16
  Nell 16–17
  Peter, Dr. C and 93–96
  question of motivation 134–135
  resistance and collusion 140–142
  Taylor 110–112
    auto-sensuous protections 111
  Zorro 84–85
Chaminade, T. 54
Chesterton, G. K. xi
Cogitations (Bion) 81, 96, 100–101
containing function
  failure in development 35
  holding and 54

infantile aspect in adult patient 90–91
maternal, Bion's concept of 39
of mind 38, 76–77
three essential components of 39–40
containing object 34, 55, 59, 67, 75, 77, 91, 99, 110, 139
Bion's model of 68
mother as 68–69
countertransference 23, 43, 51–52, 54, 56–58, 63, 98–99, 124, 135, 137, 139–141, 162 *see also* transference
Cramer, B. 158

Dartington, A. 118
de Astis, G. 171
Decety, J. 54
defensive organizations 23, 50, 93, 96, 100
delusion, creation of 186–190
Diamond, M. C. 149
Dictionary of Kleinian Thought 54
dissolution 138
dual unity 152

Eliot, T. S. 126
empathic attunement 44, 72
"Evidence" (Bion) 60
exercise of curiosity 20

Fadiga, L. 158, 168
Fairbairn, W. R. D. 57–58
Falck-Ytter, T. 158
Fauconnier, G. 162
Federn, P. 119
Ferenczi, S. 44
Fogassi, L. 158, 168
Fonagy, P. 144
Freud, S. xv–xvii, 44, 58, 60, 82, 87, 140, 150, 174–175, 186–187, 189

Frith, U. 161
frustration 61–62
Fuller, P. 43

Gaddini, E. 160
Gallese, V. 158, 168
Giannotti, A. 171
Gill, M. 102
good-enough 115
circumstances 151
infancy 57
mother 33, 170
Great Ormond Street Hospital 150
Gredebäck, G. 158
Greene, G. 123
Greenough, W. T. 149–150

Haag, G. 151, 165
hallucination, creation of 190–193
Hildebrand, P. 118
Hinshelwood, R. D. 54–55
holding function of mother 54
Houzel, D. 165
Hoxter, S. 126
Hubbard, E. M. 159–160, 163, 165–168

Iacoboni, J. M. 158–160
"I am a rock" (Simon) 107
If I Were You (Green) 174
infantile dependency, emergence of 1–17
financial considerations 7
overview 1–3
infantile sadistic act of aggression 37
interpretation 40
introjective 77–78
meaning and 91–92
of projective identification 96–97
projective 77–78
transformative sequence 91–92
introjective interpretation 77–78

James, M. 36–37, 53
Jensen, W. xv, 174, 186
job description
    analyst's 21
    patient's 21
Joseph, B. 23, 32, 58

Kanner, L. 34, 146, 152
Keats, J. 74
Klein, M. xvii, 21–24, 29–30, 33–39, 50, 54–58, 61, 81, 83, 86, 96, 101, 103, 107–108, 119, 124–125, 128, 135–136, 144, 157, 171, 174
Klein, S. 122, 124, 144
Kleinian
    Alex's definition of 23–31
    analysis and Alex 21–22
    classical 55, 57
    literature 55, 119
    model, classical 107, 136
    thinking, post- 34
    understanding of defensive organisation 86–87
Kohler, W. 163
Kohut, H. 24, 57
Krech, D. 149

Lacan, J. 42
Laufer, E. 118
Laufer, M. 118
learning from experience 2, 47, 60, 135, 150, 156, 170
Lechevalier-Haim, B. 165
LeDoux, J. E. 55
Lee, A. 175, 186–187, 190, 193
Leslie, A. 161
Levin, F. M. 158
Life of Pi (Martel) 175–177
    Pi's tale of survival, life of 185–186
The Lovely Bones (Sebold) 127

Magee, David 175
Maiello, S. 165
Mancia, M. 62, 158
Martel, Y. 173, 175–177
Martin, J. 36
Meltzer, D. 103, 126, 145, 156–157, 171
memory and desire 53, 73–79
    eschewing 75
Milner, M. 33
mirror neurons 158–164, 168
Mitrani, J. L. 13, 17, 32, 39, 44, 69, 72, 86, 88, 90–91, 118–119, 122, 126, 130, 135, 138–140, 144, 146–147, 174

nameless dread 37, 56, 153, 173
"negative capability" 74
non-psychotic aspect of the personality 106
normal infantile omnipotence 55–56
normal primary maternal preoccupation 152

Oberman, L. M. 159–160, 163, 165–168
object(s)
    idiosyncratic use of 131–132
    in the periphery 135–138
see also containing object
object lesson 78, 109, 138
Oliver, M. 121–122, 142, 144, 146
"On identification" (Klein) 174
"On loneliness" (Klein) 36
O'Shaughnessy, E. 126

Parker, Richard 177
Patel, Santosh 176
Pediatric Neuro-Psychiatric Institute of the University of Rome 148
Perfume (Suskind) 174

Pestalozzi, J. 118
Phantom of the Opera 17
Piontelli, A. 158
precocious ego development 34, 47, 53
premature awareness of bodily separateness 150–151
pre-mature depressive position 37
premature ego development 33–58
  Bion's model of container-contained 38–39
  environmental impact on 35–36
  in response to experience of mother's needs 47–48
  Klein's analysis of autistic child 34–35
  overview 33–34
  study of 36–38
  technical considerations 50–53
pre-ruth 37
privation 36
projective identification 37
  interpretation of 96–97
  realistic 59–60
projective interpretation 77–78
psychic retreats 50
psychoanalytic game 83
psychoanalytic infant observation 108
psychotic part of the personality 106, 174
  Pi's 188

Ramachandran, V. S. 159–160, 163, 165–168
realistic projective identification 59–60
refrigerator mothers 146, 152
Reid, S. 168
Rhode, M. 165
rhythm of safety 123, 131, 156, 173
Rizzolatti, G. 158, 168

The Rome studies 157
Rosenfeld, H. 102, 122
Rosenzweig, M. R. 149
Roth, P. 47–48
"reverie" 39, 44, 60, 67–69, 90–91, 139
  Bion's use of 69
rudimentary consciousness 72

Salo, F. T. 165
Schore, A. N. 55–56, 58
Sebold, A. 127
self psychology 21–23
separation 33, 56, 63, 66, 94, 108, 114, 117, 126, 133, 152
Shakespeare, W. 31
Spitz, R. A. 127
splitting 48
Stein, R. 146
Steiner, J. 50, 88, 122
Stern, D. N. 155, 179, 181, 183
Strachey, J. 91
Süskind, P. 144, 174
Symington, J. 12

taking the transference 44, 46, 59–79, 138–139
  Bion's thoughts on thinking thoughts 61–63
  empathic attunement and 72
  evidence, memory, and desire 73–79
  frustration and 61–62
  mother as containing object 68–69
  overview 59–61
Target, M. 144
Tavistock Centre 150
tolerated doubt 62
transference 2, 5, 7–8, 10–14, 24, 34, 43, 50–54, 56–58, 63, 71–73, 76–77, 88, 91, 101–103
  analyst's vulnerability and 51

-centered therapy 106, 112
immediacy of 2
infantile 17, 61, 99, 128, 140–142
negative 13–14, 72, 88
transformation(s) 39, 68–69, 90, 100, 103, 110, 139, 170
in Pi 180, 189
of a realisation 101
projective 94
Trevarthen, C. 158
Tustin, A. 19
Tustin, F. xvii, 23, 42–43, 50, 53, 55–56, 85, 88, 107–108, 110, 116–117, 122–127, 130–136, 138–140, 145–148, 150–157, 160–161, 164, 167–170, 173

The University of California 148
University of Illinois 149

Volkmar, F. R. 149
Von Hofsten, C. 158

Wallace, C. S. 150
Weddell, D. 126
Wilkinson, M. 54–55
Wing, L. 168
Winnicott, D. W. 23, 33, 37, 42, 53–57, 62, 69, 83, 102–103, 109, 125–126, 136, 145, 152, 162, 173
Wittenberg, I. 126
Wolf, K. M. 127

Zetzel, E. R. 20